THE NEW WESTERN HISTORY

The Territory Ahead

Forrest G. Robinson, Editor

THE UNIVERSITY OF ARIZONA PRESS TUCSON

The University of Arizona Press

First University of Arizona Press edition published 1998
by arrangement with *The Arizona Quarterly*.

♾ This book is printed on acid-free, archival-quality paper.
Manufactured in the United States of America
03 02 01 00 99 98 6 5 4 3 2 1

Library of Congress Cataloging-in-Publication Data

The new western history : the territory ahead / Forrest G. Robinson, editor. — 1st University of Arizona Press ed.
Published also as v. 53, no. 2, summer 1997 of the Arizona quarterly.
Includes bibliographical references and index.
ISBN 0-8165-1915-3 (cloth : acid-free). — ISBN 0-8165-1916-1 (pbk. : acid-free)
1. West (U.S.)—Historiography. I. Robinson, Forrest G. (Forrest Glen), 1940– . II. Arizona quarterly.
F591.N475 1998 98-19251
978'.007'2—dc21 CIP

British Library Cataloguing-in-Publication Data
A catalogue record for this book is available from the British Library.

CONTENTS

THE NEW WESTERN HISTORY

JEROME FRISK AND FORREST G. ROBINSON

Introduction

THE EMERGENCE of the *Old* Western History, we are often reminded, has a fixed point of inception (the Chicago convention of the American Historical Association in 1893), an authoritative founding text ("The Significance of the Frontier in American History"), and a single progenitor in the person of Frederick Jackson Turner. Perhaps not surprisingly, the *New* Western History has an "origin story" that resonates with the inflections of what some have called our postmodern condition. It may be the only "new school" yet conceived that managed to launch itself inadvertently, came into being through a questioning of its own existence, and that is obliged to consider itself the product in no small part of an academic media event. In the fall of 1989, Patricia Limerick was uncertain about the title she had chosen for an NEH symposium soon to be held in Santa Fe, New Mexico. Should it be "Trails: Toward a New Western History"; or rather, should they delete the "Toward" and thereby proclaim the existence of the fledgling school? Limerick wrote to participants to solicit their views, and received a response that in turn inquired "what the New Western History might be." When the conference was convened, Limerick distributed her answer, a brief statement entitled "What on Earth Is the New Western History? (Not a Manifesto)." Though insisting that she had no intention of founding or naming a school, Limerick concedes that something "quite understandable" occurred when several conference speakers referred to the "new western history" in their presentations, and when reporters drew on the "not a manifesto" statement to announce the formation of a new academic movement. Articles in the *Washington Post* and the *Arizona Republic*, she recalls, "started off an improbable rush of media coverage. A variety of news organizations picked up the story," and soon "the New Western History had come to exist."[1]

As the news from Santa Fe spread, this behind-the-scenes account of improbable beginnings was not, to be sure, part of the story. The "newness" of the New Western History provided the lead and focus of attention. The mythic iconography of the West was being challenged and "nobody had ever done this before"; critical histories of colonial conquest and environmental plunder were being written "for the first time." It has since become evident that such initial proclamations were not mere journalistic hyperbole. For it is above all else their claim to originality that separates the *New* Western Historians from those who have gone before them, and it is the bold newness of the revisionist narrative that holds the attention of contemporary workers in the field. There can be no doubt about it: the New Western History now dominates the center foreground of regional studies. And to the considerable extent that the West is viewed as a mirror of larger American realities, the revisionist narrative has implications that exceed regional boundaries.

It is our principal task in this volume to assess the contributions of the New Western History. First, however, it will be useful by way of introduction to identify the revisionists, and to set out the main elements of the story they have to tell. By most accounts, the leading proponents of the New Western History—sometimes referred to as "the Gang of Four"—are William Cronon, Patricia Nelson Limerick, Richard White, and Donald Worster. Other names frequently appear in association with the "school," among them Brian W. Dippie, Peggy Pascoe, Elliott West, and Michael P. Malone. Numerous other regional scholars and writers of the post-Vietnam era, virtually all of them concerned with questions of race, class, gender, and the environment, are often cited by the leaders of the movement, and may be thought of as contributing or lower-case new western historians. In the essays that follow, the phrase "New Western Historians" will refer principally to Cronon, Limerick, White, and Worster. Of course, as topics vary from chapter to chapter, different members of the Gang of Four will be drawn into the foreground. Richard White is prominent in discussions of Native Americans, for example, while Donald Worster figures centrally when attention turns to the environment. The work of other scholars will also be featured from time to time, as the specific topic dictates. Thus Peggy Pascoe's *Relations of Rescue: The Search for Female Moral Authority in the*

American West, 1874–1939 appears more prominently in the essay on women in the New Western History than anything, say, by Donald Worster.

William Cronon took a B.A. (English, History) at the University of Wisconsin, Madison in 1976, and then spent two years in England as a Rhodes Scholar. He subsequently completed an M.Phil. (American History) at Yale in 1980, a D.Phil. (British History) at Oxford the following year, and a Ph.D. (American History) at Yale in 1990. He served for more than a decade on the faculty at Yale before accepting the Frederick Jackson Turner Chair of History, Geography, and Environmental Studies at his Wisconsin alma mater in 1992. His numerous honors and awards include a Bancroft Prize for *Nature's Metropolis: Chicago and the Great West* (1991), and the very prestigious MacArthur Foundation "genius award" in 1985–1990. Cronon is something of a maverick among the leading revisionists. He stands out both for his insistence that "not all of the Turnerian legacy is worth abandoning,"[2] and, more recently, for his resoluteness in confronting the challenge of postmodernism.

Thanks in part to the success of her regional synthesis, *Legacy of Conquest: The Unbroken Past of the American West* (1987), Patricia Nelson Limerick is certainly the most "visible" of the New Western Historians. She has American Studies degrees from the University of California, Santa Cruz (B.A., 1972) and from Yale (Ph.D., 1980), and held teaching positions at Yale and Harvard before moving to the University of Colorado, Boulder, where she is a professor of history. Limerick is well known for her colorful prose style, and for the energy and humor of her lectures. She is also noted for dressing up as a Shakespearean fool and berating the world, especially the academic world, for its fatuous solemnity. "It seems pretty clear now that I am the best, most accomplished, most published fool," she has declared, "and I will not take second place to anyone."[3] A wise fool, indeed, Limerick was also appointed a MacArthur Fellow in 1995.

With the publication in 1991 of his own, now widely respected, synthesis, *"It's Your Misfortune and None of My Own": A New History of the American West*, Richard White has also achieved a certain prominence among the regional revisionists. Another graduate of the University of California, Santa Cruz (B.A., 1969), he completed his Ph.D. at the University of Washington in 1975. He has taught over the years at

Michigan State and the University of Utah, and currently resides in Seattle, where he is a professor of history at the University of Washington. White's publications have ranged widely over Native American and environmental history. In 1994 he teamed with Patricia Limerick in writing essays for the catalogue of the NEH-funded Newberry Library Exhibition on *The Frontier in American Culture*. He joined Limerick and Cronon in 1995 as the third of the New Western Historians to receive a MacArthur Fellowship.

The final member of the Gang of Four, Donald Worster, took his B.A. at the University of Kansas in 1963, and a Ph.D. in American Studies at Yale in 1971. He has held appointments at Brandeis University, the University of Hawaii, and, since 1989, at the University of Kansas, where he is the Hall Distinguished Professor of History. Worster stands out among the New Western Historians for his focused attention over two decades to environmental history. His book, *Dust Bowl: The Southern Plains in the 1930s*, was awarded the Bancroft Prize in 1980. "Beyond the Agrarian Myth," Worster's lead essay in *Trails: Toward a New Western History* (1989), is a brief, potent summation of revisionist assumptions, principles, and intentions. "The New Western History is now setting the agenda of the field," he boldly declares.[4]

Patricia Nelson Limerick directly identifies the New Western Historians with her own generation. Ray Allen Billington's "restoration of the Old Western History," she argues, was "well-adapted for carrying the ideological freight of the cold war, the revamped model of the frontier pulled out on the road again—just in time to run full tilt into the 1960s."[5] Donald Worster describes the disenchanted perspective of the now-graying newcomers who stood, nearly a quarter-century ago, in Billington's—and therefore in Turner's—way.

> A younger generation, shaken by Vietnam and other national disgraces—poverty, racism, environmental degradation—could not pretend that the only story that mattered in the West was one of stagecoach lines, treasure hunts, cattle brands, and wildcatters, nor for that matter aircraft plants, opera companies, bank deposits, or middle-class whites learning how to ski. What was missing was a frank, hard look at the violent imperialistic process by which the West was wrested from its original

> owners and the violence by which it had been secured against the continuing claims of minorities, women, and the forces of nature. . . . It was time for historians to call such violence and imperialism by their true names.[6]

The New Western Historians strive to re-tell regional history from the point of view of the oppressed, colonized, and conquered; they wish to speak out for the interests of women, minorities, and the environment. In describing the origins and purposes of *It's Your Misfortune and None of My Own*, Richard White emphasizes that "the new minority histories and the literature on gender and the environment" are the areas that now especially "deserve treatment" in any contemporary overview of the American West.[7] For historians in the Turner tradition, observes Michael L. Johnson, adult white males "*are* western history," and their story is a celebration of democracy and progress.[8] For New Western Historians, on the other hand, this Turnerian myth masks and represses the truth. Western development, Donald Worster insists, has been "plagued by racism, ethnocentrism, brutality, misunderstanding, and rage on the part of the majority and minority peoples alike, but especially marred by oppression and exploitation on the part of those holding the whip hand." Nor, he continues, have humans been the only victims. "The economic development of the West was often a ruthless assault on nature and has left behind it much death, depletion, and ruin." Worster touches here on a "populist" strain clearly discernible in the revisionist approach to what Limerick describes as the pervasive "boom/bust instability of capitalism" in the region.[9] "The western elites," Worster goes on, "have followed the old familiar tendency of those in power, to become corrupt, exploitative, and cynical towards those they dominate."[10] Richard White argues that such cynicism is also to be found among advocates of modern environmentalism who "disdain and distrust those who most obviously work in nature." White's populist commitments surface in his challenge to those who "have come to associate work—particularly heavy bodily labor—with environmental degradation."[11]

Central to the agenda of the New Western History is a shift in perspective that produces histories told from the "bottom up"—from the point of view of the margins and the marginalized. If we "look at the West from the point of view of the Indians," Worster observes, "what could it look like but a failure?"[12] This relocation of narrative "position" also entails an alteration in what Merleau Ponty calls "the intentionality of perception" (what we actively look *for*).[13] Richard White graphically illustrates this point in describing the different ways of looking at the refuse that sometimes appears along wilderness trails. "Old Western Historians looked past the garbage and saw 'nature'. . . . Many New Western Historians—particularly environmental historians—see the garbage first."[14]

Paul Ricoeur draws an apposite distinction between historical hermeneutics that are "empathetic and reconstructive," and those that are "critical and demythologizing."[15] In these terms, to be sure, the work of the New Western Historians constitutes a dedicated and even vehement variety of the latter, demythologizing mode of historical interpretation. Michael L. Johnson rightly observes that the New Western Historians have taken it as their duty to expose what they regard as the ideologically complicit "suppressions" of earlier historians in the field. "They are out to set the record straight," Johnson writes.[16] As a demythologizing hermeneutic or an ideological critique, the revisionist program swerves toward what might be called, in an inclusive sense, the New Americanism. As Michael Malone notes, the New Western History is "in large part . . . the predictable result of mainstreaming the western subdiscipline by applying to it trends in the broader field of American history and American studies."[17] More specifically, revisionist interpretive methods and agendas are at intervals in striking alignment with the widely influential writings of Sacvan Bercovitch, Fredric Jameson, and Edward Said.

We hasten to add, however, that the New Western Historians are not generally concerned with exposing the hidden economic and political interests that motivate actions, movements, and discourses. Rather, they frequently emphasize the continuities between disparate, and even apparently conflicting, historical phenomena. In *The Legacy of Conquest*, for example, Limerick's treatment of Native Americans centers on an analysis of the failed efforts of "whites intent on 'helping' the Indians." Of the "Indian reformers" of the late 1820s and early 1830s, she writes: "From the helper's point of view, the ignorance and inexperience of the Indians made them incapable of deciding their future for themselves. *Like Andrew Jackson*, Indian reformers took it upon themselves to determine the Indians' best interests and then to act—coercively if necessary—to pursue those interests. It was, of course, paternalism, but given their widely used comparison of Indians to children, paternalism was exactly what the officials had in mind."[18] Limerick shows how two ostensibly different perspectives (those of the "Indian reformers" and those of the advocates of Indian removal) actually shared racist and imperialist assumptions, and thus, predictably, produced similar results. Turning to the generation of Indian reformers that emerged in the 1880s, she continues, "the Friends of the Indian had initiated a process that took nearly two-thirds of tribal land away without doing much to assimilate Indians into a homogeneous mass of American property holders. . . . The same pattern continued to plague Indian affairs."[19]

In a more recent publication, William Cronon analyzes how "wilderness myths" and "Edenic narratives," both past and present, have functioned ideologically in a virtually uninterrupted and unbroken continuity. "By imagining that our true home is in the wilderness, we forgive ourselves the homes we actually inhabit. In its flight from history, in its siren song of escape, in its reproduction of the dangerous dualism that sets human beings outside of nature—in all of these ways, wilderness poses a serious threat to responsible environmentalism at the end of the twentieth century." What is "new" and provocative about Cronon's metahistory is his insistence that this "wilderness myth" forms a continuous legacy in American environmental discourse. Following extensive commentary on Wordsworth, Thoreau, and Muir, he concludes that "all three men are participating in the *same cultural tradition and contributing to the same myth*: the mountain as cathedral. The three may differ in the way they choose to express their piety . . . *but they agree completely about the church in which they worship.*" In Cronon's view, the myth of wilderness is the cultural product of the commingling of the myth of "the sublime" (the "broad transatlantic movement we today label romanticism") with the "more peculiarly American" myth of the frontier. "The two converged," he explains, "to remake wilderness in their own image, freighting it with moral values and cultural symbols that it carries to this day. Indeed, it is not too much to say that the modern environmental movement is itself a grandchild of romanticism and post-frontier ideology." It is thus Cronon's most urgent conclusion that the environmentalisms of Thoreau and Muir were rooted in romantic mythology, and therefore complicit with a conservative, "post-frontier ideology" which they were powerless to oppose.[20] In the upshot,

Cronon joins Limerick in producing what Worster calls a "clear-eyed, demythologized"[21] new history in which the efforts of liberal reformers are entangled with, and inadvertently perpetuate, the hegemonic ideologies of a racist and romantic frontier mythology.

When asked about his view of Hegel, Ludwig Wittgenstein responded, "No, I don't think I would get on with Hegel. Hegel seems to me to be always wanting to say that things which look different are really the same. Whereas my interest is in showing that things which look the same are really different."[22] By Wittgenstein's lights, the New Western Historians are rather thoroughgoing neo-Hegelians. Much of the persuasive force of their work, it seems, is due not only to their extraordinary productivity, but also to their bold claim to have established a new synthesis in regional studies. Richard W. Etulain concludes his *Writing Western History: Essays on Major Western Historians* with a section entitled "Total Western History: Braudel Out West." He there observes that "Braudel and likeminded historians have called for nothing less than the study of a total society or culture." Etulain concedes that "no historian has been equally ambitious in his or her prospectus for studying the American West," but adds that "a handful of western specialists have essayed broader-based thematic studies of the West, ones intended as overviews or as total histories of the region." He goes on to discuss the "total histories" of Limerick and Worster in persuasive fashion.[23] After all, at a time when—as Michael Malone puts it—"the entire discipline of history in the United States is in a state of crisis,"[24] such attempts to provide a coherent and unified overview have an enhanced appeal—an appeal, perhaps, like Ezra Pound's "great ball of crystal," which makes it all "cohere."[25]

Critical response to the New Western History has been voluminous, both in professional journals and in magazines with larger circulations. Of the latter, essays by Larry McMurtry in *The New Republic* and Alan Brinkley in *The New York Times Book Review* are perhaps fairly representative of the range of views that has emerged. McMurtry dashes cold water on the revisionists' claims to originality, and argues that their characteristic gloom and doom mentality blinds them to the romantic dreams that fueled westward expansion. "Failure Studies," he complains, "often fail themselves because they so rarely do justice to the quality of imagination that constitutes part of the truth."[26] Brinkley, by contrast, is much more attentive to what he regards as the major contributions of the New Western History. Among "their most important achievements" he includes "serious scholarship on the history of the environment," the attempt to shape a new regional identity, and an emphasis on the West's "extraordinary cultural diversity." To be sure, Brinkley shares some of McMurtry's skepticism when it comes to what is "new" in the revisionist scheme. "To academic historians in other fields," he observes, "it is sometimes difficult to understand what all the shouting is about. For much of what is new in the history of the West is not new at all to American history generally, which has been preoccupied for years now with issues of racial diversity, class conflict and gender relations, and which rejected the progressive, triumphalistic, ethnocentric assumptions of the Turner thesis two generations ago."[27] In the main, however, Brinkley's assessment is a positive one.

In light of their strong challenge to established perspectives, it is hardly surprising that the response among academics to the New Western History has been both vigorous and mixed. Robert Wooster's review of *Trails*, *It's Your Misfortune*, and *Under an Open Sky* is rather typical in this regard. "At their best," Wooster finds, "proponents of this approach offer inclusive, realistic, comprehensive analyses and narratives. Their emphasis on environment, race, class, and gender helps to fill important gaps in our knowledge and understanding of the West. On the other hand, their self-congratulatory pronouncements of triumph over Frederick Jackson Turner, Walter Prescott Webb, and Ray Allen Billington can sometimes be annoying. And their proclivity for investigating social and environmental issues occasionally proves obsessive, making it difficult to discern the West's importance to the broader past."[28]

The general critical assessment of the New Western History is rather faithfully mirrored in responses to the major interpretive syntheses set forth by Limerick in *The Legacy of Conquest* and White in *It's Your Misfortune and None of My Own*. Approving reviewers almost invariably applaud the New Western Historical emphasis on race, class, gender, and the environment. Richard Maxwell Brown commends *It's Your Misfortune* for telling "a story in which intricate relationships among various peoples and elements over time have produced the West." He goes on to add that "the book is grounded in the older, more traditional monographic literature of the field and in the much newer scholarship on minorities, the women, and the environment of the West."[29] Albert L. Hurtado is similarly impressed, and takes the view that White's book "should be required reading for all who want to know what western history is about today."[30] Joseph B. Herring, a reviewer for the *American Indian Quarterly*, describes *The Legacy of Conquest* as "a significant and powerful repudiation of the old theories and myths [which] provides the reader with a thorough understanding of the real West. More than a valuable contribution, this book is a classic in the field of American Western history."[31] John W. Bailey, writing for the same journal, is equally impressed with "the magnitude" of White's synthesis, which he describes as a "marvelous book. It is a work of mature scholarship and will be the standard study of the Far West for our generation."[32]

Generally less uniform in its focus, criticism of the revisionists is almost always accompanied by equal measures of approval. The glaring exception to this rule is a deeply troubled attack by Gerald D. Nash, in which the New Western Historians are likened to Nazis and Stalinists and condemned for their advocacy of "what in essence are totalitarian ideologies."[33] John Mark Faragher is critical of Nash's excesses, but notes nonetheless that the New Western Historians are often rather rigidly biased, and prone to exaggerate the originality of their views. "The rhetoric of 'new' and 'old' seems simply a way of distinguishing between arguments one does and does not like," he complains. "Alternative approaches to the history of the American West have existed among historians since the reconsideration of the frontier thesis began in earnest, and contrasting interpretations have less to do with 'generations' than with social theory, moral values, and the angle and breadth of historical vision."[34] Balance is also an issue for Clyde A. Milner II, who reports that Limerick's prejudices sometimes surface obliquely in her selection and interpretation of historical evidence. "Readers may find that they want to learn more about scholarly monographs which are used provocatively by Limerick," he cautions.[35] Jeanne Kay makes a kindred observation, arguing that *The Legacy of Conquest* is weighted too heavily on the side of failure, and "does not in itself provide a balanced synthesis."[36] Gerald Thompson is similarly suspicious of what he calls "the negative thesis" of the revisionists, and argues that "moving west proved beneficial for most Americans."[37] Glenda Riley meanwhile praises White for his emphasis on the role of the federal government in the development of the West, but protests that he gives too much attention to white males, and thus marginalizes women and minorities as mere victims. Granted, the Anglo men "now wear black hats instead of white ones, but their deeds continue to grab the spotlight. . . . Is this perhaps the beginning of a new mythology to replace the old?"[38]

The essays in this volume frequently echo the critical sentiments, both positive and negative, here briefly summarized. But it will be evident even to fairly casual readers that our chapters do not add up in the aggregate to a consensus report. True enough, we all agree that the New Western History is a force to be reckoned with in contemporary academic life. The revisionists have indeed set the agenda for the field. We can agree as well in approving the New Western Historical focus on race, class, gender, and the environment; as we can their emphasis on federal interventions in the West, urbanization, and regional history since 1890. On such basic elements—about which almost all reasonable students and scholars might be expected to agree—we are more or less in unison. But thereafter our views diverge, sometimes quite sharply. This is so for a number of reasons. We are the loosest kind of assemblage. We come from very different backgrounds, different universities, different academic specialties. Many of us met for the first time at a brief conference held at the University of California, Santa Cruz, just before Christmas in 1995. It was perfectly clear at that gathering that our opinions about the New Western History varied widely, and that our best course would be to learn from each other while making a virtue of dissensus. The fruits of that informal policy are on display in the chapters of this volume. We have approached our topics individually, and with the goal of evaluating in some depth leading dimensions of revisionist discourse. Our task, it has appeared to us, is to advance the lively and very important discussion that the New Western Historians have helped to set in motion.

A comprehensive bibliography of the New Western History would fill many pages, though the precise length would of course vary depending on how widely the bibliographer cast the net in identifying members of the "school." While we have made no attempt at such exhaustive coverage, the scholars involved in this project agreed at the outset to consult and generate a common list of essential or "core" texts by the principal New Western Historians. Our list does not include all of the writings of Cronon, Limerick, White, and Worster; it does not include the work of less prominent contributors to the revisionist program; nor, it should be obvious, does it include all of the materials that we consulted in forming our assessments. Opinions will doubtless vary on whether our list is properly representative. Still, we include it here both to mark the common foundation from which our varied essays first took rise, and as a guide to the further study of the New Western History. Those seeking additional bibliographical guidance will find copious references in the notes to this volume.

William Cronon

"Revisiting the Vanishing Frontier: The Legacy of Frederick Jackson Turner." *Western Historical Quarterly* 18 (1987): 157–76.

Nature's Metropolis: Chicago and the Great West. New York: Norton, 1991.

"Turner's First Stand: The Significance of Significance in American History." In *Writing Western History: Essays on Major Western Historians.* Ed. Richard W. Etulain. Albuquerque: University of New Mexico Press, 1991. 73–101.

"A Place for Stories: Nature, History, and Narrative." *Journal of American History* 78 (1992): 1347–76.

Ed., with George Miles and Jay Gitlin. *Under an Open Sky: Rethinking America's Western Past.* New York: Norton, 1992.

Ed. *Uncommon Ground: Toward Reinventing Nature.* New York: Norton, 1995. [Cronon's introduction, and his essay, "The Trouble with Wilderness; or, Getting Back to the Wrong Nature," are both relevant.]

Patricia Nelson Limerick

The Legacy of Conquest: The Unbroken Past of the American West. New York: Norton, 1987.

With Donald Worster et al. "*The Legacy of Conquest*, by Patricia Nelson Limerick: A Panel of Appraisal." *Western Historical Quarterly* 20 (1989): 303–22.

"The Trail to Santa Fe: The Unleashing of the Western Public Intellectual." In *Trails: Toward a New Western History.* Eds. Patricia Nelson Limerick, Clyde A. Milner II, and Charles E. Rankin. Lawrence: University Press of Kansas, 1991. 59–77.

"What on Earth Is the New Western History?" In *Trails*, 81–88.

"Persistent Traits and the Persistent Historian: The American Frontier and Ray Allen Billington." In *Writing Western History*, 277–310.

"Making the Most of Words: Verbal Activity and Western America." In *Under an Open Sky*, 167–84.

"The Adventures of the Frontier in the Twentieth Century." In *The Frontier in American Culture*. Ed. James R. Grossman. Berkeley: University of California Press, 1994. 66–102.

"Turnerians All: The Dream of a Helpful History in an Intelligible World." *American Historical Review* 100 (1995): 697–716.

Richard White

Land Use, Environment, and Social Change: The Shaping of Island County, Washington. Seattle: University of Washington Press, 1980.

The Roots of Dependency: Subsistence, Environment, and Social Change among the Choctaws, Pawnees, and Navajos. Lincoln: University of Nebraska Press, 1983.

"Environmental History: The Development of a New Historical Field." *Pacific Historical Review* 54 (1985): 297–335.

"It's Your Misfortune and None of My Own": A New History of the American West. Norman: University of Oklahoma Press, 1991.

"Discovering Nature in North America." *Journal of American History* 79 (1992): 874–91.

"Frederick Jackson Turner and Buffalo Bill." In *The Frontier in American Culture*, 6–65.

"'Are You an Environmentalist or Do You Work for a Living?': Work and Nature." In *Uncommon Ground*, 171–85.

Donald Worster

"History and Natural History: An Essay on Theory and Method." *Pacific Historical Review* 53 (February 1984): 1–19.

Rivers of Empire: Water, Aridity, and the Growth of the American West. New York: Pantheon Books, 1985.

Under Western Skies: Nature and History in the American West. New York: Oxford University Press, 1992.

An Unsettled Country: Changing Landscapes of the American West. Albuquerque: University of New Mexico Press, 1994.

"Nature and the Disorder of History." *Environmental History Review* 18 (1994): 1–15.

NOTES

1. "The Trail to Santa Fe: The Unleashing of the Western Public Intellectual," in *Trails: Toward a New Western History*, ed. Patricia Nelson Limerick, Clyde A. Milner II, and Charles E. Rankin (Lawrence: University Press of Kansas, 1991) 59–61.

2. "Turner's First Stand," in *Writing Western History: Essays on Major Western Historians*, ed. Richard W. Etulain (Albuquerque: Univeristy of New Mexico Press, 1991) 95.

3. *Santa Cruz Sentinel*, 3 February 1991, 3.

4. "Beyond the Agrarian Myth," in *Trails* 25.

5. "The Trail to Santa Fe," in *Trails* 63–64.

6. "Beyond the Agrarian Myth," in *Trails* 15–16.

7. *It's Your Misfortune and None of My Own* xvii.

8. *New Westers: The West in Contemporary American Culture* (Lawrence: University Press of Kansas, 1996) 69.

9. *The Legacy of Conquest: The Unbroken Past of the American West* (New York: Norton, 1987) 29.

10. "Beyond the Agrarian Myth," in *Trails* 18, 21.

11. "'Are You an Environmentalist or Do You Work for a Living?': Work and Nature," in *Uncommon Ground: Toward Reinventing Nature*, ed. William Cronon (New York: Norton, 1995) 172.

12. *San Francisco Chronicle*, 16 December 1990, 5.

13. See *Phenomenology of Perception* (London: Routledge & Kegan Paul, 1962) vii–xxi, 137, 243.

14. "Trashing the Trails," in *Trails* 27.

15. "Ethics and Culture: Habermas and Gadamer in Dialogue," *Philosophy Today* 15 (1972): 159, 162.

16. *New Westers* 78.

17. "The 'New Western History,' An Assessment," in *Trails* 99.

18. *The Legacy of Conquest* 193–94 (our emphasis).

19. *The Legacy of Conquest* 199.

20. "The Trouble with Wilderness; or, Getting Back to the Wrong Nature," in *Uncommon Ground* 72, 75, 81.

21. "Beyond the Agrarian Myth," in *Trails* 7.

22. *Recollections of Wittgenstein*, ed. Rush Rhees (Oxford: Oxford University Press, 1984) 157.

23. *Writing Western History* 344–45.

24. "Beyond the Last Frontier: Toward a New Approach to Western American History," in *Trails* 146.

25. *Ezra Pound: Selected Cantos*, ed. Ezra Pound (New York: New Directions Books, 1956) 118.

26. "How the West Was Won or Lost," *The New Republic*, 22 October 1990, 37.

27. "The Western Historians: Don't Fence Them In," *The New York Times Book Review*, 20 September 1992, 25.

28. *Southwestern Historical Quarterly* 97 (1993): 377.

29. *Journal of American History* 80 (1993): 625.

30. *American History* 22 (1994): 290.

31. *American Indian Quarterly* 13 (1989): 207.

32. *American Indian Quarterly* 17 (1993): 401.

33. *Journal of the West* 32 (1993) 4. Nash makes virtually the same case at greater length in his "Comment on the New Western History," which appears in "Symposium on the New Western History," published in *Continuity: A Journal of History* 17 (1993): 1–32. The symposium also includes contributions—all of them in varying degrees critical—from Burton W. Fulsom, Jr., Martin Ridge, Gerald Thompson, and William H. Goetzmann. See also Nash's more restrained review of *The Legacy of Conquest* in *Journal of Economic History* 48 (1988): 508.

34. "The Frontier Trail: Rethinking Turner and Reimagining the American West," *American Historical Review* 98 (1993): 111–12. See also Faragher's "Gunslingers and Bureaucrats: Some Unexpected Truths about the American West," *The New Republic*, 14 December 1992, 29–36, where he faults the revisionists for their failure to meet "the needs of the present," and calls for "a genuinely new and tolerant western history that would inspire with tales of quiet triumphs rather than the noisy clamor of the wild West" (36).

35. *American History* 17 (1989): 93.

36. *Journal of Historical Geography* 17 (1991): 110.

37. "The New Western History: A Critical Analysis," *Continuity: A Journal of History* 17 (1993): 12–13.

38. *Western Historical Quarterly* 23 (1992): 224.

JEROME FRISK

The Theoretical (Re)Positions of the New Western History

THE NEW WESTERN HISTORY is now old enough to have a history. It has secured such stature (indeed, having arguably become the now dominant reading of the West) that many New Western historians have recently initiated a self-critical reassessment of the regulative metanarratives that structure the "new synthesis" they announced in 1987. The following analysis of the theoretical perspectives assumed and marshaled by the New Western historians is thus a two-part essay. The first section evaluates the founding texts of the movement, paying particular attention to Patricia Limerick's *Legacy of Conquest*, Donald Worster's seminal essay, "Beyond the Agrarian Myth," and William Cronon's *Under an Open Sky*. I argue that such narratives are determined by a "revolutionary trope" which proclaims the newness of these stories by reductively conflating the histories of their regional precursors. And perhaps more significantly, these originating proclamations function by implicitly denying the legitimacy of alternative culturally critical histories (such as those offered by Wallace Stegner) that do not conform to the tropes, rhetorics, and political subtexts of their projects. Further, in its original apotheosis the New Western histories were conspicuously marked by their disregard for postmodern theory. The second part of this essay is focused on more recent texts in which the New Western historians have begun, in compelling and often unexpectedly incisive formulations, to both address the challenges of "theory" and to propose (contemporaneously) their self-critical reviewings of their own discursive beginnings. My effort concentrates on a selection of major essays: Limerick's "Turnerians All," Cronon's "A Place for Stories," and Richard White's "Are You an Environmentalist or Do You Work for a Living?" I argue that these interventions (though sometimes oblique, deflected, and preliminary, to be sure) both confirm previous critiques of the New Western History and, of greater consequence, illumine the repositionings of these most commanding voices in contemporary western studies. But these most current self-critical moves are as yet more promising than influential or productive. The New Western historians, in spite of the clear implications of their recent reflections, seem unwilling to offer a direct critique of their own founding texts. Thus, their belated engagement with contemporary theory often seems more strategic than consequential.[1]

I. POSITIONING THE NEW WESTERN HISTORIANS

Donald Worster's *Under Western Skies: Nature and History in the American West* (1992) contains several essays that define the New Western History by dramatically distinguishing the projects of the "new" from those of the "old" historiographies. His first chapter, "Beyond the Agrarian Myth," commands special attention as a founding text of the movement. This essay was originally presented as the opening address at the 1989 Santa Fe "Trails" conference that launched the new school, and also appears in the important collection, *Trails: Toward a New Western History* (1991). In a pivotal and typically polemical passage, Worster describes the difference between the old and the new as follows:

> During the past two decades a new western history has appeared with the express purpose of confronting and understanding those radical defects of the past. This new history has tried to put the West back into the world community, with no illusions about moral uniqueness. It has also sought to restore to memory all those unsmiling aspects that Turner wanted to leave out. *As a result, we are beginning to get a history* that is beyond myth, beyond the traditional consciousness of the white conquerors, beyond a primitive emotional need of heroes and heroines, beyond any public role of justifying or legitimating what has happened. (*Trails* 16, my emphasis)

Though Worster clearly establishes a breach between previous and current histories, does he really mean to describe all earlier discourses as "justifying or legitimating" the deeds and myths of "the white conquerors"? If only "as a result" of recent efforts are we "beginning" to move beyond an imperialistic consciousness, primitive emotional needs, and ideological practice—then how do we avoid hearing the implication that all regional histories before this new beginning are to be understood in terms that describe a near pathological condition? Because the rupture between the disciplinary past and present is the very focus of Worster's seminal essay, these questions, though seldom addressed directly, deserve special attention.

Worster recognizes, of course, that there were attempts prior to the 1960s to break through the traditional forms of historiography. The essay opens with an overview of the "radical defects of the past," as illustrated in the work of Henry Nash Smith, Richard Hofstadter, Earl Pomeroy, and Gerald Nash. He argues that these, the most significant of the earlier efforts, remained caught within ideological purviews that obscure (and therefore justify) the tragic realities of the American and western past. Prior to the late 1960s we find, at best, only failed projects—successful non-ideological interpretation begins with the work of a younger generation. The only explicit qualification Worster offers refers to those old historians who have reformed themselves by "coming around" to perspectives and insights that the younger historians presumably invented. "I do not mean to say," he writes, "that this is the whole achievement of scholars under the age of fifty; on the contrary, many of that immediate postwar generation have also come around to a more pluralistic point of view" (12). Though individual historians are thus exempted, there is no suggestion here or elsewhere that previous historiography contributed to a "more pluralistic view" of the multicultural diversity of the western region.[2] Quite the contrary.

As Worster's influential account continues, it becomes more explicitly an ideological analysis of disciplinary history and indeed, it is *as* an ideological analysis that the New Western History is defined.

> Perhaps the single most important *most distinguishing characteristic* of the new western history is its determination not to offer cover for the powers that be—not to become subservient to them, by silence or consent. A rising generation of historians insists that it is their responsibility to stand apart from power and think critically about it, as it is to think critically about

> western society as a whole, about its ideas and drives, about the contradictions it has created, about its prospects for new identities, goals and values. (15–16, my emphasis)

This trumpeting of a new moral and political stance defines the decisive attributes of this Great Awakening by postulating a radical distinction between this new critical posture and all that came before it. If distance from and resistance to "powering" is the "most distinguished characteristic" of a "rising generation of historians," then it seems precisely in terms of subservience "to the powers that be" that the old history is to be distinguished from the new. Worster, indeed, articulates an unabashed contempt for his precursors that is only matched by his seemingly untroubled and unreflected glorification of the righteousness of his comrades. It is hard not to hear biblical or theological resonances (or what Bercovitch calls "jeremiads") in the sense and rhetorical structure of the key passages of this founding essay.

> When historians fail to see themselves as critical intellectuals, as I believe historians of the West have done, they become ideological in the most dangerous sense: they become prisoners of ideology rather than masters of it. The new western history insists that scholars must perform deliberately and thoughtfully the role of cultural analyst, even to the point of presuming now and then to be a self-appointed moral conscience of their society. (16–17)

Most would agree with Worster that historical scholarship ought to be a morally responsible analysis of culture and that some previous historians, not always assuming such distance and perspective, produced interpretations that may well be called "ideological." But what is striking in Worster's statement is the absence of qualifying terms like "many" or "some" or "have not always." While commentators tend, so to speak, to insert such modifications into passages that do not have them, it may be that this very absence of qualification directly expresses the crucial sense these descriptions of the newness of the "new."[3]

While not as virulent as Worster's all but Gnostic bifurcation between the dark past and the enlightened present, Limerick's accounts are also structured by a polemical juxtaposition between the Old and the New Western Histories. Like his, her stories are regulated by a rhetorical figuration, a revolutionary trope, that marshals the compelling if well-worn metaphors of bondage, resistance, and liberation. In *The Legacy of Conquest: The Unbroken Past of the American West* (1987), often regarded as the most influential text in the New Western History, Patricia Limerick offers her version of the breach between past and present, the revolutionary event that marks the advent of the new in regional studies:

> The rigidity of the Turner Thesis left it particularly vulnerable to a great expansion of scholarship, accelerating in the 1960s and afterward. Individual historians simply set aside the Thesis and studied particular Western places, peoples, and events. The diversity and complexity those studies revealed . . . represented *an intellectual revolution*. . . . Few of the findings fit the Turnerian conceptual model. Thus a central irony: the very vitality of Western research, by exploding the model, made mainstream historians declare that the field was dead. . . . The breakdown of the old organizing idea fostered chaos; the corral built to contain Western history had been knocked apart. (22, my emphasis)

When the story is told in these familiar terms, it seems easier to hear the good news of the freedom and vitality than to see the extent of what is being portrayed as "the corral built to contain Western history." Critics like Alan Brinkley miss the full referent of such passages by noting that "central to almost all descriptions of the new history is an obligatory, almost ritualistic repudiation of Frederick Jackson Turner."[4] What is at issue here has less to do with Turner himself and more to do with an inclusive depiction of all previous western historians. A half-century of readings of the West, with no exceptions worthy of note, are described here as capitulations to the "old organizing idea." "Turner" is an allegorical trope for all pre-1960s readers of the West—the "Thesis" is a synecdoche for the Text of the West prior to this "intellectual revolution." As such, the textual landscapes these "origin stories" describe are only ostensibly restricted to the professional activities of academic history departments.

In a later essay, Limerick describes the ideological legacy of Old Western historians by focusing on "words" that are certainly also prevalent in literary, ethnographic, political, and popular discourses.

> Western historians inherit a long and sometimes embarrassing legacy from predecessors who did not keep a critical distance between themselves and the pioneers; this earlier breed of western historians adopted the terms, the point of view, and the assumptions of the people they studied. Their dependence on words like "civilization," "savagery," "frontier," and "progress" left western historians echoing, not analyzing, the thinking of Anglo-American colonizers.[5]

Presumably, these "words" are but examples; the list could be extended a good deal further, if not indefinitely. It also seems hard to avoid the conclusion that any textual "dependence on words like" these would locate the text, regardless of departmental or genre distinctions, within this ideological legacy. Further, when this passage is read as written, we once again find no suggestion that this summation applies to some, but not all, of that "earlier breed of western historians." Limerick avoids words or phrases that would even imply a difference (that makes a difference) between the western histories of Francis Parkman and Hubert Howe Bancroft, between the geographical perspectives of Herbert Eugene Bolton or Josiah Royce and Frederic Paxson, or between the sociopolitical commitments of Ray Allen Billington and Carey McWilliams or Bernard DeVoto. In spite of her recent objections, such passages construe the past as an unbroken and uncontested totality—as an uninterrupted and monological consensus.[6] It appears fair to say that the phrases Limerick used for the title to her seminal study, "legacy of conquest: the unbroken past of the American West," are coterminous with her depictions of the "long legacy" she has inherited from her "predecessors." Critics and defenders of the New Western History have certainly noted the polemical edge to this most prominent version of the movement, but their commentaries often obscure the theoretical or hermeneutical dimensions of these resolute rejections of prior histories. Otherwise said, while these historians insist on the newness of the New Western History, most assessments of the movement respond to this claim but do not take it very seriously.

Richard Bernstein and others do not engage methodological configurations when they object that previous western historians had "already subjected Turner to merciless and unfavorable scrutiny," long before the new historians rode into town.[7] Such protests imply that what is at issue here falls between academic bad manners and a distortion of the historical record. But since Worster and Limerick seem well aware of these previous criticisms of Turner, we ought rather to ask how and why some describe as "ideological subservience" what others read as "merciless and unfavorable scrutiny." Critical reviewers like Larry McMurtry also avoid such questions by taking the New Western historians to task for seeing only the tragic side of the western past, and speaking as if this "negativity" is the result of a sort of shared personality trait.[8] Though temperaments may be at play, it seems that these new interpretations have not ignored the "positive side" of the story McMurtry wants told, but rather have configured these elements within their tragic narratives as part and parcel of them. It is not so much a matter of looking at some events and not others, it seems to me, as it is a question of seeing the same events from a quite different perspective.[9] In seeking to access the regulative structures of this angle of vision, Gerald Nash points in a more useful direction. In *Creating the West* (1991), Nash concludes that Limerick's "disdain for previous interpretations" is "in part a result of New Left ideology" and in part a reflection of the historically located interests "of her own generation."[10] It is not news, of course, that Limerick and Worster stand to the Left of some Center on the conventional spectrum of political persuasions. But since this distinguishes them not much at all from their colleagues, such a mere labeling only deflects what might prove a more helpful question: with which of the contending new leftist ideologies is the New Western History, on Worster's or Limerick's account, most consistent?

Many would contest the view (which Limerick shares with Nash) that the '60s generation was forged by some common experience, and warped and woofed into a programmatic consensus of evaluative priorities and analytical strategies. Contemporary scholars generally agree that intertextual practices should be culturally critical and sociopolitically relevant, but it seems evident that there are at least two contending versions of how this professional activity should properly and most effectively engage the discursive past. Whereas most contemporary ways of reading, to be sure, appropriate strategies from both basic perspectives, we seldom have to wait until the second foot falls to see which one of the two is the regulating mode of interpretation. Some approaches, foregrounding post-structuralist procedures, stress the destabilizing and subversive elements within texts and, more generally, the contesting voices within what others have called "the tradition." Different interpretations, deploying the strategies of neo-Marxist ideological analysis, emphasize the ways in which texts neutralize any such oppositional intrusions and thus reinforce (rather than resist) the dominating mechanisms of the hegemonic apparatus of the capitalist system. According to this latter paradigm (as most influentially formulated, perhaps, by Sacvan Bercovitch and Fredric Jameson), legitimate textual subversion begins with recent neo-Marxist expositions of the ideological co-optation of all other and all previous discourses. As Forrest Robinson succinctly puts it, "For the New Americanists of Bercovitch's persuasion . . . resistance is a recent supplement to our ideology, and it is the possession of a select, correct few."[11] Worster and Limerick's analogous structuring of a radical break between the present and the past, their view of legitimate resistance as only "a recent supplement to our ideology," locates their New Western histories on the Bercovitch wing of the New Americanism. This is not to suggest that Worster and Limerick subscribe to one of several neo-Marxist modes of ideological analysis, but is rather to observe that in certain regards their postulations parallel and complement this side of the contested (left) field.[12]

In certain regards, Wallace Stegner has provided the prototypical version of what Bercovitch calls a "positive form of ideological analysis"—a culturally critical retelling of western history (markedly to the "left" of traditional versions) that stresses the contesting voices and heterodox countercurrents (432). Academic historians, with the notable exception of Richard Etulain, have not had much to say of his amateur contributions to their discipline. His biography of John Wesley Powell, *Beyond the Hundredth Meridian* (1954), is certainly an exception in this regard, and recognition of it has quite dramatically increased in recent years. But a glance at his corpus shows that the "Powell book" is but one of many, and may be regarded as a segment of an extensive historicizing of the western region. Before and after it stand his two Utah histories, *Mormon Country* (1942) and *The Gathering of Zion: The Story of the Mormon Trail* (1964), and his biography of Bernard DeVoto, *The Uneasy Chair* (1974). Further, historical narratives compose substantial portions of the essays collected in such texts as *All the Little Live Things* (1967), *The Sound of Mountain Water* (1969), *American Places* (1981), *The American West as Living Space* (1987), and most recently, *Where the*

Bluebird Sings to the Lemonade Springs (1992). To this list could be added much of *Wolf Willow* (1962), and of such historical fictions as *Joe Hill: A Biographical Novel* (1950, 1969) and *Angle of Repose* (1971)—as well as Etulain's *Conversations with Wallace Stegner on Western History and Literature* (1983, 1990), and a scattered expanse of yet to be collected articles, interviews, and prefaces. The contemporary academic movement toward cultural analysis, the rejection of conventional and arbitrary distinctions between literary and historical discourses, encourages such a reconfiguration of Stegner's texts. In short, a strong case can be made for regarding Wallace Stegner as a regional cultural historian, who also wrote some splendid literary texts.[13]

Though episodic and stylistically diffused, Stegner's histories form an internally consistent corpus that is far from fragmentary in the expansive continuity it eventually achieves. His historical studies may be read as chapters in a single narrative of an enduring legacy in the West—as confluent eddies in a regional countercurrent of radical revisioning, resistance, and rebellion. In perhaps his most significant western histories, Stegner inscribes a direct continuity between Bernard DeVoto's and John Wesley Powell's work which locates both within a "larger context of events" that reaches back to the communitarian utopianism of the Mormon heterodoxy, and that is confluent with the radical rebellions of the Wobblies as well as the Populists.[14] His biographies reveal, finally, an anti-traditional tradition that finds its most enduring and fundamental form in the long history of the American conservation-environmental movement. In his "Capsule History of Conservation," Stegner will eventually write that this swerve from traditional values was already powerful in Cooper's early nineteenth-century Westerns, and has American roots that run much deeper. "What we are working towards," he writes, "is an outlook that was frequently and sometimes eloquently expressed by the first inhabitants of this continent" (118). Stegner's regional histories, then, are illustrative episodes in a counter-discourse of mutually sustaining struggles to elucidate this revisionary outlook. By telling these stories, Stegner insists we remember that "what we are working towards" is but the contemporary manifestation of a heritage in which we, regardless of our conceits, are but the most recent participants. A few years before his death, he writes:

> Values, both those that we approve and those we don't, have roots as deep as creosote rings, and live as long, and grow as slowly. Every action is an idea before it is an action, and perhaps a feeling before an idea, and every idea rests upon other ideas that have preceded it in time. . . .
>
> *Yes, there was an environmental movement before Earth Day, a long, slow revolution in values of which contemporary environmentalism is a consequence and a continuation.* We are still in transition from the notion of man as master of the earth to the notion of man as a part of it. (117, my emphasis)

I vividly recall my own participation, as an undergraduate in the far West, in that first Earth Day in the spring of 1970. I have no doubt that we, of the now graying "younger generation," once subscribed wholeheartedly to a Worster/Limerick notion of a revolutionary breach between our own projects and those of our precursors. Stegner's essay is explicitly addressed to those among this generation who persist in their initial proclamations of newness—who, for whatever tangle of reasons, refuse to recognize their recent activity as "a consequence and a continuation" of other ideas and actions that have "preceded it in time."

Presenting Stegner's non-fictions as an alternative to the Worster/Limerick approach, underscores the point that Stegner's histories are every bit as culturally critical and politically engaged as are the recent texts of the New Western History. Worster and Limerick, to the contrary, have loudly insisted that one must either side "for them" or "against them" and that there are no viable or coherent alternatives to their "new synthesis." They claim we have but two choices: we must either remain subservient to the reactionary postulates of the old history, or must subscribe to a wholesale rejection of previous interpretations. Stegner's work demonstrates the viability of a third way or a middle trail. His way of reading salvages a useful past through a critical analysis that does not succumb to mystification. It selectively valorizes earlier textual and political protests and uses them to oppose, not sustain, the mythic and ideological forces of the "powers that be." Because they deny the existence of demythologizing discourses prior to the revolutions of the 1960s, Worster and Limerick are obliged to regard Stegner's sustained effort as but another of the befuddled attempts that remain bound by the ideological structures of the western and the

American past. In rejecting the possibility of a third way that is neither the old history nor their form of the new history, these current historians, we might say, have arbitrarily reduced the tropological possibilities that plot various discursive formations. Worster and Limerick present their tragic narrative of relentless conquest as the sole legitimate response to the traditional comic story of "triumphal procession." But it is generally agreed, of course, that there are more than two ways to tell stories about the past. If, following Hayden White, we understand irony as a "master trope" that works through "ironic reflection on the inadequacy of the characterization with respect to *the elements which resist inclusion* in the hypotactically ordered totality," then Stegner has responded to conventional comedy with an ironic alternative.[15] Whereas the Turnerian histories storied a grand synthesis, Stegner's rewriting is an ironic swerve that features "a representation of whatever contrasts or oppositions can legitimately be discerned in the totalities."[16] A recognition of Stegner's approach, as an ironic alternative or as understood in other terms, has consequences that extend well beyond whatever boundaries remain between historical and literary studies. Indeed, the opposition between the Worster/Limerick and the Stegner approach is analogous to the analytical options that have come to the fore in recent literary and cultural studies.[17]

Sacvan Bercovitch, though himself a staunch advocate of a particular mode of ideological analysis, acknowledges the significance of another method. In an overview of the essays in *Ideology and Classic American Literature* (1986), he identifies two basic forms of cultural criticism in the New American Studies. Some contemporary readers adopt a "positive mode of ideological analysis" that foregrounds the utopian and subversive dimensions of a text or corpus; other Americanists practice a "negative mode of ideological analysis," which views the literary discourse as the product or producer of the dominating controls of capitalist society (424–32). This rendition of contemporary literary debates functions surprisingly well as a description of the difference between Stegner's recovery of the anti-traditional protests that Powell and DeVoto fostered, and the Worster/Limerick subscription to a "negative mode" of ideological analysis that conflates the text and the repressive tradition that produced it. Bercovitch's graphing of the New Americanism is also strikingly parallel to Louis Montrose's account of a binary contestation within the New Historicism.

Montrose finds that there is no "systematic and authoritative paradigm for interpretation" in the New Historicism; but rather, "on one side are those who emphasize the possibilities for effective *contestation* or *subversion* of the dominant ideology," while "on the other side are those who emphasize the hegemonic capacity of the . . . state . . . to *contain* apparently subversive gestures, or even to *produce* them in order to contain them."[18] In these terms, similarly, Stegner's work is analogous to those new historicisms that "emphasize the possibilities for effective contestation," whereas the Worster/Limerick approach is clearly of a piece with the view that all "apparently subversive gestures" (failed attempts to challenge the Turner thesis) are effectively "contained" and neutralized by the ideological manipulations and "hegemonic capacity" of the "powers that be." Stephen Greenblatt's position, quite similar to my own, appears regulated by the judgment that this duality within the New Historicism (this lack of a "systematic and authoritative paradigm") is not a problem to be solved but is rather a desired and necessary condition. We neither can nor should formulate a "new synthesis," he seems to say, because the textual and cultural practices we engage are themselves ineluctably incoherent. In his well-known essay, "Towards a Poetic of Culture," he argues that the neo-Marxist analytics of Jameson and the post-structuralist interventions of Lyotard are both severely limited.[19] They see different sides or productions of the capitalist system, but neither offers a plausible account of the contradictory historical consequences that modern capitalism has somehow created. Thus the New Historicism should stubbornly refuse the either/or choice between these contending perspectives, and ought rather to keep both eyes open by persistently preserving the dialogical encounter of the both/and. It is such incommensurate historical realities, "cultural contradictions," that may be seen and analyzed when Stegner's approach is positioned as a necessary supplement to the Worster/Limerick paradigm in regional studies.[20]

A dualistic New Western History (refusing the compulsion for an authoritative paradigm) would facilitate exchanges with such discourses as those of the New Americanism and the New Historicism, but would not be without disruptive consequences. Contacts with neighboring disciplines would suggest, first of all and significantly, how the initial self-presentation of the New Western History remains framed by a conventional and increasingly irrelevant partisan polarity. The alternative "paradigms for interpretation" or "modes of ideological analysis" that Montrose and Bercovitch describe have nothing at all to do with traditional oppositions between the old/traditional/Right and the new/progressive/Left. As I have argued in regard to the Worster/Limerick and the Stegner models, these are different ways for teaching and rewriting the past in a sociopolitically committed manner. Both ways of reading share a similar vision of the future as it ought to be, but disagree on the means (discursive and pedagogical) through which this common end is most effectively attained. These two approaches become most useful, it seems, when they regard their dialogical encounter itself as the privileged site for the production of culturally critical meaning. Though formulated in other terms, similar debates have stimulated the New Western History from its origins. Only recently, however, have these bifurcations become a more conspicuous and public characteristic of the movement. The New Western History, that is, is starting to look more like the New Americanism and the New Historicism. There are now currents moving toward, as Bakhtin would have it, a more "dialogic" and less "monologic" mode of historicizing.[21] Otherwise said, there is a tilting toward Stegner, and a recognition, even in Limerick's recent work, of the contesting voices of the regional past.

The New Western History became a good deal more contested with the publication of *Under an Open Sky: Rethinking America's Western Past* (1992). This collection of essays is both a *Festschrift* for Howard Lamar and a forceful though implicit response of the Cronon wing to the revolutionary tropes of the Worster/Limerick formulation of the New Western History. Of particular import is the introductory essay, "Becoming West," authored by William Cronon, George Miles, and Jay Gitlin. The subtitle for this major position statement is no doubt carefully chosen: not "Towards a New Western History," the subtitle of the *Trails* anthology, but "Towards a New Meaning for Western History." As this reversal of terms suggests, the editors neither identify themselves as "New Western historians" nor do they explicitly mention the existence of such a school or movement in their summary chapter. In spite of their self-censoring, this article provides a rebuttal and an alternative to the more publicized manifestos of the New Western History. Underscoring the disparity between their approach and that of Worster and Limerick, the editors unabashedly reaffirm their commitments to a reconstituted form of the Turner Thesis:

> Turner's greatest achievement in defining western history as he did was to center the field not on a single region but on many regions undergoing parallel historical change. . . . Explaining how regional differences like these could emerge from common frontier processes is the key task of western history. (6–7)

They go on to summarize their six-stage schema through which a "frontier" becomes a "region," stressing different modes of regional "self-fashioning" and their ability to illumine the processes "whereby divisions of gender, class, and ethnicity reproduce themselves on the North American landscape" (22). In direct contradiction to the assertions of the "regionalist" New Western historians, this essay argues that a reconstructed form of the "frontier thesis" is fully capable of functioning as a critical ideological analysis that addresses our current concerns. Further (and as opposed to the geographical restrictions of the "regionalist" paradigm), a reformulated frontier thesis allows us to read the American West "as a chapter in the much larger story of European colonialism" (9). The hermeneutical schema the editors sketch radically rejects nationalistic notions of the uniqueness of the American "experience" and, in doing so, responds to contemporary global studies:

> Frontier areas . . . existed on the outer colonial edge of Old World empires. This suggests one important way of defining frontier settlements: as peripheries whose dependence on imperial metropoles helped define local society. Perennially short of labor and capital, frontier economies were usually extractive, transferring non industrial resources to more populous areas near the center of empire. (10)

Such a reading of the West, confluent as it is with the work of Immanuel Wallerstein and Eric Wolf, is a far cry indeed from the traditionalism of previous formulations of the frontier thesis. Therein lies the point.

The Limerick/Worster position is all but predicated upon the unqualified judgment that the New Western History does not begin until any and every version of the frontier thesis is rejected. Limerick formulated a hard-edged opposition between a frontier and a regional approach to the West, as a crucial if not decisive element in the New Western History. The proclamation that launched the movement (the

Santa Fe "not a manifesto") begins with the sentence: "New Western Historians define 'the West' primarily as a *place*—the trans-Mississippi *region* in the broadest terms, or the *region* west of the hundredth meridian" (my emphasis).[22] On this view, the very concept of a "frontier," even the very word itself, is saturated by and complicit with the imperialism, colonialism, and the various modes of conquest. As Limerick's position paper continues, "New Western Historians reject the old term 'frontier' for that process. When clearly and precisely defined, the term 'frontier' is nationalistic and often racist (in essence, the area where white people are scarce); when cleared of its ethnocentrism, the term loses meaning" (85). Cronon, Miles, and Gitlin speak sharply to this polemical formulation when they write, "Despite what some scholars seem to believe, it is no easier to define a region than a frontier, and we have no interest in pursuing what long ago became a sterile debate about the relative merits of frontier versus regional history. We have already argued that the two are in fact inextricably entangled with each other and that each is best understood when seen in the light of the other" (23). It is hard to agree that this is really a "sterile debate." The editors mean, it seems to me, that the terms in which Limerick and Worster have constructed the discussion between frontier and regional approaches—as incommensurate and mutually exclusive options—are arbitrary, if not analytically incoherent.

It is unfortunate, however, that the editors of *Under an Open Sky* do not mention Worster and Limerick by name. Having "no interest in pursuing" the debate with "some scholars," Cronon et al. lost the chance to bring the debate into the open, and to establish a public dialogue that would flesh out the differences and identities between these now-contending geo-graphics. Perhaps most significantly, the "frontier" new historians have obliged the "regionalists" to reformulate their condemnations of the frontier thesis in terms that are relevant to their contemporary colleagues. It is time to discontinue the really "sterile debate," the one the new regionalists stage against an allegorical Father—the parading of a "strawman," and the beating of a quite "dead horse." Regardless of the merits and consequences of the frontier versus regional debate itself, what is at issue here for my purposes is a fundamental disagreement over two different modes of engaging the discourses of previous western historians.[23] The Cronon wing of the New Western History, like Stegner, has appropriated the useful elements of earlier interpretations and rendered them relevant to their culturally critical interventions on the contemporary terrain. As the appearance of Limerick's *Legacy of Conquest* and Worster's *Rivers of Empire* in the mid-1980s defined the initial debates surrounding the New Western History, so *Under an Open Sky* initiated a shift in the dialogical center of gravity toward a more Stegnerian hermeneutic. A similar shift began to emerge in Limerick's work in the years following the Trails conference of 1989.

In *Legacy of Conquest*, in what may be seen as an instance of the "anxiety of influence" or "belatedness," Patricia Limerick has nothing at all to say of Henry Nash Smith.[24] It is as if *Virgin Land* (1950) had not been written and as if, for that matter, there was no such thing as American Studies. In a more recent article, "Making the Most of Words," Limerick writes of rereading and rediscovering a text she apparently has not engaged since her graduate studies some twenty years ago. In reference to the breakdown of the "Turner thesis" she now recognizes that,

> In these regards all roads lead back to *Virgin Land* and the American Studies approach it represented. Indeed *Virgin Land* may well be the essential founding book for American studies. It is, therefore, a fact full of consequence for the whole field of American Studies and cultural interpretation that *Virgin Land* is about the American West.[25]

In spite of the "weaknesses" this seminal text "passed on to both American Studies and western American history . . . Henry Nash Smith steered us towards the right goals, towards topics of lasting significance" (174). This sounds like a significantly altered version of her story—not unlike a "metaleptic retrieval" of a once repressed precursor. I do not mean to suggest that Limerick has laid down her guns or fundamentally altered her metahistorical narrative. It is hard not to read this, however, as a swerve toward a less agonistic response to her predecessors. "One must reread *Virgin Land*," she now writes, so that we may "rediscover" the contributions of its analysis of myth and symbol in the American West, we must "press on with the kind of inquiry Smith began" (173–75). The New Western History may well find that *Virgin Land* is more a representative than an exceptional text, and rediscover that more than a few others have been pressing on with Smith's "kind of inquiry" for the last half century. American Studies has been a critical analysis of American ideology that, however we assess it, has focused attention on imaginary (mythic/ideological) constructions of the very western regions where the New Western historians are now working.[26] An intertextual encounter of this sort, a renewed encounter with the textual past, encouraged the shifts that are now moving the New Western History in a more self-critical direction and toward the "Cronon side" of its own internal tensions.

II. REPOSITIONING THE NEW WESTERN HISTORIANS

It is understandable that few commentators on the New Western History have noted the significance of Limerick's reassessment of Henry Nash Smith in "Making the Most of Words." While statements like, "one must reread *Virgin Land* and rediscover that Smith is not, in fact, the culprit" seem to resonate with autobiographical inflection, the self-critical dimension of this belated (re)discovery of a significant precursor remains muted. Her recent high-profile essay, "Turnerians All" (1995), is a markedly more salient critique of her previous work. Though troubled and sometimes baffling to be sure, her paper appears to announce a fundamental turn in her thinking and propose a multidimensional challenge to the metanarrative structures of the "new synthesis" propounded by the founding texts of the New Western History. The critical passages and the regulative metaphor of "Turnerians All" are found in the middle of this arresting essay. In the previous thirteen pages Limerick argues that Frederick Jackson Turner was not only the initial critic of the Frontier Thesis, but that he indeed also formulated (in scattered publications) what Limerick calls a "Frontier Antithesis" that acknowledged the rise of industrial capitalism he otherwise and elsewhere ignored. After an astute analysis of the psychological, professional, and theoretical structures that prevented Turner from fully developing and publicly articulating his self-critical antithesis, Limerick describes how her own once confident view of the intelligibility of the present was analogously disrupted by the political events of the 1990s:

> Along with disappointment, however, came relief, and a kind of relief that Turner may not have permitted himself to feel. *When I contemplated my failure to figure out the present*, I began to wonder how I had ever fallen into the belief that such an achievement was within my reach, or within my job descrip-

> tion. And happily, as disorientation with the present increased, enthusiasm for studying the past grew proportionately. Compared to the inscrutable present, the past was an open book.
>
> *Disillusionment with presentism had the happy side effect of restoring a recognition contingency and improbability to my understanding of history. When I thought I was tracing a direct, clear line between past and present, an unhealthy fatalism crept into my thinking. Event followed event with all the drama and surprise, and spontaneity of the prearranged program of the Rose Parade.* Losing control of the pattern of present events thus offered its own form of liberation; it was as if the floats of that regimented parade suddenly started taking inexplicable right, left, and U-turns, with the General Electric float suddenly slamming into the California Fruit-Growers entry, filling the air with a rainbow of chrysanthemums and marigolds and giving the poor commentators something, at long last, to comment on. History became correspondingly more interesting as it became more chaotic. (710, my emphasis)

The text Limerick refers to here (the book in which she traces "a direct, clear line between past and present," and in which "event follows event" in a "prearranged," programmatic, and determined manner), is of course her *Legacy of Conquest* (1987). With incisive descriptions and vivid metaphorical analogy, Limerick shows herself to have become her own best critic. In likening her previous "understanding of history" to "the prearranged program of a Rose Parade," she both describes the metanarrative structure of her book and reconfigures (in a metonymic parody) its subtitle ("The Unbroken Past of the American West") in all its now admittedly absurd resonances.

Limerick, however, gives no indication here (or elsewhere in the essay) that the sustained critical commentaries of her colleagues (Richard Etulain, Michael Malone, Gerald Nash, et al.) have substantially influenced this emergent recognition of a more differentiated, complex, and elusive history of the American West. Following these pointedly self-critical paragraphs, it is not toward her critics and contemporaries but back to Turner that Limerick immediately turns. The subsequent accounts of "Turner's struggles" are analogous to "Limerick's struggles" as initially described above; and she is thus also speaking of herself (and implicitly of other new western historians) when she says of Turner:

> Turner . . . wanted to establish some control over the past. He wanted to persuade the disorderly events and people of history to submit to some kind of order. The agents and devices he used to produce that order were those reified and nearly animate concepts . . . and processes that could translate the chaos of history into patterns of clarity and manageability. (710)

As terms like "order," "chaos," and "clarity" echo those she used in describing her own previous synthesis, so she also reinscribes the very regulative metaphor (the parade) she used at the rhetorical fulcrum of her essay: "Despite his ritual declarations of tentativeness and modesty in his essays, his heart clearly melted when in the company of a rhetorically convincing generalization, with abstractions and evidence marching together in a pleasant and ordered parade toward the present" (710). Though she explicitly identifies Turner's thesis with the antithesis she offered in *Legacy of Conquest* (both describing an "ordered parade toward the present"), and though it is clearly her "heart" as well as his that "melted when in the company of a rhetorically convincing generalization"—Limerick continues on in an ostensible analysis of Turner that persistently alludes to a Limerick/Turner identity that is not, even now, fully articulated as such.

As she rejected her previous understanding of history for lacking "drama, surprise, and spontaneity," so she says of Turner that, "success in this venture, though, carried a great price: the more effectively Turner identified and arranged the determinants of history, the more he sacrificed drama, as well as realism. The complexity of historical evidence was silenced and squeezed in order to fit into the tight categories Turner built for it" (710–11). A few sentences later the paragraph concludes with a sentence that is yet again and quite literally a gloss on the self-depiction she offered on the previous page: "And when this parade . . . picked itself up and reappeared to march, in identical order, through the South Pass in Wyoming, a large share of the contingency, improbability and interest of historical change seemed to have been surrendered" (711). By another repetition of the key terms and metaphors she used above to reject her own founding thesis (the "contingency," "improbability," and "interest" that is lost when history is viewed/constructed as a "parade")—the transgenerational horizons of her analysis come into better focus. We begin to see that these repeated terms and metaphors refer to the work of both old and new American historians, and that Limerick really means what she says when she titles her essay, "Turnerians *ALL*" (my emphasis).

Turner's recalcitrant commitment to the deterministic metanarrative of the Frontier Thesis was in crucial part the consequence of what Limerick calls a "faith in presentism"—and it is this conviction, and its congruent mode of interpretation, that unites the New Western historians to their much maligned precursor. Limerick defines "presentism" as follows:

> One could, the theory went, get a grasp on the fundamental patterns of ones own times. . . . In examining the events of ones time, one applied the same kind of pattern-finding to the present that one applied to the past; and, when one had identified the outcome, or the past's product, one was in a much improved position to trace and understand the whole story, primarily because one could now identify the path of significant change, distinguishing the consequential events from the inconsequential. *It was as clear and linear a matter as if the movement from the past to the present were a railroad track.* Once one had identified and inspected the point of arrival, it was an easy matter to follow the track back to its origin. (704, my emphasis)

Here, as throughout the essay, Limerick has coined the term "presentism" to refer to a conventional mode of analysis that others have called "the metaphysics of presence," "logocentrism," "instrumental reason," "essentialism," "foundationalism," "metanarrative," and so on. "Turnerians All" may be read as a post-structuralist or post-modernist critique of the "scientism" and "determinism" that unites (into an "all") the hermeneutical projects of the Old and the New Western historians. But it is a critique (however forceful, effervescent, and consequential it may be or become) which seems compromised and deflated by Limerick's unwillingness or inability to acknowledge her debt to "theory." However indirect her engagement with academic postmodernism may be, her critique of "presentism" is very much a recapitulation of contemporary theory—and her failure to locate her most recent reflections on this landscape does little service to the persuasiveness of her mea culpa. While Limerick is certainly not obligated to follow Cronon's lead and respond directly to the challenge of postmodern theory, it seems that the very sense of her essay (as an attempt to candidly describe the events of the present that disrupted her previous formulations) requires at least an acknowledgment of the pervasive theoretical movements that explicitly direct their subversive force toward traditional historical constructs that assume, as Limerick writes, "it was as clear and linear a matter as if the movement from the past to the present were a railroad track." Nevertheless, as the essay continues her commentary on Turner becomes more deeply perceptive, and it becomes increasingly evident that "Turnerians All" is an ambitious effort to assess the conditions and failures of her generation of western American historians.

In what could well be considered a statement of the subtextual purpose of her paper as a whole, she writes, "the point is to learn from his example and to use it as an occasion to ask ourselves, 'What are *our* blind spots? What are the elements of our social identity that limit our vision as sternly as racial assumptions limited Turner's vision?'" (715, her emphasis). Were it not by now such a commonplace as to have become all but a definitive trope of postmodern academic writing (this call for self-critical assessments that neither begins its own project nor offers any explicit indication of the direction in which we/they should proceed), one could well protest that Limerick has undermined the credibility of her critique of Turner. Turner has been chastised for not saying what he really thinks, for seeing his own "blind spots" but not having the courage to publicly articulate what he has seen. Though Limerick insists that we must do better and do otherwise, that historians must engage "the project" of "self-understanding and self-disclosure," she remains silent at precisely that point where one would think she would be most inclined or obliged to speak. How can it be that she has no substantive reflections that address her own crucial question, "what are the elements of social identity that limit our vision?" If she is certain that she herself and her compatriots of the '60s generation do indeed have significant "blind spots," then how can it be that she has no lamp to hold that would illumine these prejudices, myopics, and perspectival confusions? But as an autobiographical reflection that dances and shimmers between moments of concealment and revelation, it may well be that Limerick, however suggestively, has indeed done much to illumine the "elements of social identity that limit our vision."

The "social identity" and thus the "blind spots" to which Limerick gestures can only refer to American academics of a particular generation who were decisively influenced by the "official codes" that regulated their historically located and politically over-determined era. Though Limerick does not say so directly, the following is surely a cursory account of the "social identity" to which she alludes:

> By the time I entered graduate school in 1972, the historian's right to a faith in progress was greatly, and appropriately, constricted. . . . In the graduate schools of the late twentieth century, the phrase "Whiggish history" was in common usage, deployed to indicate that the speaker or writer was too well trained to believe in the old fantasy of progress, too sophisticated to believe in a world in which the transition from past to present was a transition of improvement. . . . Just beneath the surface of those declarations of cynicism (and in some ways protected and insulated by the official code of cynicism) was a faith that matched that of Frederick Jackson Turner. By this faith, historians could be useful, and useful in a way that might actually help to produce progress. (713)

In the American academic community, in other words, the official code of public and discursive conduct (the ideological agreed-upon to which one would either subscribe or endure the consequences) urged all to propagate a critical, dissuasive, and cynical view of claims that meaningful progress was discernible in the story of American history. Affirmations of the past were condemned as "Whiggish," politically conservative, and reactionary perspectives. To engage the past (to write history) in any other manner was not only to associate oneself with reactionary politics, but was also to render one's professional training and intellectual sophistication suspect.

As Turner encouraged historians to address present problems so that "history may hold the lamp to conservative reform," so Limerick acknowledges that "I myself, along with many of my contemporaries, would have to 'hold the lamp' for somewhat less cautious reform, but we certainly had no objection to the notion that historical understanding might lead to wiser and more benevolent action in our time" (714).

The point, however, ought not to be that the true believers of Limerick's generation merely "had no objection" to the regulative Turnerian assumptions (that historical trajectories can become translucent and that substantial change can be fostered by such historical knowledge). The situation seems rather, as Limerick implies, that the faith of the '60s generation in both their analytical abilities and in the possibilities of sociopolitical change was indeed far greater (and correspondingly less self-critical) than that of their precursors. In a significant sense, then, the young anti-Turnerians were more Turnerian than the Turnerians. While posturing themselves as radicals and rebels, they were really or also conservative (even reactionary) in their intensified reinscription of two fundamental propositions: (1) a near scientistic or deterministic belief that historical patterns and events were knowable, and (2) an all but theological faith in the possibility of profound changes (even eschatological and utopian visions) in the near future. If so, then the academic metahistory a generation of American historians have told to themselves about themselves stands in need of a rather thorough-going revisionary retelling.

But Limerick, at least publicly, is not particularly troubled with the theoretical confusions of her generation. She is more deeply affected by the pedagogical, practical, and political disruptions of the present, and how, specifically, the 1994 elections have altered the credibility, relevance, and usefulness of the academic strategies and agendas of her colleagues. As the official codes of the institutional "disciplinary apparatus" required the young scholar to regard previous notions of progress as ideological mystifications, and rewarded those who were most able to expose the "Whiggishness" of "the old fantasy of progress," so too a near-religious faith in the utopian possibilities of a non-capitalist future was taken to provide a viable and effective political alternative. Though this was certainly "a faith that matched that of Frederick Jackson Turner," it was also a "faith" that greatly exceeded his notions of realistic expectations and his preferences for gradual rather than revolutionary transformations. The "faith" in question for Limerick and her colleagues was the conviction that a more fundamental and even revolutionary transformation was both possible and desirable. This particular mode of "presentism" has been so "betrayed by the present" that those who wish to remain (or become) what Limerick calls "public intellectuals" must explore and fashion different views, mark new trails, and learn to tell other stories. They must do so, that is, if they wish to work effectively and to begin to actualize what Limerick nicely calls, in her subtitle to "Turnerians All," the "Dream of a Helpful History."

By acknowledging precursors like Hofstadter, Smith, and Turner himself, Limerick has illumined and creatively reformulated a central element of the "blind spot" of her social identity as a New Left American historian, and has done much to challenge the "official code" that obligated scholars of her generation to assume a cynical posture toward the "fantasies" of the past. Yet "Turnerians All" is itself not unlike the sort of carnivalesque swerving and dissociations of Limerick's new perspective on the Rose parade of western history. For whatever profusion of motives, Limerick has identified the Old and ostensibly New Western History in an extraordinarily lucid and incisively critical manner—she has acknowledged her own failures and confusions (however obliquely) in such a way as to address the "field imaginary" of an entire generation of American historians in particular and Americanists in general. Limerick speaks not only of her previous work but also of the regulative mentality (the Symbolic Order and Weltanschauung of her generation) when she says, "an unhealthy fatalism crept into my thinking. . . . I was tracing a direct line between past and present . . . event followed event with all the drama, surprise, and spontaneity of the prearranged program of the Rose parade" (710). She offers a cogent and unexpected reassessment, a provocative and timely critique of the deterministic heuristics of the *Legacy of Conquest* and other founding texts of the New Western History in particular, and of the modes of "presentism" (essentialism, scientism, and determinism) often propagated by the now-graying '60s generation of academic professionals in general. Though Limerick's is perhaps the most compelling voice in the current re-positionings by the most notable of the New Western historians, recent essays by William Cronon and Richard White have sounded similar reviewings of the hermeneutics and projects of the "new synthesis" announced at the 1987 "Trails" conference. Like Limerick's "Turnerians All," their current interventions are motivated by an attempt to rethink and reconstruct the no longer self-evident and agreed-upon purposes, perspectives, and projects of the New Western History.

William Cronon's "A Place for Stories: Nature, History, and Narrative" (1992), announces itself as a major attempt to address the problems raised for environmentalist historians by contemporary developments in postmodern theory. Cronon informs the reader that his essay has been formulated in no less than four versions and has received "comments and suggestions" from Kai Erikson, Peter Gay, Howard Lamar, Patricia Limerick, Paul Taylor, Richard White, Donald Worster, and no less than twenty-seven other listed eminent scholars who "read and critiqued various versions of the essay" (1347). Having notified the reader of what he will subsequently call the "process of production" of his essay, Cronon begins by describing a paradigmatic instance of the conflicting historical narratives:

> In 1979, two books were published about the long drought that struck the Great Plains during the 1930s. The two had nearly identical titles: one, by Paul Bonnifield, was called *The Dust Bowl*; the other, by Donald Worster, *Dust Bowl.* The two authors dealt with virtually the same subject, had researched many of the same documents, and agreed upon most of their facts, and yet their conclusions could hardly have been more different. (1347)

Bonnifield's history is conservative and comic; "nature had made a mess, and human beings cleaned it up," telling of, that is, a successful struggle that "was a triumph of individual and community spirit" (1348). Worster's narrative of the same events is radical, tragic, and "paints a bleaker picture." The Dust Bowl was "one of the three worst ecological blunders in history," and "the inevitable outcome of a (capitalist) culture that deliberately, self-consciously, set itself the task of dominating and exploiting the land for all it was worth" (1348). Cronon initially poses the problem as one of identifying the origins of these divergent stories:

> But it is not merely their *conclusions* that differ . . . they tell two entirely different stories. In both texts, the story is inextricably bound to its conclusion, and the historical analysis derives much of its force from the upward or downward sweep of the plot. So we must eventually ask a more basic question: where did the stories come from? (1348)

In the body of his essay Cronon shows how the major histories of the Great Plains "come from" the political commitments of their authors. He describes how James Malin "wrote in the wake of the New Deal and was a staunch conservative opponent of everything it represented," and thus how his "positive" narratives "expressed his own horror of collectivism by resisting the New Deal story at virtually every turn" (1361). And similarly, "it is James Malin's anti–New Deal narrative that informs Paul Bonnifield's *The Dust Bowl*. Writing in the late 1970s, at a time when conservative critiques of the welfare state were becoming a dominant feature of American political discourse, Bonnifield argues less urgently and polemically than Malin, but he tells essentially the same story" (1362). Cronon's analysis of the various versions of the other basic metanarrative (what he alternatively calls the "negative," "tragic," or "declensionist" form) also reveals the regulative function of political judgments. Of New Deal histories he says, "the political subtext of this story is not hard to find . . . the New Dealers constructed their stories so as to place themselves on center stage. . . . The New Dealers' affection for stories in which nature and society were metaphorically cast as organisms only revealed their own hostility to individualism and their flirtation with communist notions of the state" (1361–62). In this critical regard (how contesting histories are structured), Cronon finds, so to speak, nothing new in Worster's New Western History: "If Bonnifield elaborates the optimistic Dust Bowl narrative of a conservative critic of the New Deal, Donald Worster returns to the New Deal plot and deepens its tragic possibilities," and argues "that the Plains were actually a paradigmatic case in a larger story that might be called 'the rise and fall of capitalism'" (163).

But if both "upward" and "downward sweeping" historical narratives are analogously motivated by their "political subtexts," then what are the legitimate means by which one of these two metanarratives (given the "relativism" that postmodern theory seems to endorse) can be deemed "better" than the other? The problems raised by theory, as Cronon tells us early in his essay, are ones that New Western historians are obliged to address:

> When we choose a plot to order our environmental histories, we give them a unity that neither nature nor the past possesses so clearly. In doing so, we move well beyond nature into the intensely human realm of value. There, we cannot avoid encountering the postmodernist assault on narrative, which calls into question not just the stories we tell but the deeper purpose

> that motivated us in the first place: trying to make sense of nature's place in the human past. (1349)

Cronon does not hesitate in formulating this unavoidable encounter in the full gravity of its challenge. He is certainly referring to both Old and New historians when he says that "the uneasiness many historians feel in confronting the postmodernist challenge comes down to this basic concern, which potentially seems to shake the very foundations of our enterprise. If our choice of narratives reflects only our power to impose our preferred version of reality on a past that cannot resist us, then what is left of history?" (1370–71). Cronon is clearly describing his own views when he writes that, "most practicing historians, of course, do not believe that all stories about the past are equally good, even if we are not very articulate in explaining why one is better than the other" (1371). Yet the sense of this suggestion is hardly clear: is the problem really that historians are not "very articulate" (as if a more expert command of academic discourse could solve the conundrums postmodernism has raised); or is it rather that historians, however "articulate" they become, can no longer legitimately claim access to objective or agreed-upon criteria that would ground and justify their metanarratives?

Cronon states the issue more incisively when he says (after enumerating such "criteria" as "depth," "inclusiveness," "coherence," and "original reading") that:

> All these are possible criteria, and most of us would agree that they play a part in helping us to recognize good history when we see it. The trouble, obviously, is that they themselves can all too easily become objects of disagreement and struggle. . . . It is not at all clear that they would help us very much in deciding whether Webb or Worster or Bonnifield or Plenty Coups is the better narrator of Great Plains history. If the criteria we use in deciding the relative merits of historical narratives are open to the same sorts of value judgments as the narratives themselves, then we have hardly escaped the dilemma that postmodernist theory has posed for us. We still seem to be rudderless in an endless sea of stories. (1371)

In a sense, one version of this important essay concludes with this "endless sea of stories." Cronon pauses here to say, "before going any further,

I should probably confess my own uncertainty about how to navigate from here to a safe harbor, wherever it might be" (1371). Only after describing how his essay has gone through four different versions, how different groups of readers persuaded him each time that his "efforts to find safe harbor had failed," and how thus the essay itself "recapitulated the very problems it set out to solve," does Cronon begin his concluding reflections with a much qualified suggestion:

> But perhaps there lies hidden in this seemingly frustrating fact a partial solution to the narrative dilemma. (Watch: I try one more tack to seek some shelter in this theoretical storm.) The same process of criticism that shaped the various versions of this essay typifies the production and consumption of all historical texts. (1372)

Cronon ventures a partial solution to the postmodernist dilemma by describing three factors that limit the power of historical storytelling for environmental historians: first, these narratives "cannot contravene known facts about the past," second, they "must make ecological sense," finally and most significantly, historical stories are bounded and constrained by the fact that historians "do not tell stories by themselves. We write as members of . . . a community of other scholars" (1372–73).

However idealized, the following account of the self-critical functions of the academic community in the production and consumption of histories must be taken most seriously—for it is this limitation "on our power to impose our preferred versions of reality" that bears the burden of providing a safe shelter from the "assault" of theory. The community of critical readers will, Cronon writes,

> remind me of the excluded facts and wrong headed interpretations that my own biases, self-delusion, and lack of diligence have kept me from acknowledging . . . [others] will evaluate the accuracy . . . the fairness and truth of what we say . . . we cannot afford to be arbitrary in deciding whether a fact does or does not belong in our stories . . . [because] some among our readers will eventually inform us of our failings. (1373)

Such an account, however, seems to bracket a central concern his essay has raised—and indeed, avoids the thrust of any number of postmodern and cultural studies critical theories.

Most who have been influenced by theory, that is, would subscribe to the view that located discursive communities are to some extent driven by agreed-upon projects and assumptions that are not immediately evident to them. They would also acknowledge that some voices and views have a great deal more power than others, that it is naïve at best to obscure the institutional and "disciplinary" force of the "power/knowledge apparatus"—and many would hold that to do so risks enforcing the traditional ideology that mystifies the academic community as an egalitarian and democratic forum. (Indeed, in this regard as elsewhere, Limerick's "Turnerians All" functions effectively as a pointed critique of Cronon's idealized depiction of the contemporary academic community.) It is only in the final sentence of his optimistic description of scholarly self-criticism, however, that Cronon qualifies the safety of his harbor. "Criticism can sometimes do more harm than good—burying strong arguments underneath nit-picking caveats, *reinforcing conventional wisdom at the expense of new and radical insights*, and murdering passion—but it can also keep us honest by forcing us to confront contradictory evidence and counternarratives" (1373, my emphasis). Since the focus of his essay becomes what might be called the problems and possibilities of self-criticism in the New Western History, it is pertinent to consider the critical function of the text itself within the discursive community of its intended audience and "ideal" readers.

Inasmuch as "A Place for Stories" is addressed to New Western historians in particular, it seems more than fair to ask in what ways does it "force" its professional readers to "confront contradictory evidence and counternarratives," and thus itself provide the sort of critical operations it proposes as not only desirable but necessary in these stormy times? In other words, does Cronon mean to criticize Donald Worster, in particular, when he concludes his essay with the imperative injunction that "we must learn to use it (narrative) consciously, responsibly, and self-critically" (1376)? There seems to be a permeating and even structuring ambiguity in Cronon's essay, a hesitancy or deflection that leaves the reader uncertain as to how Worster's history of the Great Plains (also, White's, Limerick's, and Cronon's previous stories) is to be evaluated when we finally get our "partial solution" to the problem of narrative. On one hand, Cronon's analysis of Worster seems to reveal an instance (even a paradigmatic episode) of unselfconscious and unself-critical storytelling:

> For Worster, the refusal to recognize natural limits is one of the defining characteristics of a capitalist ethos and economy. He is therefore drawn to a narrative in which the same facts that beckoned progress for Webb and Malin become signs of declension and of the compounding contradictions of capitalist expansion. The scene of the story is world historical, only this time the plot leads toward catastrophe. . . . By this reading, the chief agent of the story is not "the pioneers" or "civilization" or "man"; it is capitalism. The plot leads from the origins of that economic system, through a series of crises, towards the future environmental cataclysm when the system will finally collapse.

As the reader is presumably expected to recall such accounts when encountering the concluding injunctions for a self-critical use of stories, so also, when here as elsewhere Cronon exposes the fundamental (narrative) identity between Worster's and Bonnifield's texts, the reader is seemingly encouraged to remember the critical dimension of his initial analysis of "the two large groups of possible plots." We subsequently learn that Cronon is speaking of Worster as well as Turner and Bonnifield when he says:

> Their plots are cultural constructions so deeply embedded in our language that they resonate far beyond the Great Plains. Historians did not invent them, and their very familiarity encourages us to shape our storytelling to fit their patterns. Placed in a particular historical or ideological context, neither group of plots is innocent: both have hidden agendas that influence what the narrative includes and excludes. So powerful are these agendas that not even the historian as author entirely controls them. (1352)

But why, given that Worster is a contemporary historian of the highest stature and Bonnifield relatively anonymous, does not Cronon more explicitly direct his analysis toward the work of his colleague and compatriot? More to the point, if it is contemporary historians (not their precursors) who are obliged to meet the challenge of postmodernism, then why does Cronon explicitly say so very little of the founding texts of the New Western History? It seems at odds with the sense of the essay, that is, for the reader to be left with the project of assessing how

Limerick's *Legacy of Conquest*, for example, might provide a current example of the "declensionist" writing, of the workings of the "political subtexts," and of "hidden agendas" that unselfconsciously determine (meta)narrative constructions. It seems understandable, perhaps all too understandable, that Cronon is here unwilling to directly critique the more recent work of his fellow New Western historians. But his reluctance does not bode well for the security of the harbor he proposes. The efficacy of his "partial solution" (inasmuch as it requires ready and forthright critical responses of scholars to work in their field) seems troubled by his own essay's failure to fully engage this very process. The questions here, no doubt, are related to the emphasis placed on the necessity of moral and political commitment in the concluding pages of the text.

However seriously Cronon takes postmodernism, he comes close to saying that, finally, moral and political concerns ought to override whatever theoretical quandaries historians may encounter from their reading of Hayden White, Martin Heidegger, or Jacques Derrida:

> However serious the epistemological problems it creates, this commitment to teleology and narrative gives environmental history—all history—its moral center. Because stories concern the consequences of actions that are potentially valued in quite different ways, whether by agent, narrator, or audience, we can achieve no neutral objectivity in writing them. . . . Within the field of our narratives we too—as narrators—are moral agents and political actors. (1370)

Cronon quite persuasively argues that the "special task of environmental history is to assert that stories about the past are better, all other things being equal, if they increase our attention to nature and the place of people within it," and if they do so in a politically committed manner that is both motivated by and engenders "an engaged moral life" (1375). In this regard, to be sure, Donald Worster is an exemplary environmental historian. But is it then that those who share each other's engagements—who are comrades as "moral agents and political actors"—are predictably (and legitimately) disinclined to confront each other's texts in a rigorously critical manner?

"A Place for Stories" provokes such urgent but seldom-asked questions, but is perhaps so regulated by constraints of binary analytical components that it cannot easily explore the terrain it so well opens. Postmodernism, of course, has also had much to say about the workings of such binaries: how they conflate differences into identities, ineluctably become hierarchical, dominating, and hegemonic—and how, in their privileging of one side over the other, they foster and reinforce the agonisms of "us" against "them" bifurcations. Further, there may also be a related slippage in Cronon's persistent identification of "moral agents and political actors." It might be persuasively argued that moral engagement and political commitment are not as Cronon suggests so seamlessly conjoined or congruent. His compelling convictions regarding an "engaged moral life" (that "to try to escape the value judgments that accompany storytelling is to miss the point of history itself, for the stories we tell, like the questions we ask, are all finally about value" [1376]), become less convincing when we substitute the terms "political actions" for "value judgments." Moral agents (and historical narrators) can share regulative value judgments, but hold different and even contrary views regarding the sorts of political actions that seem best suited to further these common goals. Confluent value judgments (and long-term sociopolitical purposes), in other words, can engender different narrative and metanarrative productions. If so, then we are urged beyond binaries to (at least) quaternaries in offering typologies of story emplotments. If so, then the questions which come to the forefront of discussions in our various communities of scholars ought to be those which bring political subtexts to full light. Among the most urgent questions, that is, would be those which debate the viability of certain political actions and commitments (and their attending narratives) as strategic means to actualize shared values. In this sense, then, the problem with the New Western historians is not that we/they have become too political, but rather that we/they are not political enough—must learn, so to speak, to become political in a more conscious, responsible, and self-critical manner. This is what Cronon could have meant when he said that "we are not very articulate in explaining why one (story about the past) is better or worse than another." Both Cronon's and Richard White's more recent contributions to *Uncommon Ground* give the New Western and environmental historians a good hard push in this direction.

Though Cronon and White balk back from acknowledging, to use Limerick's terms, the "unhealthy fatalism" (the evasion or repression of "contingency and improbability") of their previous work, the troubling present has disrupted antecedent clarities and has stimulated a less stable and more stormy vision of the western past. While Limerick writes of the disorienting force of the unexpected political events of 1994, for Cronon, it is contemporary theoretical developments that have dislocated all claims to comprehend history (and configure the natural world) in an objective, unprejudiced, clear, and distinct manner. Cronon, that is, continues to struggle with the recognition that historical discourses are suspect to the extent that they claim to be, in Limerick's self-critical terms, "tracing a direct, clear line between past and present." Introducing *Uncommon Ground*, and describing the "central dilemma" that preoccupied the NEH seminar group of high-profile scholars he had assembled at UC Irvine, Cronon writes:

> The second of our two starting insights was perhaps even more challenging to popular conceptions of nature, and it soon emerged as the central dilemma to which our research group kept returning. *The work of literary scholars, anthropologists, cultural historians, and critical theorists over the past several decades has yielded abundant evidence that "nature" is not nearly so natural as it seems. Instead, it is a profoundly human construction.* This is not to say that the non-human world is somehow unreal or a mere figment of our imaginations—far from it. *But the way we describe and understand that world is so entangled with our own values and assumptions that the two can never be separated.* What we mean when we use the word "nature" says as much about ourselves as about the things we label with that word. (25, my emphasis)

It is telling that Cronon's initial description of the impact of contemporary "theory" is phrased in language that confounds the answer to an arguably critical question: which views have been challenged by the current "evidence" that has uncovered the cultural construction of all "realities" and the evaluative dimension of all representations? Though the text specifically states that contemporary insights are "challenging to our *popular conceptions* of nature," it seems evident that academic conceptions of nature cannot be excluded or sequestered from the challenges of "theory."

Indeed, in the following paragraph Cronon designates a seemingly inclusive terrain that is structurally altered when the perspectival nature of consciousness is acknowledged:

> What happens to environmental politics, environmental ethics, and environmentalism in general once we acknowledge the deeply troubling truth that we can never know at first hand the world "out there"—the "nature" we seek to understand and protect—but instead must always encounter that world through the lens of our ideas and imaginings? (25)

Though on one hand much of the work of the New Western historians, and Cronon's own work in particular, must be included in the above-designated category "environmentalism in general," there is here no directly self-critical reference to New Western environmental historians. Rather and quite otherwise, a puzzling distinction between popular views and academic discourses is underscored. "Our emphasis throughout," Cronon continues, "is primarily on environmental ideas in American popular culture rather than on the more systematic thinking of those who have devoted their professional lives to understanding the environment (people whose ideas have in fact profoundly shaped our own thinking in writing this book)" (25).

But neither Cronon's own essays nor others he here anthologizes can persuasively maintain this analytical disjunction between popular environmentalist discourses and those of a select (but unspecified) cadre of academics. In Cronon's own contribution, "The Trouble With Wilderness," he convincingly demystifies and deconstructs the "idea of Wilderness" (the construction of nature as a pristine and untouched refuge), but provides only an ambiguous sense of to what and to whom he attributes this ostensibly dominating ideational and iconographic configuration. It is unclear if Cronon is speaking of American "popular culture," or of "American environmentalism" in general (Thoreau through Muir to Leopold and Stegner to the New Western historians of the present), or if he is referring to, as he sometimes also says, the "modern environmentalism" of only certain recent texts like Bill McKibben's *The End of Nature* (1989). It seems undeniable, however, that Cronon's most recent essays (like his earlier "A Places for Stories" [1992]) may quite usefully be applied to the environmentalist views of the New Western historians.

Similarly, Richard White's contribution to *Uncommon Ground*, "Are You an Environmentalist or Do You Work for a Living?" leaves the reader wondering how the critical thrust of this essay could not be directed, at least in substantial part, toward the previous work of Cronon, Worster, Limerick, and White himself. Like Cronon, White is sharply critical of "American environmentalism" for having postulated binary oppositions, which are theoretically untenable and politically dysfunctional, and pushes hard for the development of alternative environmentalist perspectives that pursue what Cronon called a "middle way." White's essay begins:

> In Forks, Washington, a logging town badly crippled by both over-cutting and the spotted owl controversy, you can buy a bumper sticker that reads "Are You an Environmentalist or Do You Work for a Living?" It is an interesting insult, and one that poses some equally interesting questions. How is it that environmentalism seems opposed to work? And how is it that work has come to play such a small role in American environmentalism? (171)

Continuing, he introduces positions and perspectives that may be located within the Agrarian Populist tradition. "Humans," he writes,

> have known nature by digging in the earth, planting seeds, and harvesting plants. They have known nature by feeling heat and cold, sweating as they went uphill, sinking into mud. They have known nature by shaping stone and wood, by living with animals, nurturing them, and killing them. . . . Modern environmentalism lacks an adequate consideration of this work. Most environmentalists disdain and distrust those who most obviously work in nature. (172)

By denigrating agrarian workers, contemporary environmentalists have not only postured themselves as "self-righteous, privileged, and arrogant," but have propagated a political discourse that has inadvertently supported the environmentally destructive policies of the "wise-use movement." The critique of the sociopolitical consequences of such environmentalisms could not be more incisively stated than the following:

> By failing to examine and claim work within nature, environmentalists have ceded to the so-called wise-use movement valuable cultural terrain. The loss of the natural terrain can only follow. . . . As long as environmentalism refuses to engage questions of modern work and labor, wise-use will prosper and our children, in the end, will suffer. (172)

But of whom does White speak when he asserts that "most environmentalists disdain and distrust those who most obviously work in nature," and, for having done so, "have ceded to the so-called wise-use movement valuable cultural terrain"? Such pleas and protests, much needed and long in coming, seem to have more than a little relevance to the texts of White's colleagues. For the New Western historians, the blue-collar workers of the American West (the farmers, ranchers, miners, loggers, agricultural and hydraulic workers) have been generally portrayed as mere cogs in the machinery of conquest—as complacent victims of hegemonic forces they can neither understand nor influence. If blue-collar workers in nature may be called "agrarian workers," then it is pertinent to note that Agrarian Populism has hardly been a preoccupation of the New Western historians. In Ostler and Johnston's unpublished essay, "The Politics and AntiPolitics of Western History" (1995), it is, for example, specifically to the Agrarian Populists that they refer when they strenuously take Cronon and Worster to task for "marginalizing" these radical agrarian movements and having "consigned the Populists to historical oblivion" (18). Though the "self-critical" inflections of this important paper are problematically veiled, White's effort to subvert elitist posturings and recapture the historical/political force of western agrarian populism, moves his current version of the New Western History into an unexpected confluence with the Old/New Western histories and politics of the "Stegnerian" tradition. White's essay, that is, belongs to the politically and environmentally engaged heterodoxy Wallace Stegner's historical narratives have storied: the culturally critical contributions of precursors like Henry George, John Wesley Powell, John Muir, Carey McWilliams, Bernard DeVoto, and Wendell Berry.

Of greater consequence, by my lights, is the manner in which White here foregrounds the necessity of what might be called a public textualizing of the "political subtexts" and "hidden agendas" that have long regulated the efforts of the New Western historians in a less than (as Cronon phrases it in another regard) fully "conscious, responsible, and self-critical manner." Like Limerick and Cronon, White's recent intervention may be read as a sharply self-critical reassessment of the founding texts (his own included) of the New Western History. His repositioning assumes Cronon's justification of value judgments and political engagements, and goes on to ask, so to speak, "well, what then?" If our politically motivated narratives have not contributed, in the most effective manner possible, to the political ends they value, then what good reasons could we possibly offer for maintaining rather than reformulating them? Thus, if we intertextualize the most recent essays of Limerick, Cronon, and White, it becomes clear that the New Western History, in regard to both its theoretical constructs and political positionings, has opened itself to a polyphonic and indeterminate reassessment of what it means to be a self-conscious historical storyteller and, in Cronon's words, a "moral agent and political actor." But if so, then for what reasons have the New Western historians so consistently obscured, deflected, and misdirected their own self-critical reflections? It is not approximately but precisely this consideration that focuses and structures Limerick's essay, "Turnerians All." The regulative question of this paper, in other words, is this: why and how is it that Turner—though he knew well that his "Thesis" was fundamentally flawed—muted or diffracted his self-critical reflections and carried on (allowing himself to be glorified and lauded) as if there were no compelling objections to this account of the American state of affairs? Limerick writes of herself, her colleagues, and her precursor:

> The passage of time offered this particular historical explorer many *chances to rethink his earlier impressions*. . . . And yet, except in brief and indirect suggestions of the Frontier Antithesis, *Turner consistently refused those opportunities*. . . . Why? Here we return to Turner's standing as the representative historian, a central player in the routinizing and professionalizing of the academic historians activities. . . . *Turner was triumphant*. But he was also trapped: trapped, in part, by a host of impossible book-writing obligations brought to him by the success of the Frontier Thesis, *but also trapped by the fact that his career and status now rested on his identification with the 1893 thesis*. . . . It (the

> academic success of his work) *brought many benefits:* the presidency of the American Historical Association, a position at Harvard, *many followers and devotees, and a happy package of status, prestige, visibility, and name recognition.* . . . (But) *when one was the established authority in one's field, the pleasures of rebellion are considerably diminished. Turner could not frankly discuss the flaws of the 1893 essay because it formed the foundation his career, his prestige, and his sense of personal achievement. The choice not to do so set precedent from which the profession has never broken fully free.* (703–4, my emphasis)

Indeed.

University of California, Santa Cruz

NOTES

1. For full citations, see "Introduction" of this volume, 12–13.

2. More interesting than such partial qualifications is the tension to be found between Worster's recent meta-historical configurations and his own earlier historical studies. In *Rivers of Empire*, Worster wrote enough of the Powell-DeVoto-Stegner tradition to trouble his own more recent portrayals of a revolutionary breach between the past and the present. More graphically, in his *Nature's Economy: A History of Ecological Ideas* (1977), Worster challenges the contemporary conceits of the environmentalist movement in very much the same way that I would criticize his recent presentations of the New Western historians. "The Age of Ecology," he wrote, "is inevitably the outcome of its long and complex intellectual history, *regardless of how strongly it believes in its own novelty*. Failing to accept this, or to realize how diverse and contradictory that past has been, we will not make much headway toward a true understanding of our current ideas about nature" (347, my emphasis). I can come up with no better language to describe what I find wrong-minded in the strong beliefs of the New Western History "in its own novelty." Further, since much of the New Western History is very much a part of this "Age of Ecology," it would certainly seem that Worster refers above to a "long and complex intellectual history" that both hold in common.

3. Perhaps we misunderstand what is "new" in these recent histories unless we see the inclusive damnation of previous interpretations of the West as a basic and even necessary postulate of these self-definitions. But how do we take such pronouncements seriously when it is hard to see a motivation, much less a methodological imperative, for such virulent denigrations? This may become less puzzling when we recall what Worster said above of the "most distinguishing characteristic" of the new history. Adamant denunciations of the old histories are required, perhaps, by the "most important . . . determination not to cover up for the powers that

be" (*Under Western Skies* 15–16). It could well be that the rebuke of the textual past becomes obligatory because a failure to do so would also constitute, by its "silence or consent," an act of ideologically complicit capitulation.

4. Alan Brinkley, "The Western Historians: Don't Fence Them In," *The New York Times Book Review*, 20 September 1992, 22.

5. Patricia Limerick, "Making the Most of Words," *Under an Open Sky* 168.

6. Limerick sometimes suggests that she has often been misunderstood, and that the problem resides with her readers: their "heavy emotional investment in the mythic West" is so deep that her effort to describe the West as a "muddled mixture" of the "positive and the negative" that has "the same moral complexity as every other part of the planet" is wrongly construed as depressing, negative, and "devoid of light" (74). Journalistic misrepresentations are understandable, but "why some professional historians" read her work in this fashion, she writes, "remains a puzzle to me" (73). Her puzzlement is itself more than a little bewildering, because both sympathetic and critical commentators seem to have similarly "misread" her in this rather significant manner. Michael Malone's essay in *Trails*, the much-reviewed text that Limerick herself edited, is a case in point. Whereas Limerick understands herself to have written of the West as a region that has "the same moral complexity as every other part of the planet," Malone says of *Legacy of Conquest*, "One may or may not accept *this book's main contention*, that the West is the American region *most marked* by a legacy of human and environmental conquest" (150, my emphasis). Peggy Pascoe is evidently also confused when she writes, "If, as Patty Limerick has convincingly argued, *the central theme* of the history of the American West is conquest, we need to come to terms with the ways that conquest shaped intercultural relations in the region" ("Westering Women at the Cultural Crossroads," also in *Trails* 53, my emphasis).

7. Richard Bernstein, "The Old West," *New York Times Magazine*, 18 March 1990, 56.

8. Larry McMurtry, "How the West Was Won or Lost," *New Republic*, 22 October 1990.

9. In his *Trails* essay, appropriately titled "Trashing the Trails," Richard White writes that:

> much of the difference between the New and Old Western Historians is revealed by what they make of the garbage so lavishly strewn along the trails. Old Western Historians looked past the garbage and saw "nature." . . . Many New Western Historians—particularly environmental historians—see garbage first. (26–27)

But why is it that some see the garbage and others see the nature? White often implies a fully traditional hermeneutic (in spite of his tropological suggestions), with such statements as, "All these things are visible on the New Western History trail rather than that of the Old Western History because the New Western Historians have abandoned frontier blinders that restricted their view" (31). I would have said: they have replaced an old set of "frontier blinders" with a new set of "frontier blinders," and that all views remain "restricted." *On my view*, as Berger and Luckmann said long ago now, "reality is a 'social construct,'" and ineluctably remains a cultural production in spite of (indeed, by means of) our attempts to revise and re-vision our response to it. See Peter Berger and Thomas Luckmann's *The Social Construction of Reality* (New York: Doubleday, 1967) for an earlier and in some ways more radical formulation of the now common-place stress on the "social construction" or the "cultural production" of our "realities." It is unfortunate that there are few sustained attempts to examine the similarities, differences, and historical connections between what we now call Cultural Analysis or Cultural Studies and the Berger/Luckmann presentation of the phenomenological analysis of social constructs (Merleau-Ponty, Alfred Schutz et al.) that re-reads, through Edmund Husserl, the sociology of knowledge tradition of Weber, Mead, and others. See Wuthnow et al., ed. *Cultural Analysis: Phenomenology, Cultural Anthropology, Neo-Structuralism, Critical Theory* (London: Routledge & Kegan Paul, 1984), for an uncommon example and a promising beginning.

10. Gerald Nash, *Creating the West: Historical Interpretations, 1890–1990* (Albuquerque: University of New Mexico Press, 1991) 200.

11. Forrest Robinson, "The New Historicism and the Old West," *Western American Literature* 25 (1990): 120.

12. Perhaps the clearest statement of Bercovitch's neo-Marxist ideological analysis is found in his commentaries in *Ideology and Classic American Literature* (New York: Cambridge University Press, 1986). Jameson's major text remains *The Political Unconscious* (1981); and a particularly lucid account of his analytical practice is found in his influential essay, "Reification and Utopia in Mass Culture" (*Social Text*, 1979). I do not mean to ignore the important contributions of Louis Althusser, Antonio Gramsci, Raymond Williams, Terry Eagleton, and many others, but rather to suggest that Bercovitch and Jameson are particularly cogent in formulating the hermeneutical procedures I am concerned with above. I would suggest, however, that Gramsci and (especially) Williams are more usefully understood as "post-" precisely because of their stress on what Gramsci called "counter-" Marxists or "alternative" hegemonies and Williams' sustained insistence that "at any time, forms of alternative or directly oppositional politics and culture exist as significant elements in the society" (*Marxism and Literature* [New York: Oxford University Press, 1977] 113).

13. In this regard, our views of Stegner's contributions may well have been altered had he not hesitated in writing the bio-historical study he planned on John Muir. In response to Etulain's inquiry about this unwritten text, Stegner explains that, while he dallied, "Now it has been sensibly done by a gentleman named Fox." Stegner is referring here to Stephen Fox's *John Muir and His Legacy: The American Conservation Movement* (1981); and he goes on to suggest that, like Fox, he would have storied "Muir as a kind of kick-off for a history of the whole conservation-environmental movement" (Richard W. Etulain, *Conversations with Wallace Stegner on Western Literature* [Salt Lake City: University of Utah Press, 1983] 194–95). Though I argue that Stegner eventually wrote a "capsule" version of this book in his 1990 essay, "A Capsule History of Conservation" (*Where the Bluebird Sings to the Lemonade Springs* [New York: Penguin, 1993] 117–132), a major study of Muir and

his context, standing with and between his works on Powell and DeVoto, would have provided a markedly historical stature to his corpus.

14. Whatever may be said of the "traditionalism" of DeVoto's western histories, or any distinction advocates of the new western history might want to draw between DeVoto's historical narratives and his historical commentaries in public journals, would be much beside the point. Worster and Limerick are clearly portraying their precursors and presenting themselves in regard to the absence or presence of sociopolitical interventions, and their calls for publicly engaged intellectuals promotes an overcoming of traditional boundaries between discursive genres. Indeed, one way to rephrase the thrust of the Worster/Limerick critique is to say that the old historians allowed themselves to be constrained by the conventional "disciplinary apparatus" that obliged them to write "academic" histories and to distance themselves from political commentary and cultural analysis. Thus, for them to argue that DeVoto's journalistic writings and his public activities are outside the parameters of their depictions of old western historians would be to strategically reinscribe the very textual/genre/verbal activity distinctions that they have so adamantly rejected and critiqued.

15. Hayden White, *Tropics of Discourse: Essays in Cultural Criticism* (Baltimore: Johns Hopkins University Press, 1978) 6, my emphasis.

16. White, *Tropics of Discourse* 5.

17. An ironic focus on resistances to forced unities fosters a perspectivalism—a self-reflexive posture that implies a recognition of itself (and each other mode) as "only one of a number of possible perspectives on history" (Hayden White, *Metahistory: The Historical Imagination in Nineteenth-Century Europe* [Baltimore: Johns Hopkins University Press, 1973] 434). The ironic insistence on difference does not entail a passive or disengaged relativism, but is rather critical intervention that actively subverts the synthetic totalities and meta-narrative posturings. It might also be suggested that Stegner's ironic narratives imply a sub-regionalist geography—a cultural cartography of differences within an ostensibly meta-regional configuration of the "West." Stegner, though it took him a while, eventually advocated such a sub-regionalist graphing of the various cultural landscapes of the western regions.

18. Louis Montrose, "Professing the Renaissance: The Poetics and Politics of Culture," *The New Historicism*, ed. Veeser (New York: Routledge, 1989) 21, his emphasis.

19. Stephen Greenblatt, "Towards a Poetics of Culture," in Veeser's *The New Historicism* 1–14.

20. This fundamental binary is by no means restricted to literary studies and is not an invention of the New Historicism and the New Americanism. Intervening in a once well-publicized debate between Hans Gadamer and Jürgen Habermas, Paul Ricoeur distinguished between two different modes of engaging historical traditions in a quite similar fashion. He described Gadamer's as a "hermeneutics of reconstruction," Habermas' as a "hermeneutics of demystification," and argued that both proposed legitimate ways of responding to the past so as to re-evaluate the present. See Ricoeur's essay, "Ethics and Culture: Habermas and Gadamer in Dialogue," in *Philosophy Today* (1972). Mikhail Bakhtin's distinction between "dia-

logic" and "monologic" modes of reading (as I note below) is but one of many earlier configurations of analogous hermeneutical binaries. Importantly, there is also such a split in neo-Marxist studies in general and British Cultural Studies in particular: see Stuart Hall's "Cultural Studies: To Paradigms," in Dicks et al., ed., *Culture/Power/History* (Princeton: Princeton University Press, 1994) 520–38. See Raymond Williams' *Marxism and Literature* for a particularly cogent exposition of the sort of (post)Marxism that associates Williams (and his reading of Gramsci) with the Gadamer, Bakhtin, Stegner side of this binary. Williams' *The Country and the City* (Oxford: Oxford University Press, 1973) is an especially relevant (and often forgotten) contribution to both (post)Marxist cultural/literary analysis and to what might be called Rural Studies.

21. Mikhail Bakhtin distinguishes between "dialogic" and "monologic" forms of reading. As Kramer writes in *The New Cultural History*, Biersack and Hunt, eds. (Berkeley: University of California Press, 1989), the significance of Bakhtin's work is by no means restricted to literature and literary history:

> This attention to the dialogical process in great literature becomes relevant to the historical analysis of other texts and contexts in that it *stresses the importance of contestatory voices*. The texts or social realities of past societies evolve through constant dialogues that can not be reduced to a single monologic meaning. The dialogic approach to history would therefore open up the discussion between opposing categories on a number of different levels: the dialogue between opposing ideas within specific texts, the dialogue between historians and the past, or the dialogue between texts and contexts. (114, my emphasis)

In these terms, Worster and Limerick practice "monologic" rather than "dialogic" approaches to regional history and its discursive interpretations. Through their persistent marginalization of "contestatory voices" and their tendency to collapse historical texts into the sociopolitical context from which they emerged, they close the sort of discussions Stegner's reading opens in this "dialogic" attention to "the importance of contestatory voices." See especially Bakhtin's *The Dialogical Imagination*, ed. Michael Holquist, trans. Emerson and Holquist (Austin: University of Texas Press, 1981) and Clark and Holquist's *Mikhail Bakhtin* (Cambridge: Harvard University Press, 1984).

22. Patricia Limerick, "What on Earth Is the New Western History?" in *Trails* 85.

23. My point here should not be misunderstood as an advocacy of the "frontier" rather than the "regionalist" side of the productive debate between the current versions of these western purviews. Though I find both helpful, both tend to force us, in spite of their intentions, back where we began with the old western history—to the wide and open spaces, and still stuck in the middle of the Hollywood chronotope. You see something of this in the titles of their current texts, "under western skies" and "under an open sky"—in too many regards we are offered a choice between Buffalo Bill (for the "regionalist" model) and Daniel Boone (for the "frontier model") as the allegorical synecdoches for western history. For both, what Earl

Pomeroy called the "Pacific Slope" is finally regarded as a subregion that was once part of the West, but which somehow and unaccountably became something quite different. See Pomeroy's *The Pacific Slope* (New York: Knopf, 1965). I would call it the "New West," and suggest that we are left, then, with the rather troubling conclusion that the New Western History, in either of its prominent versions, has very little at all to say of New Western History. See Nash's *The American West in the Twentieth Century* (Englewood Cliffs: Prentice Hall, 1973) and Nash and Etulain, ed., *The Twentieth-Century West: Historical Interpretations* (Albuquerque: University of New Mexico Press, 1989) for a sense of what is curtailed rather than furthered by the younger historians. I am more compelled by pluralistic paradigms—somewhere between Stegner's subregionalism and the more localized heuristic geography (the communitarian [riparian] politics) that Charles Wilkinson describes in his splendid essay, "Toward an Ethic of Place," in *The Eagle Bird: Mapping a New West* (New York: Pantheon, 1992).

24. These terms are from Harold Bloom's psycho-rhetorical poetics, and I take him seriously when he suggests their more general applications. In his *Map of Misreading* (New York: Oxford University Press, 1975), Bloom contends that every reading/writing begins in a vulnerable posture—in an "anxiety of influence" or of "belatedness" in the face of the voluminous mass of the textual past. Being late on the scene and weak before the recalcitrant firmness of the pre-given, the new reading/young writing is initially "compelled to assert its uniqueness, its totality, its truth," to insist "that the meaning it finds is exclusive and accurate" and belongs to itself alone (69–70). This involves the denial and the misreading of previous texts and what Bloom calls an "agonistic response to its own precursors." From this "initial scene," the writing may progress through five stages of rhetorical tropings and corresponding psychic defenses. In the final stage, those readings/writings that are "strongest" and most healthy engage in a "metaleptic retrieval" of the lost, forgotten, or repressed voices of their discursive predecessors (101–3). The initial "anxiety of influence" becomes here, for some, an acknowledgment of influence. But Bloom's account gives us no convincing reasons for assessing the value of a discourse in terms of its "health" or its literary strength and stature. I find Bloom's cartography most useful when it is configured horizontally rather than vertically, when it is used as a descriptive rather than as an evaluative hermeneutical schematization.

25. Patricia Limerick, "Making the Most of Words," in *Under an Open Sky* 170.

26. In *Reading America: Essays on American Literature* (New York: Knopf, 1987), Denis Donoghue recalls an American Studies conference in 1975, and after naming the canonical studies, the dozen texts, he and his colleagues "relied upon" in their discussions, he continues:

> These were the books we took as indicating that American experience was indeed exceptional, and that it was best understood as involving a refusal, upon principle, of values derived from history and society. The American hero, these books encouraged us to see, enters into a fellowship with nature—with a continent barely domesticated, still in its essence a

> wilderness—to forestall the constraints that in every other respect would be enforced by considerations of politics and economics, money and greed . . . his essential self is spiritual, and it finds its true place in the wilderness. (7–8)

If Donoghue is at all right in this, then the "reading of America" pursued by a previous generation seems complementary to the mode of culturally critical ideological analysis the New Western historians are promoting. This seems particularly the case because the pervasive and definitive escape from "reality" described above is directed toward and into the western regions.

The (ideological) American hero, that is, enacts a "refusal" of historical and economic constraints (reality), attempts a flight into mystical "fellowship with nature," which is viewed here, as Donoghue quotes Poirier, as "an essentially imaginative environment" (8).

FORREST G. ROBINSON

Clio Bereft of Calliope: Literature and the New Western History

> If we are to have any new thoughts, if we are to have an intellectual identity of our own, we must make the effort to distinguish ourselves from those who preceded us, and perhaps pre-eminently from those to whom we once had the greatest indebtedness.
>
> Richard Hofstadter[1]

> I suppose . . . that the root of my uneasiness with the Western revisionism generally is that the revisionists would like us to believe that they were more or less the first to notice, or at least to emphasize, how violent, how terrible, and how hard winning the West actually was. My own reading, as well as my boyhood among the old-timers, leads me to exactly the opposite conclusion: everyone noticed how hard it was.
>
> Larry McMurtry[2]

E. L. DOCTOROW'S NOVEL, *Welcome to Hard Times*, is set in a small town on the Western mining frontier. Life in Hard Times *is* hard. Men and women alike—merchants, miners, prostitutes—are caught up in a precarious struggle for survival. The environment is arid, exposed, and hostile, while the settlers are rootless, disenchanted, and desperately venal. Pervasive frustration and failure are centrally represented in a furiously destructive bad man who descends at regular intervals to lay waste to the town. This rapist and murderer, Doctorow suggests, is the concentrated embodiment of the human perversity everywhere at large in Hard Times. He is the recurrent disaster which the fallen little community brings upon itself.

The narrator of *Welcome to Hard Times*, a man named Blue, is by far the most fully developed of the novel's characters. Doctorow's emphasis on the teller of the tale is his way of underscoring the essential constructedness of the very familiar, if extreme, Western scene that he sets before us. Blue is strangely bland and matter of fact in describing a sordid, violent, doomed society. To the very end he keeps ledgers, written accounts of events as they unfold. The writing seems to provide a measure of control, distance, and hope; and it reinforces Blue's sense of himself as an embattled innocent. Yet all of this, Doctorow makes clear, is false. The only things under control in the town of Hard Times are the narrator's carefully cultivated illusions. Blue is in fact deeply implicated in the hopeless world he surveys. His optimism is groundless, and his innocence is a sham, a cover for spineless evasions and an imperfectly repressed fascination with the bloodletting.

Blue's self-deception, his recoil from the destructive reality of his experience into a consoling but utterly fabricated web of words, is the leading element in Doctorow's emergent assessment of the frontier myth. To the extent that the myth, endlessly reproduced in history and fiction, film and television, involves a triumphal narrative of Euro-American enterprise, endurance, and progress toward the fruition of democratic ideals, it is not—the novel suggests—merely a fabrication, but a flagrant lie. Doctorow's inspiration for *Welcome to Hard Times* arose out of the drudgery of reading "lousy" Western screenplays for a film company. "From reading all those screenplays and being forced to think about the use of Western myth, I developed a kind of contrapuntal idea of what the West must really have been like. Finally one day I thought, 'I can lie better than these people.'"[3] It is in Blue that Doctorow gives voice to his understanding of the way in which Western myths are generated and sustained. "Like the West, like my life," Blue reflects, "the color dazzles us, but when it's too late we see what a fraud it is, what a poor pinched-out claim." Bitter experience notwithstanding, he is also convinced that "a person cannot live without looking for good signs," and goes on to add that "if a good sign is so important you can just as soon make one up and fool yourself that way." Newcomers are especially welcome to Blue, because "anyone new helped bury the past."[4]

An ingenious literary critic of the proper regional persuasion might, upon first reading *Welcome to Hard Times*, take it as a *roman à thèse* designed to illustrate the leading doctrines of the New Western History. Central to the program of the "school" is an assault on outworn Western myth, associated most familiarly with Frederick Jackson Turner, which links westward expansion to progress, fails properly to represent women and minorities, and has tended to foster the exploitation of the land and its resources. The true story of the West, argues Patricia Nelson Limerick, like the true story of the South as told by C. Vann Woodward, has been characterized by frustration, failure, and defeat. But the tragic burden of the regional past has been submerged in the Turner myth. "Western American history," Limerick observes,

> used to be what I will call, not altogether kindly, Happy Face History. Have a Nice Day History, because it was so firmly centered on Anglo-Americans, and because it seemed to end so well, with white people in charge of the continent and with a lot of natural resources converted into cash in white people's pockets. This is not the version of Western American history we teach now.[5]

Donald Worster is equally emphatic in declaring it "the express purpose" of the New Western History to overthrow the frontier myth by "confronting and understanding [the] radical defects of the past." Thanks to such efforts, he is pleased to report, "the truth is breaking in, driving out myth and self-deception."[6]

Our critic would undoubtedly begin by observing that Doctorow and the New Western historians are both bent on replacing the triumphal Turner myth with a story of violent conquest undertaken by white men in pursuit of easy wealth. Attention would also be drawn to kindred views on the abuse of women (who are virtually all prostitutes in Hard Times), the neglect or mistreatment of minorities (John Bear, an Indian, is the victim of prejudice in the novel), and the destruction of the land (the merchants in Hard Times plan to profit from nearby mining operations). Finally, Blue's habitual evasiveness, most clearly on display in the groundless optimism of his constructions of events, would be offered as evidence of a shared perspective on the self-serving illusions advanced in Western myth. Blue's ledgers and Turner histories, in short, might be construed as parallel texts.

Were the ingenious critic to press much further, however, important differences between Doctorow and the New Western historians would begin to surface. It would be necessary to observe, for example, that no one is taken in by Blue's evasions, not even Blue himself. "And now I've put down what happened, everything that happened from one end to the other," he concludes. "And it scares me more than death scares me that it may show the truth."[7] Blue is a fully self-conscious mythmaker, moved in his fabrications not by complacent self-interest, but by a profound fear of encroaching disorder. In the example of Blue's terror, Doctorow seems to be suggesting that the ways and means of Western myth are at once more complex, more darkly fraught, and more universal than anything contemplated by the New Western historians. I say "universal" because Doctorow is not inclined, as the New Western historians are, to draw a clear line between myths and realities, between lies like Blue's and the "truth" of contemporary historical narrative. "The world in which we live is still to be formed," Doctorow has observed; "reality is amenable to any construction that is placed upon it."[8] It follows that narratives of all kinds are to be distinguished not so much by their truth content as by their success as aides in the amelioration of the human condition. Blue knows that he is lying, but in his panicky retreat from disorder he has taken refuge in a rigid, hopelessly maladaptive optimism. The historical narrative contained in his ledgers is defective, then, not because it is false (as a New Western historian would have it), but because it is a construction of reality that inhibits change.

Viewed in this light, the fact that the novel's villain is named Turner takes on a certain critical sense. At the very least, Doctorow is suggesting that there was more to the preeminent historian of the West than the "Happy Face History" assigned to him by Patricia Nelson Limerick. Turner is the agent of the destruction which Blue's false optimism makes inevitable; he is the tragic return on the town's investment in illusions of innocence and progress. He is thus kindred to the portrait of Turner the historian drawn by those who—in contrast with Limerick and company—perceive a strain of pessimism in his view of the West. "The Significance of the Frontier in American History," it will be recalled, concludes on a rather ominous note. The frontier has been closed; free land has run out; America must face the future bereft of its most precious moral resource. Will rugged independence and the democratic spirit go into decline as the result? Turner is not sure, though his tone in describing what he regards as an epochal transformation is markedly grave. Richard Hofstadter is prominent among the many who have drawn attention to "the latent pessimism" of Turner's position. "If the frontier was the making of America," he asks, "what could ever replace it?"[9] Harold P. Simonson has gone further in this vein, arguing that "the closed frontier" provides "the necessary climate for tragedy—specifically, for American tragedy." Shielded as he was by an "inveterate optimism," Turner was not fully aware of his dark drift toward "the tragic sense that darkened Henry Adams' prophetic vision." Still, his frontier "thesis" clearly "suggested that the West was no longer another Eden, the Westerner no longer another Adam."[10]

So regarded, the frontier thesis finds America poised for a fall. This is to suggest that the New Western historians are not after all so new, and that their claims to originality rest on a partial, blandly monochromatic reading of Turner. Michael Steiner is one among several critics to have advanced this view. "Far from being a triumphant tale of continuing conquest spun by the ever-smiling Norman Vincent Peale of American history," he argues, "the frontier-regional thesis is a more somber lesson in limits tempered by tragedies in Turner's own life."[11] Advocates of this perspective often go further, to insist that Turner is not the only legitimate precursor to have been overlooked by the current revisionists. Why don't we hear more about Royce and McWilliams, Bolton and Malin, DeVoto and Stegner? Whatever the explanation for such conspicuous omissions, it is widely recognized—as John Mack Faragher points out—that "alternative approaches to the history of the American West have existed among historians since the reconsideration of the frontier thesis began in earnest." Indeed, Faragher is quite blunt in faulting the revisionists for their failure to observe "one of the cardinal rules of history: close attention to antecedents."[12]

But it is not the neglect of earlier historians that concerns me here (that topic is eloquently considered in the essay by Jerome Frisk that precedes this one). Rather, I want to reflect on the fact that the New Western historians have been even more neglectful of the Western literary tradition. *Welcome to Hard Times* is entirely apposite in this regard—though I will argue that Doctorow's novel is hardly unique among literary texts in anticipating the regional revisionists. Why, we may reasonably inquire, would Western historians of a gravely moralizing and tragic bent turn a blind eye to similar sentiments as they are everywhere to be found in the literature of their region? There is of course the complaint, familiar enough among New Western historians, that imaginative writing does not qualify as evidence in historical discourse. Richard White is skeptical in drawing on novels by Sandoz, Smedley, Le Sueur, and Olsen, for example, because of doubts that they are "at all indicative of actual social attitudes."[13] But this representative objection, I will argue, rationalizes an over-determined and finally indefensible refusal to come to terms with Western literature.

At one level, we are here witness to the New Western historians' more general reluctance to acknowledge legitimate precursors—in this case, *literary precursors*. For as any student of Western literature knows, writers from Cooper to McCarthy, and including—among many others—Twain, Cather, Rolvaag, Sandoz, Steinbeck, and Stegner, share a strong inclination to represent the regional past in mingled and often tragic lights. Virtually everyone "noticed," as Larry McMurtry points out, "how hard it was." To read Western literature, in short, is to read a story similar in its gravity of tone, its thematic preoccupations, and its historical trajectory, to the one the revisionists claim to be telling for the first time.

But the neglect of fictional writing, I want to argue, is also grounded in resistance to the example of Western literature *as history*. Doctorow is once again apposite. For *Welcome to Hard Times* is highly self-reflexive, and perfectly self-conscious in featuring its own constructedness, and its intertextuality with earlier fictional and historical narratives (Frederick Jackson Turner's prominent among them). The past, Doctorow makes clear, is unknowable save in discursive terms. History is a story among other stories, subject to the vagaries of language and ineluctably shaped by context, convention, and the pressure of authorial interest. As we have seen, Blue is acutely aware of himself as fabricator. He is equally alert to the pervasive mingling of good and evil in the world he surveys. The destruction of Hard Times, he reflects, is to some extent a disaster that the local people bring on themselves. "Could you really know what was coming?" he wonders. "Or did it come because you knew it? Were you smarter than the life, or did the life depend on you?"[14] Doctorow thus answers Limerick's demand that we acknowledge "the moral complexity of Western history." But this is not, as she goes on to claim, a uniquely contemporary development brought on in good part by historians of her persuasion. "Stories of men and women who both entered and created a moral wilderness" have *not*, as she argues, just "begun to replace the simple contests of savagery and civilization, cowboys and Indians, white hats and black hats."[15] As D. H. Lawrence long ago observed, such stories are surely there in the Leatherstocking Tales, and in numberless other literary texts that have appeared in the nearly two centuries since Cooper's time.

In what follows I want to set out in a bit more detail the position of the leading New Western historians with respect to our regional literature. Along the way, I will analyze a selection of literary texts, with a special eye to qualities—moral complexity and the tragic impulse prominent among them—that the revisionist historians seem to have overlooked. Finally, I will review recent gestures among New Western historians toward postmodernism. What kinds of changes are such gestures likely to produce in their view of literature? and, by extension, in their approach to the history of the West?

When Donald Worster observes that the West has "emerged from the old clouds of myth and romance and now seems for the first time honestly revealed," his terms appear to include literature in their field of reference.[16] Myth and romance, he goes on to indicate, are the sorts of things that Henry Nash Smith studies in *Virgin Land.* Featuring visions of peace and plenty on the land, and an idyllic escape from the evils of the Old World, myth and romance represent the West as a prelapsarian garden. Such fanciful and even dangerous notions are widely influential in American culture, thanks to their currency in popular history, literature, and film. Most vitally for Worster's purposes, myth and romance are to the New Western History as falsehood is to truth.

By contrast, William Cronon, who stands out among the major revisionists for his balanced assessment of Turner,[17] has not gravitated to broad binary juxtapositions of old myth and new history. His most celebrated book, *Nature's Metropolis: Chicago and the Great West*, displays a supple readiness to "cross over" from history to literature. This is not to suggest that Cronon takes major interpretive cues from fiction, or that his narrative is notably literary in its attention to language and form. But on several occasions he illustrates his points by alluding to well known novels. Frank Norris' *The Pit*, for example, provides him with an index to Chicago's ambiguous power. Evidence of a similarly mingled mood turns up in the writing of Hamlin Garland, newcomer to Chicago from rural Iowa. An even darker picture emerges from Robert Herrick's *The Gospel of Freedom*, in which ominous, unnatural energies seem to drive the city. The book also serves Cronon as a reminder that personal history both intersects with and influences his narrative. "Herrick's dark praise for Chicago's conquest of nature," he reflects, "carries me back to my own youthful revulsion at the city."[18] Fictions thus give vital color and accent to Cronon's writing, and at the same time draw attention to his own informing perspective on the great metropolis.

Patricia Nelson Limerick betrays no such partiality to literature. In an essay entitled "Making the Most of Words: Verbal Activity and Western America," she admits that she came to her "topic with a resigned feeling that I was off to the literary wars, off to the trenches to reread Cooper's *Leatherstocking Tales* and to keep track of the plots of dime novels. This topic seemed to me, in other words, to give marching orders that directed me to the periphery, away from the daylight zone of political, economic, and social behavior and off to the twilight zone of myth and symbol."[19] Limerick's impatience with "literary history" (which she equates with the analysis of myth and symbol) is emphatically clear. The problem, she goes on, is that literary analysis as conducted by Henry Nash Smith, like history as conducted by Frederick Jackson Turner, is much too abstract. Smith studied myths and symbols rather than real things; likewise Turner viewed the West as "a process, not a place: a concept, not an actual geographical location." As the punishment for his errand into abstractions, Limerick recalls, she and her graduate student peers condemned Smith's *Virgin Land* as "the most pernicious book ever written in American Studies."[20]

It is telling of course that Limerick came to the study of history convinced that it gave her unmediated access to real things, real events, real people, and not to their constructions in thought and word. Graduate student convictions notwithstanding, she went on to write a dissertation—subsequently her first book, *Desert Passages*—devoted, as she puts it, to the "myth and symbol of deserts." Had she somehow fallen into the clutches of the "pernicious" Smith? Happily enough, she was spared this embarrassment by a timely *rereading* of *Virgin Land*, which revealed that the book's abstractions were in fact anchored in "real" historical soil (it was the verb tenses that originally led her astray), and which thus vindicated the inadvertent sagacity of her own lapse into myths and symbols. Yet even as she now praises Smith for his "straightforward, down-to-earth method," Limerick scorns "the conceptually sophisticated and obscurely written offerings of some of his followers and critics." Thus she contrives to hold on to the self-approval earned by her revaluation of *Virgin Land*, but continues at the same time to reject myth and symbol studies, except as they are practiced by people like Smith and herself, who aim "directly at the point of intersection between language and events."[21]

Which brings us back to Limerick's faith, unshaken since graduate school, in the power of language to directly engage "real things." Where exactly does she locate "the point of intersection between language and events?" In her first example, it resides in "a central fact of western American life," as observed in the 1830s by Richard Henry Dana, that there were several languages spoken in Mexican California. In praising Dana for his signal perspicacity, Limerick neglects to mention that linguistic variety illustrates nothing so well as the constructed nature of language. Dana in fact found himself at the intersection of arbitrary systems of symbols: the event, the Babel of words, had only such meaning as he assigned to it. But of course his interest was taken up in other matters, among them the prospects for American conquest in Alta California. The setting, climate, and natural resources of the region, he observes, "all fit it for a place of great importance." To such opportunities, the native inhabitants—given as they are to idleness and excess—show little save indifference. But "in the hands of an enterprising people," Dana reflects, "what a country this might be!"[22] How perfectly ironic that in dwelling at length on language, Limerick misses altogether this profoundly meaningful forecast of events to come. What Dana "saw taking shape on the San Diego beach," she insists, "was no Turnerian wave of Anglo-Americans relentlessly pushing a frontier line westward."[23] But of course that is precisely what he saw.

The timely reappraisal of Henry Nash Smith is a good example of what we may as well designate The Limerick Maneuver. A leading element in this recurrent strategy is the exemplary admission that a major precursor has been overlooked or misunderstood. Josiah Royce goes entirely unmentioned in *The Legacy of Conquest*, Limerick confesses, because "an awful Freudian slip of omission shows me bending under the anxiety of influence."[24] Wallace Stegner, she has very recently discovered, anticipated by several decades the New Western Historical attention to minorities.[25] Most striking of all, perhaps, Limerick in 1995 came to what she describes as "a greater awareness" of Richard Hofstadter's 1968 critique of Turner in *The Progressive Historians*.[26] If present trends are to be trusted, she will soon announce her discovery that Mary Austin is missing from the all-male gallery in *Desert Passages*, that Bernard DeVoto had a thing or two to say about the environment, and that Carey McWilliams anticipated the New Western Historical emphasis on racial minorities by about a half-century.

I use the adjective "exemplary" to describe Limerick's periodic *mea culpas* because it is frequently implied that the courage on display in such admissions more than outweighs the intellectual transgressions which give them rise. Such is the case in her reappraisal of Henry Nash Smith, as it is, even more explicitly, in the recent "Turnerians All: The Dream of a Helpful History in an Intelligible World." Limerick here admits that she has for years misrepresented Turner, but goes on to contrast the courage of that confession with what she regards as his failures of intellectual integrity. "Turner's unwillingness to scrutinize himself and put his own earlier, career-establishing ideas through a process of critical examination has become a luxury we can envy but no longer afford," she declares, going on with evident complacency to describe her own "self-understanding and self-disclosure."[27]

Such proffered impressions of unprecedented intellectual "character" are often accompanied by the suggestion that Limerick's scholarly transgressions are in fact of scant import. While Royce's omission from *The Legacy of Conquest* is acknowledged, for example, the significance of his absence—a topic to which I will return—goes unexplained. In like fashion, Limerick has no sooner admitted overlooking Hofstadter's critique of Turner than she proclaims—as if to make a startling revelation, and at the same time to convict Hofstadter of an oversight at least the equal of her own—that Turner was in many ways his own first and best critic. Finally, she softens her rejection of myth and symbol studies only to the limited extent strategically required for the justification of her own practice.

We will come back in due course to the realism of Limerick's epistemology, and to its defining impress on her sense of the relationship between history and literature. Richard White is equally determined to maintain the boundary between the sister disciplines, though he has come to the task with rather more theoretical self-consciousness. As early as 1985, White declared his opposition to those branches of environmental history which "presume an entity—whether an American mind or national character—which does not demonstrably exist, and even if it does, there is no guarantee that the sources under consideration reveal its content." This rejection of intellectual, cultural, and literary history has its foundation in the deep suspicion of any approach that reduces nature to "an intellectual construct." Allowing that the reign of environmental determinism has passed, White concedes that "nature does not dictate" the human discourse about it. "But," he insists, "physical nature does, at any given time, set limits on what is humanly possible. Humans may *think* what they want; they cannot always *do* what they want."[28]

White's rather muscular and affective allegiance to "the real"—which he sets in opposition to ephemeral social constructions of nature—is more broadly manifest in his recent *"It's Your Misfortune and None of My Own": A New History of the American West.* Dedicated to Vernon Carstensen—who taught White "to think deeply about the West while always distrusting deep thinkers"[29]—the book bristles with the conviction that the real West, the place, like much of what has really happened there, is obscured in fanciful human constructions, in myths. "The West that Americans recognize in the twentieth century is their own work," he declares at the outset. "In the imagination of modern America, the West has come to stand for independence, self-reliance, and individualism. Rhetorically, at least, modern westerners see themselves as part of a lineage that conquered a wilderness and transformed the land; they spring from a people who carved out their own destiny and remained beholden to no one."[30] This is a startling proposition, it will be conceded, coming from a scholar who sternly rejects entities such as the "American mind." Still, White's confidence that most Americans are and always have been wrong about the West is entirely compatible with his equally confident sense that he and a few others are in possession of a new and true story about the region. "The American West," he declares, clearly echoing Limerick, "is a product of conquest and of the mixing of diverse groups of peoples."[31] Such presumably is the import of the book's title, bearing as it does the suggestion that white men have indeed conquered the West, but only as the result of their brutal mistreatment of women, minorities, and the environment—crimes for which they refuse to accept responsibility. It is to the revolutionary truth of this view, we must suppose, that the book's subtitle—*A New History of the American West*—directs our attention.

The oppositional patterning of old and new, myth and history, wrong and right, serves as a reminder that White's concessions to the constructedness of "nature," and of historical narrative, are in tension with a potent commitment to the real and the true. Beyond "nature" there is, White assures us, something real that stands in opposition to human constructions: just so, beyond what most people believe about the past there is a truth that stands in opposition to myth. White has it both ways here; for even as he concedes the inherent discursiveness of knowledge, he lays claim to a privileged apprehension of the true reality toward which language strains. As he puts it in an opening statement on method, "I will use relatively simple criteria in deciding which events are pertinent to the creation of the West and thus deciding when Western history begins."[32]

White's claim to a privileged perspective on the West has a direct bearing on his view of the place of literature in historical narrative. Because it is preeminently fictional, literature is aligned with myth—with the old, false triumphal story of white male conquest that the New (and True) Western History puts to rest. This means, of course, that literature cannot possibly tell, or even significantly anticipate, the story that White and the other revisionists have to offer. But if, as White seems to concede, all narrative is a construction, then how is it possible to maintain a distinction between fiction and history as approaches to what he calls "the creation of the West"? He turns to this question at the very end of *It's Your Misfortune*, in a brief chapter entitled "The Imagined West."

White begins by describing the West as "the most strongly *imagined* section of the United States," and by acknowledging that in addition to their "gluttonous consumption of fictions about the West . . . Americans have also actively imagined their own Wests." Given its pervasiveness and authority, we may ask, why has consideration of "the imagined West" been put off until the very end of the book? Because, White argues, "it would have been potentially confusing to interrupt each chapter to analyze how various imagined Wests have shaped the topics of discussion." Yet the question remains, what is "the relationship between the variety of publicly imagined Wests—the mythic Wests—and the historic West?" White is quick to declare that question "misleading, for it implies that the two can be easily separated." But what then are we to make of the fact that the two have been kept separate in *It's Your Misfortune* for more than 600 pages? Quite evidently, White's commitment in theory to a constructionist conception of narrative has scant influence on his practice, where a strong impulse to separate false "publicly imagined Wests" from the true "historic West" prevails.[33]

White goes on to elaborate a distinction between mythmakers—"professional writers, journalists, and filmmakers who are often located outside the West itself or in that peculiar corner of it, Hollywood"—and historians (whose geographical locations he does not specify). Both "aspire to derive meaning from the past," though mythmakers take greater liberties with characters and events. But "historians also draw from history, and they, too, are selective." Once again, there is a startling ambiguity in White's language. For even as he concedes that historians construct their narratives in much the same manner as mythmakers do, he also insists on something prior to those narratives which he calls "history." Hence historians do not compose or construct history: they "draw" from it. By this definition, history is not a narrative at all; rather, it is facts. These exist independently and await the historian or mythmaker when they set to work. Historians "select from among numerous available facts," narrowing their data until they arrive at a pool of "largely agreed upon facts"; then they argue about the "relationship between facts," but on the understanding that they may not "reorder facts or invent new ones." Mythmakers do the same thing, albeit with greater license. But both draw selectively on history to construct narratives.[34]

White's equation of "history" with "facts" testifies to his enduring assumption that historical narrative is anchored in something real. But it also begs the question of what he refers to in passing as "conceptual difficulties over what a fact is." Though he does not develop the point, it is evident that if facts are themselves constructions, then their "reality" is compromised, and the distinction between myth and history collapses. Unwilling to debate further the precise status of facts, White in effect abandons his opening gambit and turns instead to a consideration of time as the key to distinguishing myth and history. Drawing on the writings of Richard Slotkin, he argues that by contrast to history, in myth "time brings no essential change. The past and the present are not only connected, they are also metaphorically identical. The lessons of a story from the past apply equally well to the present. . . . Myths are thus antihistory, for history above all depends on context."[35]

White does not pause to elaborate on this definition, and thus misses the chance to address the questions to which it gives rise. For example, if the precise status of facts is in doubt—and if therefore the difference between history and myth is equally uncertain—then on what basis shall we privilege the historian's evocation of context? Moreover, what evidence shall we draw upon to demonstrate that mythical narratives collapse time and therefore apply to the present, while historical narratives do not? White seems to contradict himself in a recent publication, where he praises Turner and Wild Bill Cody as creators of Western stories that "accept change and conflict as givens."[36] We may go further in this vein to ask how exactly a novel like *Giants in the Earth* "rips events out of context and drains them of their historicity."[37] The same may be asked of *Roughing It*, *The Professor's House*, *The Big Rock Candy Mountain*, *Lonesome Dove*, and many other books that qualify as myth in White's lexicon. On the other hand, how are we to enforce the boundary between past and present concerns, especially when historians themselves fail to honor it? Granted, *The Virginian* spoke to American preoccupations at the turn of the century; but so, in much the same way, did Roosevelt's *The Winning of the West*. More recently, the revisionists have themselves emphasized that their historical preoccupations arise directly out of their experiences as students and scholars in disenchanted modern America. The context most vital to their enterprise is the present, not the past.

As if to acknowledge that the boundary between fact and fiction will not hold, White concludes his brief theoretical excursus by emphasizing their complex interpenetration. "The mythic West imagined by Americans," he writes, "has shaped the West of history just as the West of history has helped create the West Americans have imagined. The two cannot be easily severed." Myths are thus valuable "historical sources reflecting the values and concerns of the period and people who produced them." Cognate sentiments turn up in the brief survey of Western myth that follows. Fictions have an important part to play in shaping "popular consciousness," we read, and in producing "visions of what an American social order should look like." This being the case, myths have evident historical value as "a national mirror."[38] Such remarks are relevant here not only because they reinforce our impression that White's distinction between fact and fiction will not hold, but also because of their direct implications for the overriding distinction between the old, false, triumphal narrative of myth on one side, and the new, true, tragic historical narrative of the revisionists, on the other. For as the boundary between fact and fiction erodes, so does the boundary between old and new, false and true.

All this being the case, we are brought back to the question why myth—and, more particularly, literature—is excluded from serious consideration in the New Western History. If history and myth "cannot be neatly severed," then why continue to insist on a clear separation between them? If the imagined West and the historic West merge into one another, then why continue to use the terms "myth" and "history" as though they referred to distinct—and even sharply contrasting—entities? If what White calls myth—as it is embodied in literature, journalism, and film—is indeed a historically revealing "national mirror," then why are the New Western historians so reluctant to look into it?

At one level, the answer is perfectly obvious. Like many members of their discipline, the New Western historians hold on rather jealously to the notion that their contributions to knowledge are readily distinguishable from those of scholars in adjacent fields. Anxiety on this score has run pretty high in recent years, largely because of assaults on the disciplinary integrity of history coming from theorists within the field, and from others in areas such as literature and philosophy. At the very heart of the historian's self-defense is an insistence that the reality of the past is accessible in empirical evidence which is gathered and then synthesized in historical narratives. Departures from this "scientific" procedure are said to produce varieties of falsehood. The involvement of the New Western historians in this ongoing debate is of course perfectly evident—witness White's attempt to separate historians from mythmakers, and Limerick's rejection of literary history, with the concomitant juxtaposition of "idea people" with "fact people."[39]

Persistence in the defense of such unstable positions suggests that there is more at stake here than the maintenance of disciplinary boundaries. Indirect support for such a surmise is to be found in the willingness among New Western historians to exempt certain contemporary regional novelists from the usual strictures against myth. Elliott West, a contributor to *Trails*, takes the view that there is "a 'new fiction' that has grown up alongside the new history. The novels and short fiction of Douglas Unger, James Welch, Patricia Henley, Craig Lesley, Kent Haruf, William Kittredge, Louise Erdrich, and David Quammen" especially catch his eye, because they are "stories of disappointment and persistence, grudging accommodations, the ghost of traditions. Just as the new historians look hard at the romantic idealism of earlier works, these writers break with the easy heroism of the traditional western novel."[40] White echoes Elliott. "During the 1970s and 1980s," he observes in *It's Your Misfortune*, "the West has produced probably the most skilled and compelling group of writers in its history. James Welch, Larry McMurtry, Leslie Silko, Louise Erdrich, Charles Bowden, Richard Ford, Ivan Doig, William DeBuys, Judith Freeman, William Kittredge, and others have produced western fictions and memoirs that have in common an interplay of an earlier imagined West and a modern West that at once reflects and fails to live up to those imaginings."[41]

Evidently enough, the strong appeal of such recent regional writers is their gravitation to what Elliott refers to in the title of his essay as a "longer, grimmer," but for that a "more interesting" story about the West. White in turn approves of Welch, McMurtry, Silko, and company because in their stories he hears his own. The new western mythmakers, like the New Western historians, are properly attentive to disillusionment and failure, and thus there is no impulse to fault them for the mismanagement of facts and contexts. In the face of a pleasing if grave consensus, the straining after theoretical distinctions is suspended and the boundary patrols take leave. History and myth, fact and fiction, are virtually as one so long as the correct story—featuring disappointment, failure, and tragedy—gets told.

But are Westerners the fatuous optimists, hopelessly inured to "Happy Face History," that the revisionists describe? Consider some familiar names: Junipero Serra, Meriwether Lewis, Natty Bummpo, Stephen Austin, the Jibbenainosay, the Donner Party, Joaquin Murietta, the Mountain Meadows Massacre, Ramona, Clarence King, Geronimo, Mark Twain, Wounded Knee, Wolf Larsen, John Muir, Willa Cather, Isadora Duncan, Bo Mason, the Joads. As this patchwork list surely suggests, the tragic perspective on the Western experience is hardly new. It is not new to the historical record, nor, as I have indicated more than once, is it new to the literary record. Quite to the contrary, from Cooper and Twain on down to Ivan Doig, Leslie Marmon Silko, James

Welch, William Kittredge, and Marilyn Robinson, the Western novel has set forth a rich tapestry of hope and failure, triumph and defeat, comedy and tragedy, the whole mixed record of human endeavor in this region. To be sure, women and minorities are more visible in the story as it is told today, and we are now more attentive to the environment than in the past. But women and minorities have never been entirely absent from the canvas, and concern for the environment has always been a prominent feature of Western writing. Donald Worster complains that Westerners have only recently accepted the fact that their region "is inextricably part of a flawed world."[42] In the same vein, Patricia Nelson Limerick congratulates the New Western historians for at last making "it clear that in western American history, heroism and villainy, virtue and vice, and nobility and shoddiness appear in roughly the same proportions as they appear in any other subject of human history."[43] But as any survey of the literary tradition will surely demonstrate, Western writers have inhabited a mingled, flawed world right from the beginning.[44]

Consider, for example, Cooper's profoundly troubled account of the advance of "civilization" in The Leatherstocking Tales. These are the most traditional of Western novels, and yet there is nothing in Natty Bummpo of what Elliott describes as "easy heroism." The same may be said for Bird's *Nick of the Woods*. Let us be mindful as well of the rough realism of Joseph Kirkland and Edward Eggleston, and of Hamlin Garland's many volumes on the hardship and frustration of farm life in the Middle West. Vardis Fisher's novels of frontier Utah are studies in moral and spiritual suffocation; frontier Nebraska is no less hostile to youthful aspiration in Mari Sandoz's *Old Jules*. What of Euro-American triumphalism in King's regressive "The Newtys of Pike"? There is of course the harsh anti-romanticism of Crane's "The Blue Hotel" and "The Bride Comes to Yellow Sky." Variations on the theme of disenchantment are also to be found in London's *Martin Eden* and in Norris' *The Octopus*; of declension in *The Sea-Wolf* and *McTeague*. The deflation of illusion is prominently thematized in the work of Nathaniel West, and in Clark's *The Ox-Bow Incident*, while D'Arcy McNickle's novels dramatize the tragic impasses of Indian-white relations.

Such examples well illustrate what Jeffrey Ostler and Robert Johnston have described as the more general failure among New Western historians to properly recognize the role of resistance in the regional past.[45] There is scant support here for the notion that the West has been in thrall to a myth of triumphant white conquest; to the contrary, virtually all of the writing presents a challenge to that familiar revisionist claim. Nor have I come close to exhausting the relevant evidence. Mark Twain's *Roughing It*, for example, a seminal Western text, sets forth a darkly complex analysis of the mining frontier. Life in Washoe is very hard indeed, and the hardship almost invariably arises out of the painful contrast between glittering expectations and grim realities. *Roughing It* evokes the romantic myth of easy wealth, but only to subvert it utterly.[46] Henry Steele Commager found the same basic message in O. E. Rolvaag's *Giants in the Earth* when it appeared in 1927. In Rolvaag's hands, he observed, the westward movement "ceases to be the proud epic of man's conquest of earth and becomes the tragedy of earth's humbling of man."[47] Twenty years later, in *The Mountain Lion*, Jean Stafford gave unblinking expression to the equally tragic impoverishment of female lives out West. Willa Cather was of course intensely alive to the hardships endured by women (and others) in the West, witness *O Pioneers!*, *My Ántonia*, and *A Lost Lady*. And what of Steinbeck's *The Grapes of Wrath*, not to mention *In Dubious Battle*, *Of Mice and Men*, and *The Long Valley*? Again, none of these works contribute to the kind of triumphal myth that the revisionists have in mind.

Nor do the California writings of Josiah Royce, whose omission from *The Legacy of Conquest* provoked belated admissions of a Freudian slip and surrender to the anxiety of influence. Though Limerick does not venture an explanation for her stunning oversight, we can begin to understand it better in the framework of the Western literary tradition. Once again, none of the works that I have mentioned contribute to the kind of triumphal myth that the revisionists describe as the norm. Put another way, all of these works portray in some substantial measure the hardship, failure, and tragedy that the New Western historians applaud in the mythmakers of their own time. Yet they are mysteriously left out of the record. Why? For the same reason, I believe, that Royce is conspicuously omitted from *The Legacy of Conquest*—because, obviously and yet paradoxically, he tells a story that Limerick can approve, but that she wants to claim as her own. To include him, and others like him, would be to acknowledge that the self-proclaimed New Western historians are fundamentally misnamed.

Royce wrote from intimate experience of the frontier. His mother, Sarah Royce, the "California Pioneer of 1849" to whom Josiah dedicated his history of the state, composed her own *Recollections of the Gold Rush and Early California* with her son's work in mind. The record of no little hardship and tragedy, Sarah's narrative, with its alternating currents of failure and hope, selfishness and sacrifice, individualism and community, was clearly an influence on Josiah's equally mingled *California: From the Conquest in 1846 to the Second Vigilance Committee in San Francisco*, published in 1886. Drawing in part on his knowledge of the mining frontier, Royce was suspicious of the doctrine of progress, and more generally of romantic and teleological approaches to history. Loyalty and service to the community were paramount in his moral scheme, and these were hardly on display in early California. Rather, Royce's backward glance settled on the failures of the frontier—on Fremont's dangerous folly and the hypocrisy of the Bear Flag revolt; on the crime of lynch law; on pervasive racial injustice; on the mistreatment of women; and on the triumph of grasping individualism over the claims of family and community. In all of this, he anticipated the New Western historians. The same may be said for his habitual moralizing, and his conviction that hope for the future has its surest foundation in a candid reckoning with happy illusions about the past. "Whoever wants merely a eulogistic story of the glories of the pioneer life of California must not look for it in history," he warns; "and whoever is too tender-souled to see any moral beauty or significance in events that involve much foolishness, drunkenness, brutality, and lust must find his innocent interests satisfied elsewhere."[48]

In acknowledging her failure to properly recognize Josiah Royce, Limerick confers upon him "his deserved status as the father of western history; he had, after all, the chronological jump on Turner."[49] But in fact the oversight is hardly repaired in this definitive example of The Limerick Maneuver. Consider that "conquest" is Limerick's talismanic word; it is to her historical project what the word "frontier" is to Turner's. "The history of the West," she writes, "is a study of a place undergoing conquest and never fully escaping its consequences." It is "conquest," and not "frontier," that "forms the historical bedrock of the whole nation."[50] But Royce surely beat Limerick to "the conquest thesis." The subtitle of his history of California—*From the Conquest in*

1846 to the Second Vigilance Committee in San Francisco—marks his bold and unequivocal refusal to deal in terms such as "progress," "revolution," and "manifest destiny." And as my brief overview of Royce's history surely suggests, this continuity in key words is merely one of numerous unacknowledged but very significant links to be drawn between Limerick and her predecessor. Did Royce have "the jump on Turner"? Was he the "father of western history"? By seeming to repay Royce with such praise, Limerick in fact conceals the much deeper indebtedness that a comparison of their work brings to light.[51]

It is important to emphasize the complex dynamics of the "anxiety of influence" on display here. In declining to mention the clear and fundamental continuities between Royce's *California* and *The Legacy of Conquest*, Limerick holds rather tenuously to the illusion of her own originality. It is the further price of this evasion that she sacrifices the opportunity to reinforce her own western story with the authority of Royce's. Her loss is the greater for the fact that the symptomatic neglect of historical precursors has its corollary in the characteristic failure to make use of literary evidence—in this case, Royce's California novel, *The Feud of Oakfield Creek*, which gives dramatic expression to his historical vision of California, and at the same time enriches our understanding of the moral and psychological legacies of conquest among the conquerors and their offspring.

The action of *The Feud of Oakfield Creek* centers on the conflict between two old pioneer friends, Alonzo Eldon and Alf Escott. Veterans of service under Fremont, of Indian wars in Washoe, and of the vigilante movements of the 1850s, the pair embody much that Royce condemned in California's past. In the three decades and more since statehood, Eldon has morally compromised himself even further in amassing a great fortune, while Escott has remained pure in principle, but relatively poor in the things of the world. Driven by an impulse to submerge his guilt in benevolence, Eldon plans to endow a vast museum and research center inspired by the writings of Henry George, and dedicated to the study of higher socialism. But in attempting to purchase atonement, he repeats the errors of his past, crosses swords with Escott, and brings tragedy to himself and the community. Eldon's example bears out Royce's conviction that hope for the future of California must be grounded in dramatic changes of heart and behavior, not in vainglorious gestures. Redemption will commence only with the banishment of inflated frontier mythologies, and with the full embrace of the tragic errors of the past. Otherwise, Californians will continue to labor—as Royce's characters labor—in a world of strife, clouded by uncertainty and frustration, and burdened with remorse.

Donald Worster declares, as part of his "program of the New Western Historians," that we must "find ourselves prefigured in our ancestors and find in them the origin of the problems and questions that plague us today." In pursuit of that goal, we must free ourselves from the "unthinking acceptance of official and unofficial myths and explanations."[52] Limerick makes the identical case, arguing "that we cannot take ourselves and our present challenges seriously until we take our history seriously. We cannot live responsibly in the American West until we have made a responsible and thorough assessment of our common past."[53] Josiah Royce undertook just such an assessment, both in history and fiction, more than a century ago. Limerick has herself in mind when, at the very outset of *The Legacy of Conquest*, she asserts that "the West need[s] someone comparable to C. Vann Woodward to write *The Burden of Western History*."[54] Kevin Starr, meanwhile, in declaring that "the crucial issue of *The Feud of Oakfield Creek* is the burden of California history," also clearly recognizes—as Limerick does not—that Royce's vision of the West anticipated Woodward's much later treatment of the South.[55]It is perfectly ironic that Limerick should seize upon the tragic example of Woodward's South while rejecting the same thing in Royce's West. The Woodward connection is of course flattering, and it lends a certain girth to what the revisionists regard as the thinly "comic" myth of the frontier. More crucial, perhaps, the appropriation of Woodward is offered as an enhancement of the originality of the New Western program, while recognition of Royce would have the opposite result. It may be replied, of course, that Royce's books were not widely influential at the time of their publication. This is true, though it is vital to add that both *California* and *The Feud of Oakfield Creek* were rejected in good part because they failed to conform to reigning regional mythologies. Royce learned, as Kevin Starr has observed, that "Californians . . . preferred their history uncorrected."[56] In taking arms against a complacent, well-entrenched establishment, Royce displayed the kind of intellectual courage that the New Western historians often claim for themselves. Limerick associates the founding of her "school" of history with a momentous "unleashing" of public intellectuals who have met the demand "for courage and heroism in the West today."[57] She casts herself in "the role of rebel against the standing models of western history," implies that she and the other revisionists "care about their subjects" with unexampled intensity, and declares it her moral duty "to put that concern on record."[58] Donald Worster projects an equally intrepid self-image, declaring that "the single most important, most distinguishing characteristic of the New Western History is its determination not to offer cover for the powers that be—not to become subservient, by silence or consent, to them." Traditional Western historians, he observes, have been "prisoners of ideology," while the members of his school are "masters of it," and therefore quite properly, the "self-appointed moral conscience of their society."[59] But how, in the matter of valiant commitment, real impact, and personal sacrifice do these self-proclaimed moral crusaders—who have enjoyed rapid academic promotion, big book sales, celebrity status, and three MacArthur Foundation genius awards as the yield on their intrepid, myth-busting defiance of the establishment—stack up against such earlier Western warriors as John Wesley Powell, John Muir, Royce himself, Aldo Leopold, Rachel Carson, Bernard DeVoto, Wallace Stegner, and Carey McWilliams?

E. L. Doctorow, I have observed, betrays in *Welcome to Hard Times* an inclination to regard all narrative as "composed," as an "interested" and partial construction of reality. As one corollary of this characteristically postmodern posture, the traditional boundary separating history and literature is brought down. By contrast, I also observe, the New Western historians have resisted postmodern incursions, insisting on a distinction between "true" history of the kind they write, and false history, or myth, which includes literature. I have viewed this resistance as obliquely expressive of the revisionist determination to insist not only on the "truth" of their story about the West, but also on its originality. The rejection of postmodernism preserves the history/myth distinction and at the same time justifies the refusal to take seriously the tragic narrative widely at large in Western literature. Quite ironically, then, the dismissal of earlier Western narratives as evasive is itself anchored in evasions.

Doctorow is hardly alone among Western writers in recognizing the constructedness of "history" set forth in their narratives of the past. Cooper was well aware that fact and fiction merged in indistinguishable ways in *The Last of the Mohicans*. The possessive pronoun in the title of *My Ántonia* is one clue among many that the book—featuring the highly subjective memories of a fictional narrator, Jim Burden, which are in turn based on Cather's actual but equally subjective memories of a "real" Bohemian girl—is a meditation on the ways and means of its own construction. Self-reflexivity of a rather different type is everywhere on display in Mark Twain's literary fabrications of self and world. Nor are the traces of such ostensible sophistication wanting in so-called mass cultural texts. Consider, for example, the way in which *The Virginian* thematizes the potently informing attraction of its tenderfoot narrator for the handsome cowboy. Jack Shaefer's *Shane* dramatizes an even more complex pattern of attraction and resistance in its boy-narrator's evolving perspective on the hero. The central mythic figure in both texts is offered up not as an iconic *fait accompli*, but as a narrative construction—an ambiguous figure taking shape in the eyes of an interested, idiosyncratic beholder.[60]

This is not, of course, to argue that such earlier texts are in any full or conscious sense postmodern. But it is to note the strong tendency in literary texts, Western and otherwise, to dramatize their own constructedness. Novelists and poets are much more prone than historians to the view, rather baldly formulated by Doctorow, that ours "is a world made for liars," and that writers—*all* writers—"are born liars."[61] Having said this much, it is important to recognize that what Robert Berkhofer calls "the postmodernist challenge to traditional history" has been a reality of academic life for a full generation now. Most historians, it is true, have been inclined to dismiss postmodernism as a kind of transient theoretical virus, and to carry on with business pretty much as usual. In their espousal of a realist epistemology and the concomitant distinction between history and myth, the New Western historians have in the past adopted a mainstream position on this issue. In a handful of recent publications, however, there has been evidence of a willingness among revisionists to consider alternative perspectives. Are such signs of interest in "theory" likely to produce significant changes in historical practice? and, rather more narrowly, in the willingness of New Western historians to consult and learn from the regional literary tradition?

To the first, more general question, I am strongly inclined to follow the lead of Jerome Frisk, whose clear and fully elaborated argument issues in a qualified negative. To date, at any rate, while all four of the major New Western historians have reconnoitered postmodern territory; and while each has returned prepared in some degree to recognize what William Cronon describes as "the human artifice that lies at the heart of even the most 'natural' of narratives,"[62] none has shown any interest in reflecting on the significance of postmodernism for their own historical projects. Rather predictably, Cronon, most especially in discussing the potent Marxian subtext driving Donald Worster's *Dust Bowl*, has gone further in this direction than his associates. But, as Frisk points out, Cronon fails to elaborate the larger implications of his analysis, both as they apply to Worster's work, and to the New Western History more generally. Rather, and quite in spite of the "human artifice" at large in all narrative, Cronon admits that "like most practicing historians," he is "only willing to follow the postmodernists so far." With commendable candor on the score of his own uncertainty, Cronon in effect jettisons the logic of his analysis in order to keep the listing ship of history afloat.[63]

The New Western historians have characteristically had it both ways with postmodernism, acknowledging its challenge on one hand, but implicitly denying its implications for their own work on the other. Donald Worster's recent essay, "Nature and the Disorder of History," is a case in point. Worster traces the modern "emphasis on change and disorder" in conceptions of history and nature to origins in capitalism. With its vision of "ceaseless change, infinite possibilities, and boundless creativity," capitalism dissolves "any fragmentary notions of stability, order, or normality left to us." Postmodernism—which Worster describes as "a degenerate worldview"—of course arises in such circumstances to dominate "modern historical consciousness." Fortunately, however, historians have it within them to "transcend our present-day circumstances," and thereby to arrive at conclusions that "seem objectively true." From among such truths, Worster reveals three—the principles of interdependency, rule-governed behavior, and enlightened change—as essential to survival.[64]

Thus even as he acknowledges the force and authority of the postmodern challenge, Worster retreats to a defensive position behind the walls of historical truth. The world around him has succumbed to degeneracy, but in Worster's perspective nothing has really changed at all. Capitalism, as he has long insisted, is the disease; and a "green" variety of Marxian socialism is still the cure. So armed in truth, the historian puts the world of postmodernism behind him—though he concedes that were the truth to fail him, he would still "be looking for a way back to some prehistorical or premodern consciousness, some folk or vernacular worldview that antedates modern historical thinking." In the upshot, historical knowledge is no more than a handmaiden to Worster's faith in a myth of premodern innocence, and serves merely to confirm his unshakable belief that modern life, like the postmodernism pathology it has spawned, is contemptible not least in its powerlessness to grasp the saving truth. We are doomed to self-destruction, he predicts, sounding more like Calvin than Marx, because though "we have more knowledge of the past than ever before . . . folly is still our old familiar companion."[65]

Worster comes to terms with the postmodern challenge to history by treating it as a symptom of the modern madness that threatens to destroy us all. Patricia Limerick approaches the problem in less direct and apocalyptic manner, but nonetheless contrives in her own fashion to have things both ways. Her recent essay, "Turnerians All: The Dream of a Helpful History in an Intelligible World," is the quintessential Limerick Maneuver, a labyrinth of retractions and rationalizations designed, one feels, to foster an illusion of change where none in fact has occurred. It is the crowning irony of the essay, as Frisk suggests, that even as she faults Turner for his failure to publicly amend his own work, Limerick fails in the same way to amend her own. "Turner," she argues, "could not frankly discuss the flaws of the 1893 essay because it formed the foundation of his career, his prestige, and his sense of personal achievement."[66] Limerick's motives are not nearly so transparent to us as Turner's are to her; still, one may reasonably surmise that she has a substantial personal and professional investment in *The Legacy of Conquest.* Thus we may be impressed when she admits in "Turnerians All" to having stumbled here and there along the way. In confessing that she neglected Hofstadter's critique of Turner, for example, or that she overlooked Turner's piecemeal self-criticism, Limerick sets herself in virtuous contrast to her hypocritical predecessor. But despite such concessions—as piecemeal, after all, as Turner's—there is nothing in the essay to suggest that Limerick recognizes in postmodernism a challenge to the towering abstraction—conquest—which gives focus and provides boundaries to her own work. It is one secret to the longevity of the Turner thesis, she jests, that it was like "the Pillsbury Dough Boy, it bent momentarily to absorb challenges and then instantly resumed its previous shape."[67] Quite ironically, the "conquest thesis" in "Turnerians All" bends and reinflates in just the same way.

Limerick has Turner to thank for having drawn her to the threshold of a postmodern perspective on history. It all began with the famous doctrine of "presentism," summarized in Turner's declaration that "each age writes the history of the past anew with reference to the conditions uppermost in its own time."[68] Limerick settled on this pronouncement as the epigraph for *The Legacy of Conquest*, but subsequently discovered the folly of assuming that the meaning of the present might somehow be known—the folly, as she puts it, of supposing that her "effort to write a happy ending to western history" was warranted by the trajectory of contemporary events. Things were improving for minorities, women, and the environment; or so it seemed to Limerick in the 1980s. But more recent political developments have produced a total reversal in view, and with it a chastened historiography. The old confidence that the past and present are knowable has given way to "a recognition of contingency and improbability" in history, to a reckoning with "chaos." Gone is the old realist epistemology, and the confident assumption that it is possible to draw "a direct, clear line between past and present." In their place is a strikingly postmodernist conception of historical narrative as the attempt to "translate the chaos of history into patterns of clarity and manageability." We are duly cautioned against the potency of our desire "to establish some control over the past." "Turner's hunger for ideas that would hold a fragmented world together was palpable and urgent." It was also his undoing.[69]

"A historian who goes around declaring that an understanding of the present will deepen our understanding of the past," Limerick has learned, "is a historian who will eventually have to eat crow." Thanks to her lapse into presentism, she has been served "a generous helping of this unattractive substance" and obliged to eat it "in public." But the plate of crow is hardly a mark of humiliation. Carefully framed against Turner's alleged refusal to admit and amend his intellectual errors, it is offered as testimony to Limerick's contrasting courage and intellectual integrity. Readers impressed by this display of magnanimity may be forgiven for failing to recognize that it produces no answering adjustments in the historian's view of the Western past. Limerick generously declines to fault Turner for his "failure of self-consciousness," and urges instead that we ask, "'What are *our* blind spots? What are the elements of our social identity that limit our vision?'"[70] What significance, more particularly, does the passage from presentism to a version of postmodern theory have for the conquest thesis? What bearing does the encounter with contingency and improbability and chaos in history have on the confident, truth-telling tone of *The Legacy of Conquest*? What is the significance of postmodern theory for pervasive, normative distinctions between fact and fiction, history and myth, the old Western story and the new one? "Turnerians All" avoids such issues, and in doing so leaves the impression that the experience it records has served not to undermine Limerick's somber reading of the past, but rather to confirm it. For in giving up on the "happy ending" that she had in mind for her regional story, Limerick links the bleakly "Unbroken Past of the American West" (so confidently described in the subtitle of her major book) to an equally bleak present.

If, as Limerick reports, political developments in the 1990s soured her optimism, then we may reasonably suppose that evidence of her now vanquished hopefulness will turn up in *The Legacy of Conquest*. Readers will recall, however, that there is nothing at all sanguine about the book's disposition, either to the past or the present. The final chapter invokes C. Vann Woodward in its title, "The Burdens of Western History," and takes the dark continuities between past and present as its principal theme. Despite the efforts of historians to displace it, the old triumphal frontier myth of "freedom, opportunity, abundance, and success" continues to flourish, most notably perhaps in presidential rhetoric. The Mormons are mired in controversy and denial; the blundering injustice of federal Indian policy persists, reinforced by "selective amnesia" among whites; the treatment of illegal Hispanic immigrants "brings to mind the famous three-fifths compromise of the U.S. Constitution." In closing, Limerick laments that racial hostility forms a "disturbing element of continuity in Western history. . . . One would be happy to consign this pattern of thought to the old frontier West," she observes gravely, "but the quarantine would not hold."[71] Granting the plausibility of much that Limerick has to say, there is no trace here of the impulse "to write a happy ending." To the contrary, *The Legacy of Conquest* ends by affirming that the tragedy of the Western past is everywhere manifest in the Western present.

By why, then, does Limerick insist on her former optimism? Why, against the overwhelming evidence of her published writing, does she project hopefulness onto a narrative of unrelenting greed, violence, and self-deception? In part, perhaps, because she recognizes that the unmingled gloom of her account of the West is patently incomplete, ignoring as it does the fabulous opportunity, enterprise, and human fulfillment that the region has witnessed in the past two centuries. But in greater part her phantom optimism serves as the nexus of a multiform contrast with Turner. He erred in refusing to admit that things had gotten worse, while Limerick erred in hoping they would get better. His error, grounded in pride and selfishness, is ignominious; hers, expressing an excess of virtue, is laudable. By admitting her error, she displays the kind of "character" that he, in denying his, conspicuously lacked. The failure of Turner's frontier thesis to keep pace with change was intellectually disastrous; on the other side, because she was never prone to optimism in the first place, Limerick relinquished nothing of intellectual substance in seeming to give it up. Quite the opposite, in fact, for the rather staged collapse of her hope serves in yet another way as the occasion for an equally rhetorical encounter with postmodern theory. I say "rhetorical" because the brief address to contingency and chaos in "Turnerians All" forms no challenge to the "truth" of *The Legacy of Conquest*, but rather contributes—quite paradoxically—to its reinforcement. Thus the more things change, the more they stay the same. Postmodernism, like Turner, presentism, and the error of optimism, is absorbed into the supple conquest thesis, which further expands its dominion over the Western story, past and present.[72]

The tragic burden of Western history, I have argued, is on record in much Western history and, even more emphatically perhaps, in much Western literature. I have also argued that the reflex refusal to consult this background is part and parcel with the revisionists' ambition to be perceived as bold iconoclasts taking arms as none have before against entrenched interests and outworn traditions. Their belated and uneasy truce with postmodernism has a kindred explanation. Postmodern theory, emphasizing the textuality of all sources and the interestedness of all points of view, bears with it an obligation to approach all stories with something like an equal eye. It makes it harder to ignore or dismiss precursors; it highlights the informing role of language, other texts, and received structures in the creation of historical reality; and, most vitally for present purposes, it erodes to the point of collapse the boundaries separating history and literature. As the work of Hayden White and Dominick LaCapra has made clear, the failure of historians to consult literature—either as a source of information, a model for historical interpretation, or a laboratory on language and meaning—is not easily defended. If we agree with White that "there is no such thing as a *single* correct view of any object under study," but rather "*many* correct views, each requiring its own style of representation," then historians must surely embrace literature as a valued source and model.[73]

It is precisely the crisis of the New Western History that it can neither accept the postmodern challenge to embrace the literary tradition, nor justify denying it. The assent to postmodernism threatens the revisionists' claim to truth; likewise, the postmodern valorization of all varieties of narrative, including literature, poses a threat to their claim to originality. Little wonder that their response to contemporary theory has been guarded. While none of the New Western historians has flatly denied the force of the postmodern challenge to history, all have contrived in various ways to evade or deflect a reckoning with its implications for their own work. Thus they may plausibly claim to have "come to terms" with the enemy, but without yielding ground in the process. In the upshot, their *de facto* embargo on theory virtually ensures that the revisionists will continue to draw the line between history and literature. As a result, the crisis of the New Western History, arising out of indefensible claims to originality and truth, will likely persist.

The New Western History has certainly enriched our perspective on the past; but it has also seriously impoverished it. By moving to a place at the center and foreground of regional studies, the revisionists have effectively obscured a rich tradition of historical and literary discourse. This is hardly an accident, for it is often the first gambit in New Western Historical works to dismiss virtually all previous writing on a given subject as ideology or myth. Literature of all varieties, popular and canonical, is invariably lumped together and discarded with the rest. Readers are thus encouraged to believe that they have nothing to learn from earlier installments on the Western story; it is all triumphal puffery and mystification, to be studied, if at all, as a species of propaganda. Cooper, Parkman, Royce, Cather, McWilliams, DeVoto, Stegner, and many, many others are made marginal to the conversation about the past and present. If you doubt that this is so, run your eye through the spacious indexes to *The Legacy of Conquest* and *"It's Your Misfortune and*

None of My Own." Cooper appears in neither; Cather, Royce, McWilliams, and DeVoto appear but once; Parkman gets two entries; Stegner is not mentioned.

Stegner is not mentioned! These books, celebrated on their covers as "all-embracing," "an excellent new synthesis," "the most talked about and influential book in Western history in years," find no place in their aggregate 1,040 pages for Wallace Stegner! As well leave John Muir out of the story of Yosemite. Stegner is of course not completely excluded. His name turns up from time to time in articles by Cronon, Worster, White, and Limerick. But it is nonetheless to recoil in amazement at the extent to which his enormous contributions as historian, novelist, journalist, teacher, and public servant are effaced in the work of the revisionists.

The explanation for this gaping omission forms a variation on a by-now-familiar paradox. Stegner is marginalized in the revisionist reckoning, it seems clear, because his Western story so thoroughly anticipates the one they want to claim as their own. To properly acknowledge the startling originality of Stegner's contribution—about which he was invariably modest—would bring with it an apparently intolerable loss of luster. From the beginning, Stegner challenged Western myths. *The Big Rock Candy Mountain* (1943), an autobiographical family saga, sets out the unequivocally critical view of footloose individualism and the heedless pursuit of the main chance that Stegner came back to again and again in the course of his long career. The novel gives ample space to the role of women in the West, a theme that persists, and often dominates, in Stegner's later fiction. *One Nation* (1945) surveys racial and religious intolerance in America at war's end. *Mormon Country* (1942) and *The Gathering of Zion* (1964) offer sympathetic portraits of another group that suffered from prejudice. Meanwhile, *Beyond the Hundredth Meridian: John Wesley Powell and the Second Opening of the West* (1954) at once promotes the cause of the environment and lends visibility to one of its earliest and worthiest advocates. In Powell Stegner found inspiration for a lifetime's commitment to promoting the appreciation and preservation of the land.

Stegner's views on race, gender, and the environment were not in all respects the same as those currently in favor. But of course it would be egregiously ahistorical to expect them to be. Stegner was confident that the issues he attended to were the important ones. But he knew as well that his views on such issues, however balanced and well informed, had no final purchase on the truth. He was not, let it be said, a postmodernist by sensibility or intellectual inclination. Traditional culture was precious to him; he believed that certain human truths had abiding validity. It was for this reason, among others, that he demanded of Western writers that they strive to articulate the continuities between past and present, avoiding the pitfalls of nostalgia and cynicism along the way. Success in this demanding venture involved the achievement of what he called "the middle ground" between history and fiction, Clio and Calliope. Like prose fiction, Stegner reasoned, history deals with persons, places, and events; it shapes itself in narrative; it is not a science, but a branch of literature. Like history, novels are grounded in social reality; but thanks to their imaginative liberty, they often illuminate the past in ways that strictly factual accounts cannot. Stegner acknowledges in *Wolf Willow*, for example, that he has "occasionally warped fact a little in order to reach for the fictional or poetic truth" that he ranks "a little above history."[74] The volume achieves the middle ground, in other words, precisely because it acknowledges that history and literature overlap, and because it exploits their merging in the attempt to arrive at the imaginative truth.

Stegner made much of the obstacles that confront those who aspire to the middle ground. "I share the nostalgia that I have attributed to most writers of the West," he concedes. "I share their frequent distaste for the uglified and over-engineered and small-spirited civilization that threatens to turn us into one gigantic anthill. But," he cautions, "I do not think we can forget the one or turn away from the other."[75] Stegner recognizes as well that the desired balance is never easily or fully or permanently achieved. Such is the leading moral to be drawn from *Angle of Repose*, his fictional treatment of the life of Mary Hallock Foote (1847–1938), which won a Pulitzer Prize in 1971. The story is told from the point of view of Foote's grandson, Lyman Ward, a prominent historian whose world is abruptly overturned by a series of unforeseen personal disasters. Lyman is struck by a painful, progressive arthritic condition which calcifies his skeleton and leads to the amputation of a leg. While he recuperates, his wife runs off with his surgeon, leaving him bitter, rigid in mind and body. Bereft in an unbearable present, and looking to the past for clarity and consolation, Lyman decides to write the biography of his grandparents. "This world of 1970 is no more an extension of my grandparents' world," he assures himself, "this West is no more a development of the West they helped build, than the sea over Santorin is an extension of that once-island of rock and olives."[76] There is no continuity in Lyman's view of history, and therefore no middle ground. *Angle of Repose* records his halting progress toward just the opposite perspective.

Lyman has no illusions about the distortions inherent in any attempt to reconstruct the past. In coming to terms with the challenge of composing historical narrative, he invokes the Doppler Effect. "The sound of anything coming at you—a train, say, or the future—has a higher pitch than the sound of the same thing going away." It is his ambition as historian to leap imaginatively from a diminished perspective on experience as it recedes to a fresh, head-on encounter with the world gone by. "I would like to hear your life as *you* heard it," he protests, reflecting on his grandparents, "coming at you, instead of hearing it as I do, a sober sound of expectations reduced, desires blunted, hopes deferred or abandoned, chances lost, defeats accepted, griefs borne."[77] Lyman is not yet ready to accept what his words surely hint at—that the past he conjures cannot be finally separated from the present he rejects. A similarly theoretical reckoning with historical distortion surfaces in his comical reunion with his old friend Al Sutton. Because of his weak eyes, Al is forced to wear thick glasses in performing his chores as an appliance repairman. Lyman is quick to apply the visual analogy to the challenge facing him, a bitter invalid, writing history. "Space being curved, tunnel vision and the rigid neck could leave a man focused on the back of his own head. I don't know what the effect of quadruple focals on a historian might be—nausea, maybe—but there might be a virtue in trying them on." After all, he reflects, "Whose head *isn't* inside a Bendix?"[78]

The more he learns about his grandparents, the more Lyman learns about himself. It is the harder truth of his sage reflections on historical method that life was as frustrating and morally precarious for his admired forbears as it has been for him. They erred; they suffered; they lived with consequences that had little about them of simple justice. In coming to accept such painful continuities, and thus in arriving at the middle ground, Lyman recognizes as well that the truth of the past will always exceed his grasp. On one side, he acknowledges that "living a day in his grandparents' life" allows him "to avoid paying too much attention to his own." On the other, he admits that "there is some history that I want not to have happened."[79] Lyman thus expresses Stegner's belief that historians operate in the partial darkness of their own very human limitations. Lyman speaks even more clearly for his maker when he decides on *Angle of Repose* as the title for the life he is writing. Such conscious self-reflexiveness bears home Stegner's admission that he shares his fictional historian's blindness, and that his novel is quite as imperfect and anguished as Lyman's biography.

Angle of Repose is a celebrated novel. It is also a brilliant—if controversial[80]—biographical rendering of the life of a major Western figure. Finally, it dramatizes in powerful and plausible ways important aspects of the history of the period in which it is set. Students with an interest in the American mining frontier, irrigation in arid country, life as it presented itself to gentlewomen coming West, Victorian sexual mores, and late nineteenth-century cultural and literary developments will be stimulated and enlightened by what Stegner has written. *Angle of Repose* is as true about much in the Western past as any historical narrative can be. And it is this in good part *because* it is a novel, and not in spite of it. The book fully exploits the imaginative resources of its genre. It takes full advantage of the license to supplement fragmentary and disconnected factual information with plausible reconstructions of incident, motive, and emotion. Finally, it dramatizes not only the life and times of Mary Hallock Foote, but also the complex and fallible human processes by which that story is seized upon, studied, and finally shaped into narrative. These are historical strengths that cannot be separated from what is literary in *Angle of Repose*. Stegner knew this, as his doctrine of the middle ground clearly suggests. His novel vividly demonstrates—what the New Western historians have so far been reluctant to acknowledge—that Clio and Calliope can ill afford to part company.

University of California, Santa Cruz

NOTES

1. *The Progressive Historians* (New York: Knopf, 1968) xiv.
2. "How the West Was Won or Lost," *The New Republic*, 22 October 1990, 35.
3. Interview with Larry McCaffery, in *Essays and Conversations*, ed. Richard Trenner (Princeton, NJ: Ontario Review Press, 1983) 33–34.
4. *Welcome to Hard Times* (New York: Bantam, 1975) 186, 89, 124.

5. "Progress or Decline? Judging the History of Western Expansion," in *A Society to Match the Scenery*, ed. Gary Holthaus, Patricia Nelson Limerick, Charles F. Wilkinson, and Eve Stryder Munson (Boulder: University of Colorado Press, 1991) 46. For the references to C. Vann Woodward and the South, see "Haunted by Rhyolite: Learning from the Landscape of Failure," in *The Big Empty: Essays on the Land as Narrative*, ed. Leonard Engel (Albuquerque: University of New Mexico Press, 1994) 41; and *The Legacy of Conquest: The Unbroken Past of the American West* (New York: Norton, 1987) 9, 18–19.

6. "Beyond the Agrarian Myth," in *Trails: Toward a New Western History*, ed. Patricia Nelson Limerick, Clyde A. Milner II, and Charles E. Rankin (Lawrence: University Press of Kansas, 1991) 16, 19.

7. *Welcome to Hard Times* 213.

8. "False Documents," in *Essays and Conversations* 16.

9. *The Progressive Historians* 61.

10. *Beyond the Frontier: Writers, Western Regionalism and a Sense of Place* (Fort Worth: Texas Christian University Press, 1989) 55.

11. "From Frontier to Region: Frederick Jackson Turner and the New Western History," *Pacific Historical Review* 64 (1995): 487. Steiner goes on to add that "today's anti-Turnerians unconsciously affirm much of his larger theory" (499).

12. "The Frontier Trail: Rethinking Turner and Reimagining the American West," *American Historical Review* 98 (1993): 111–12.

13. *"It's Your Misfortune and None of My Own": A New History of the American West* (Norman: University of Oklahoma Press, 1991) 332.

14. *Welcome to Hard Times* 7, 149.

15. *The Legacy of Conquest* 54.

16. "Beyond the Agrarian Myth" 6.

17. See especially "Revisiting the Vanishing Frontier: The Legacy of Frederick Jackson Turner," *Western Historical Quarterly* 18 (1987): 157–76; "Turner's First Stand: The Significance of Significance in American History," in *Writing Western History: Essays on Major Western Historians*, ed. Richard W. Etulain (Albuquerque: University of New Mexico Press, 1991) 73–101; and "Becoming West: Toward a New Meaning for Western History" (with George Miles and Jay Gitlin), in *Under an Open Sky: Rethinking America's Western Past*, ed. Cronon, Miles, and Gitlin (New York: Norton, 1992) 3–27.

18. *Nature's Metropolis: Chicago and the Great West* (New York: Norton, 1991) 3, 9–11, 14–15. Later on in the book (366), Cronon makes brief reference to works by Ignatius Donnelly, Henry Blake Fuller, and William T. Stead.

19. "Making the Most of Words: Verbal Activity and Western America," in *Under an Open Sky: Rethinking America's Western Past* 169.

20. *Under an Open Sky* 171, 173.

21. *Under an Open Sky* 173, 175.

22. *Two Years Before the Mast* (New York: Washington Square Press, 1968) 216, 161.

23. *Under an Open Sky* 175.

24. Donald Worster, Susan Armitage, Michael P. Malone, David J. Weber, and Patricia Nelson Limerick, "*The Legacy of Conquest*, by Patricia Nelson Limerick: A Panel of Appraisal," *Western Historical Quarterly* 20 (1989): 317.

25. "Precedents to Wisdom," in *The Geography of Hope: A Tribute to Wallace Stegner*, eds. Page Stegner and Mary Stegner (San Francisco: Sierra Club Books, 1996) 21–28.

26. "Turnerians All: The Dream of a Helpful History in an Intelligible World," *American History Review* 100 (1995): 698.

27. "Turnerians All" 715.

28. "American Environmental History: The Development of a New Historical Field," *Pacific Historical Review* 54 (1985): 305, 335.

29. *"It's Your Misfortune"* v.

30. *"It's Your Misfortune"* 57.

31. *"It's Your Misfortune"* 4.

32. *"It's Your Misfortune"* 4.

33. *"It's Your Misfortune"* 613.

34. *"It's Your Misfortune"* 615–16.

35. *"It's Your Misfortune"* 616.

36. *The Frontier in American Culture*, ed. James R. Grossman (Berkeley: University of California Press, 1994) 55.

37. *"It's Your Misfortune"* 616.

38. *"It's Your Misfortune"* 616, 623, 625.

39. "Making the Most of Words" 171. For a recent, thorough, and illuminating overview of the disciplinary wars of truth, see Robert F. Berkhofer, Jr., *Beyond the Great Story: History as Text and Discourse* (Cambridge: Harvard University Press, 1995).

40. "A Longer, Grimmer, But More Interesting Story," in *Trails* 110.

41. *"It's Your Misfortune"* 629.

42. "Beyond the Agrarian Myth" 25.

43. "What on Earth Is the New Western History?" in *Trails* 86.

44. See, for example, Richard Slotkin, *Regeneration Through Violence: The Mythology of the American Frontier, 1600–1860* (Middletown: Wesleyan University Press, 1973); Lee Clark Mitchell, *Witness to a Vanishing America* (Princeton: Princeton University Press, 1981); Jane Tompkins, *West of Everything: The Inner Life of Westerns* (New York: Oxford University Press, 1992); Michael Denning, *Mechanic Accents: Dime Novels and Working-Class Culture in America* (New York: Verso, 1987); and my own *Having It Both Ways: Self-Subversion in Western Popular Classics* (Albuquerque: University of New Mexico Press, 1993).

45. "The Politics and Antipolitics of Western History," unpublished paper delivered at the Western History Association Conference, Denver, 1995, 7, 17–18, 23.

46. Henry Nash Smith defined the terms of subsequent critical discussion in "Mark Twain as an Interpreter of the Far West: The Structure of *Roughing It*," in *The Frontier in Perspective*, ed. Walker D. Wyman and Clifton B. Kroeber (Madison:

University of Wisconsin Press, 1965) 205–28; compare also my "Seeing the Elephant: Some Perspectives on Mark Twain's *Roughing It*," *American Studies* 21 (1980): 43–64.

47. "The Literature of the Pioneer West," *Minnesota History* 8 (1927): 319.

48. *California: From the Conquest in 1846 to the Second Vigilance Committee in San Francisco* (Boston: Houghton, Mifflin & Company, 1886) 175. See also Sarah Royce, *A Frontier Lady, Recollections of the Gold Rush and Early California*, ed. Ralph Henry Gabriel (New Haven: Yale University Press, 1932). I have benefited in my thinking about Royce from Kevin Starr's "'Because I Am a Californian': The Loyalties of Josiah Royce," in *Americans and the California Dream, 1850–1915* (New York: Oxford University Press, 1973) 142–71; and Earl Pomeroy, "Josiah Royce, Historian in Quest of Community," *Pacific Historical Review* 40 (1971): 1–20.

49. "*The Legacy of Conquest* . . . A Panel of Appraisal" 317.

50. *The Legacy of Conquest* 26–27.

51. It is of interest in this regard that Limerick comments at some length in *The Legacy of Conquest* on Charles Howard Shinn, a contemporary and acquaintance of Royce, whose *Mining Camps: A Study in American Frontier Government*, published in 1884, argues that frontier California gave "happy proof"—as Limerick observes—"of an inherent Anglo-Saxon and Teutonic instinct for order" (63). Shinn turns up in *Legacy* as an example of the false optimism often found in regional history. But she does not mention that Royce took Shinn to task for just such derelictions—a point brought home quite emphatically by Rodman Wilson Paul in his introduction to the edition of *Mining Camps* (New York: Harper and Row, 1965) xviii–xxi, cited in *Legacy*. For instances of Royce's courteous but firm disagreements with Shinn, see *California* 220, 235, 247–49, and 266–68.

52. "Beyond the Agrarian Myth," in *Trails* 24–25.

53. "What on Earth Is the New Western History?" in *Trails* 87.

54. *The Legacy of Conquest* 9.

55. *Americans and the California Dream, 1850–1915* 165.

56. *Americans and the California Dream* 164. See also Robert V. Hine, *Josiah Royce: From Grass Valley to Harvard* (Norman: University of Oklahoma Press, 1992) 143–65; and John Clendenning, *The Life and Thought of Josiah Royce* (Madison: University of Wisconsin Press, 1985) 144–63.

57. "The Unleashing of the Western Public Intellectual," in *Trails* 77.

58. "What on Earth Is the New Western History?" in *Trails* 82, 87.

59. "Beyond the Agrarian Myth," in *Trails* 22–23.

60. For a fuller discussion, see my *Having It Both Ways: Self-Subversion in Western Popular Classics*, passim.

61. "False Documents," in *Essays and Conversations* 16.

62. "A Place for Stories: Nature, History, and Narrative," *The Journal of American History* 78 (1992): 1367.

63. See also Cronon's Introduction to *Uncommon Ground: Toward Reinventing Nature* (New York: Norton, 1995), and his essay, "The Trouble with Wilderness: or, Getting Back to the Wrong Nature," in the same volume. The essay later appeared in *Environmental History* 1 (1996), along with wide-ranging responses from Samuel

P. Hays, Michael P. Cohen, and Thomas Dunlap. While these writings offer additional evidence of Cronon's attention to contemporary theory, they do not elaborate on how such theory might bear on the New Western History.

64. "Nature and the Disorder of History," *Environmental History Review* 18 (Summer 1994): 9–14.

65. "Nature and the Disorder of History" 13, 15.

66. "Turnerians All" 703.

67. "Turnerians All" 698.

68. Frederick Jackson Turner, "The Significance of History," in *The Early Writings of Frederick Jackson Turner*, ed. Everett E. Edwards (Madison: University of Wisconsin Press, 1938) 52.

69. "Turnerians All" 709–10.

70. "Turnerians All" 709, 715.

71. *The Legacy of Conquest* 322–49.

72. In order to conserve space, I have excluded Richard White from the discussion of the New Western History and postmodernism. White has recently acknowledged "the power of the postmodern critique," but emphasizes that it neglects the physical, tangible world, a world of substantial bodies, and trivializes our experience in it" ("Discovering Nature in North America," *Journal of American History* 79 [1992]: 874). See also his discussion of the social constructedness of "nature" in "'Are You an Environmentalist or Do You Work for a Living?': Work and Nature," in *Uncommon Ground: Toward Reinventing Nature*, ed. William Cronon (New York: Norton, 1995) 171–85. There is nothing in either essay to indicate a major shift in White's position, or an inclination to subject his work to postmodern scrutiny.

73. Hayden White, *Tropics of Discourse: Essays in Cultural Criticism* (Baltimore: Johns Hopkins University Press, 1978) 46–47. I am more generally influenced in my thinking by White, *Metahistory: The Historical Imagination in Nineteenth-Century Europe* (Baltimore: Johns Hopkins University Press, 1973), and *The Content of the Form: Narrative Discourse and Historical Representation* (Baltimore: Johns Hopkins University Press, 1987); Dominick LaCapra, *Rethinking Intellectual History: Texts, Contexts, Language* (Ithaca: Cornell University Press, 1983), and *History and Criticism* (Ithaca: Cornell University Press, 1985); John E. Toews, "Intellectual History After the Linguistic Turn: The Autonomy of Meaning and the Irreducibility of Experience," *American Historical Review* 92 (1987): 879–907; Lloyd S. Kramer, "Literature, Criticism, and Historical Imagination: The Literary Challenge of Hayden White and Dominick LaCapra," in *The New Cultural History*, ed. Lynn Hunt (Berkeley: University of California Press, 1989) 97–128; and Berkhofer, *Beyond the Great Story*.

74. *Wolf Willow: A History, a Story, and a Memory of the Last Plains Frontier* (New York: Viking, 1962) 307. Stegner develops his ideas on the middle ground in three essays, "Born a Square," "History, Myth, and the Western Writer," and "On the Writing of History," which appear as chapters in *The Sound of Mountain Water* (New York: Doubleday, 1969). For a critical elaboration, see my (with Margaret G. Robinson) *Wallace Stegner* (Boston: Twayne, 1977) 51–52, 66–67, 93–95, 151–52.

75. *The Sound of Mountain Water* 201.

76. *Angle of Repose* (New York: Doubleday, 1971) 18.
77. *Angle of Repose* 24–25.
78. *Angle of Repose* 77.
79. *Angle of Repose* 409, 512.
80. For a thorough description of Stegner's debts to the papers of Mary Hallock Foote, and a discussion of the ethical issues involved in his treatment of her life, see Mary Ellen Williams Walsh, "*Angle of Repose* and the Writings of Mary Hallock Foote: A Source Study," in *Critical Essays on Wallace Stegner*, ed. Anthony Arthur (Boston: G. K. Hall, 1982) 184–209.

KRISTA COMER

Literature, Gender Studies, and the New Western History

IT IS NO COINCIDENCE that one of the earliest and most visible critics of the New Western History, Larry McMurtry, is a writer.[1] Or that one of McMurtry's principal targets, Patricia Limerick, is a white woman. At issue in the McMurtry/Limerick debate is the embattled status of "the imaginative" in revisionist history. Also at issue is the absence of prior revisionists in recent accounts of the western past. But something more is going on. That "something" has to do with the status of the white *literary* man in western history, the man who has critiqued western Anglo masculinity in ways that anticipate the New Western History by as much as a half-century. What kind of revisionism is this, McMurtry wonders, that bites off the hand that feeds it? A good question. And a strategically important one for anyone invested in promoting feminist politics within Western Studies.

Now if the McMurtry/Limerick controversy is no long *au courant* in New Western History discussions, it nonetheless raises questions about the realm of "the imaginative" which seem of continuing importance to New Western historians. One often hears in informal scholarly conversation a lot of open struggle and confusion about "stories," and the role that storytelling plays or should play in revisionist history. Historians speak, moreover, of their desires to tell "new stories" which also must be "multiple stories" of the western past. These questions, issues, and desires would seem to return us to the status of "the imaginative." They would seem to be illuminated by an inquiry into the structures or tropes which govern narrative organization, or by sophisticated consideration of the role that culture or cultural production plays in the making of history.[2]

But few of these provocative topics earn much sustained thought. Part of the reason for the non-attention owes to the fact that, notwithstanding notable exceptions, the New Western History is quite conservative when it comes to narrative issues.[3] This is not so surprising, of course, for professional history at large is similarly conservative. The point I wish to emphasize, however, is that the New Western History has its own very western reasons to be so, and those reasons have to do with the conservative role that culture—especially western mythology—is perceived to have played in western expansion, conquest, and history. That myth justified and in fact produced, so the broad assumption goes, every kind of racist, male supremacist, imperialist, and anti-nature politic under the western sun. Revisionist western history has thus been premised on a repudiation of western myth. From its inception, the New Western History dedicated itself to the production of a "realist" discourse that operates as counter-discourse to that of myth. Its legitimacy derives, at least in part, from the distance it claims between its own narratives and those which are "mythic."

As the reader will have intuited, I wish in this essay to question the repudiation of western "myth," not because I would retain it or valorize it in any simple way, nor because I dispute the fact that a vague but pervasive white male centeredness dominates the regional imaginary. But as someone more familiar with the cultural side of the New Western history project, I have come to believe that this "mythic West" that so many discussions depart from (including often my own) is something of a bogeyman, a straw man, gendered language intended. When one looks at it up close, it does not stand as still, or look as categorically fixed, as it seemed at first glance. More, as both historical and political thinkers, we impoverish our analyses if we over-rely on the supposed all-encompassing power of this myth to write history and popular opinion about the western past and present.

If classic myth-producing texts like Cooper's *The Last of the Mohicans* or Wister's *The Virginian* do indeed perform very conservative cultural works, they are also shot through with all kinds of subversions of and challenges to white and male supremacy, female sexlessness, Indian "savagery," environmental ruin, the invisibility of women of color, the heterosexist imperative, and so on.[4] I therefore begin this essay from the premise that, at the outset, the primary producers of mythic discourse shaped a complex, dialogic narrative which was as full of tension, dissent, self-doubt, and taboo desire, as it was a triumphal narrative of white male progress in the western wilds. Popular engagement with mythic discourse, thus, is an engagement with a cultural logic which sustains the consolidation of empire at the same time it questions and undermines that logic.

CROSSING THE HISTORY/LITERATURE DIVIDE

As champions of a mythbusting, complex, anti-romantic, anti-progressive narrative about the western past, the New Western History has made many friends among western literary critics. Although I see few signs that New Western historians are aware of this, western critics have themselves been engaged in a similar "realist" project since the early 1960s when the Western Literature Association was founded. That is, like the New Western History, western criticism has also hoped to "save us from myth." So it has come as something of a surprise to watch the New Western History emerge as a discourse that by and large does not call upon literary sources, or western literary criticism, in its revision of "western business as usual." There are exceptions, yes, most of them in women's history. And I will attend to the implications of this fact later. In all, however, western writers, especially male writers, play virtually no role in the New Western History's portrait of "the West." If you doubt this, look through a sampling of your favorite New Western History texts and see if you can find the names of a few "serious" writers. I doubt you will find many.

If writers are generally irrelevant, literary critics are invisible. Consider as example an essay by Walter Nugent, "Where Is the American West?"[5] Nugent's question, even if historians understandably tire of addressing it, is of first importance for the theoretical, epistemological, and political subjects it raises. But those issues don't get addressed in a really sophisticated way because Nugent doesn't structure *in* to his survey any capable alternative voices. We get three groups of sources: historians, publishing professionals, and members of Western Writers of America. Generally, Nugent finds, historians define the location of the West in topographic terms. By contrast, western writers, whom Nugent defines explicitly as myth-makers, "believe the West is myth, and they write about and perpetuate the myth"; well, one already knows where they locate the West, right?[16] Publishing professionals are in the middle of the place/idea divide. My questions here is, why not query the Western Literature Association (WLA), too, when Nugent's investigative logic was to query organizations like WHA and WWA? Did Nugent not know about WLA? Did he not consider that critics' work lives are dedicated to exploring these questions?

This erasure of critics was recently re-enacted, rather astonishingly, at the 1996 WLA/WHA annual conferences, where for the first time, the two associations met jointly. Several panels were organized to facilitate the acquaintance including the keynote plenary on history and literature. But who spoke on this panel? Three historians, three writers. No critics. If critics had been participants, an actual conversation among scholarly peers about the relationship between literature and history would have been unavoidable. Instead, we got a public fiction reading which prominent New Western historians officiated. This point about historians "officiating" is not professional sour grapes. Rather it goes to the fact that historians know something about the current literary regionalism, because it is perceived to be part and parcel of the New Western History social and public history phenomenon. No doubt many classrooms devoted to New Western History issues use literary texts by some of the new regionalists from the unconscious conviction that they, too, are part of the New Western History *as* a public history phenomenon.

The new literary regionalists participate quite self-consciously in debates about the New Western History. Think of Louise Erdrich, Leslie Silko, N. Scott Momaday, James Welch, Garrett Hongo, Maxine Hong Kingston, Fae Ng, Lisa See, Frank Chin, Sandra Cisneros, Gloria Anzaldúa, Cherrie Moraga, Rudolfo Anaya, Richard Rodriguez, Gary Soto, Ivan Doig, Norman Maclean, William Kittredge, Mary Clearman Blew, Teresa Jordan, Terry Tempest Williams, Barbara Kingsolver, Pam Houston, Gretel Erlich, Wanda Coleman, Sherley Anne Williams, Wilma Elizabeth McDaniels, and Gerry Haslam. These writers see themselves as activists whose public medium is literature. Indeed, many of them are far more invested in rewriting western history than in writing something like a Great American Novel.

The media represent these writers as public historians, too. *Newsweek* (and other popular magazines), in its early coverage of the *West as*

America controversy, pictured writers like Terry Tempest Williams alongside historian Patricia Limerick.[7] Recently the PBS "NewsHour with Jim Lehrer" featured Terry Tempest Williams on environmental issues, and, in a different broadcast, Barbara Kingsolver, in an interview with the very prominent David Gergen, about what is means to be a Southwestern American. The books these writers write, the representations of history these books communicate, all contribute to the basic project of the New Western History—to rewrite the individualistic (male-centered) heroic tale of days past with a new postmodern one, in which there are many interdependent protagonists in the story of Western history.

Let me build on this sensibility, then, to make one of the basic claims of this essay: the complex educational work performed today *by* literary discourse, *about* history, is hardly new. Something like it has long gone on in Western history. If this were a working premise of the New Western History, we would not have overheard the eminently learned and respected Elliott West remark during the recent plenary, from the podium, that when he was younger there was no one around the likes of Norman Maclean for him to read. There indeed were plenty of "Norman Macleans" around in the 1940s, 1950s, and 1960s, as we shall see. They just have not yet been written *into* the New Western History.

The first point structuring this essay, then, is that the New Western History thinks of itself in opposition to mythical projects, which has meant, implicitly, an anxiety about and mistrust of the realm of "the imaginative." To battle the mythic, the New Western History articulated its narrative identity through "realist" rhetoric. It assumed that realist narratives have a trustworthy (mimetic) relationship to narrative and to the realm of the imaginative, as well as an inherent political progressivism. We begin our discussion of the relationship of literature and history, consequently, with the notion that historians deal in "reality" which suggests also progressive politics, and that writers deal in the "imaginative" and in "myth" which suggest regressive or conservative politics. In this particular political bargain, most of Western literature has been jettisoned as "myth," or at the least, as irrelevant to a progressive revisionist history. Critics, as thinkers associated with culture and not "reality," have been summarily dealt out of revisionist history, too.

To have a discussion about the relationship between literature and history which does not privilege the above assumptions, or that in fact is able to consider some of the questions about "stories" that preoccupy many scholars, requires, I hope it is clear, a reformulation of the discussion. The first re-frame is to undo this line between "realist" narrative and "mythic" or "fictive" narratives; and to undo, too, the implicit assumption that "realist" politics are inherently progressive. That undoing would undo further the conflation of myth with literature (and indeed undo their status as opposites), and would also re-position the New Western History so it is not in opposition to both. The need for such an undoing is pressing, as I hope the following example will demonstrate.

The new literary regionalism is, of course, a conspicuous exception to historians' disregard for literature. The advent of this movement probably even brought the recent WHA and WLA conferences together. Patricia Limerick in particular has promoted the new regionalist literature, and one of her reasons for doing so, specifically, is because of her support of its "realist" and, hence New Western historicist, character.[8] Now I have no wish to take the major promoter of literature in the New Western History to task, because I am behind Limerick's intent and admire the range of her intellectual energies. But we should consider carefully the pitfalls of predetermining what counts as "good imagination" (realism) versus "bad imagination" (other imaginative genres). For many of the new regionalists are assuredly *not* realists. They are postmodernists, and their embrace of postmodern form is linked, importantly, to their very ability to *tell* "new stories" like those of female and minoritarian history.[9] Think of Gloria Anzaldúa, Maxine Hong Kingston, Tomás Rivera, N. Scott Momaday, Sandra Cisneros, to name but some of the most luminary. Further, most of the new regionalist writers who are indeed "realists" are white writers whose imagined West is the most conventional of Wests: the Rocky Mountain West. I take up this topic elsewhere, but here I suggest only that dismissal of nonrealist narrative strategies, out of hand, has complications for political progressivism that perhaps have not yet been fathomed.[10]

I hope it is clear, thus, that the call I make here for a more flexible embrace of the realm of "the imaginative" comes not on theoretical, but rather on political grounds. The reality/myth divide that the New Western History rather unconsciously assumes is not only facile, and something of a theoretical embarrassment, not only does it lead to erroneous thinking about cultural history, but more important, it maintains the disciplinary divide between literary and historical renderings of the West. This absence of coalition between literary and historical studies is something that political progressives, to my mind, should lament and redress. For the reality/myth divide hangs up Western Studies where we have much in common, and where we are most vulnerable and cannot afford disunity—namely, *in our joint commitment to a reconstruction of Western masculinity*.

Now how did we get to a "reconstruction of Western masculinity" when the New Western History remains fairly obtuse about marking the category of masculinity *as* a gendered category?[11] The most sweeping evidence that makes the case for "reconstruction" is that the men under discussion in the New Western History "canon," from the beginning, were not predominantly white men.[12] This fact is, of course, a critique of the racialized bent to western history, which is well known. Given the implicit white racialist agenda of neoconservatives in the 1980s, this critique is quite culturally significant.[13] But the critique also applies to the masculinist character (in its racialized dimensions) of the western past. As welcome and necessary and radical as this move is, however, one wishes for a more self-conscious commitment to highlighting masculinity as a gendered construct, especially given that the New Western History is a movement whose stated goals are those of social justice. We need explicit, not implicit analysis of the gendering of male historical subjects. And I want to suggest here that were western literature by white men a regular source for New Western historians, its content would enable, and even force, scholars to consider the historical processes by which white men become gendered subjects. More on this in a moment.

Now if one reads (perhaps too generously) a progressive politic in the history canon's focus on masculine identity, one cannot escape the fact that that focus serves to marginalize female actors of all races in western history. Even if one re-articulates male history in less racially monolithic terms, male-centered stories, like men themselves, end up, however inadvertently, representing "normative" history and "universal" experience. Sometimes the New Western History canon departs from this organizational center—as moments in Cronon's and White's works suggest.[14] And since the publication of *Legacy of Conquest*, Patricia Limerick has bent over backwards to acknowledge that text's neglect of women. Nonetheless, women's history in canonical New Western History texts is not much of an overt "player," a regrettable fact when one considers the wide textbook circulation of *It's Your Misfortune and None of My Own* and *Legacy of Conquest*, in particular. These texts pass on to new generations of undergraduates the impression that gender relations are not every bit as much at the center of western history as are race or class relations.

Indeed, in the New Western History at large, gender analysis continues to be pretty much the province of women's studies scholars. That is, gender continues to mean "women." This observation is hardly news. Feminist historians have repeatedly expressed their own disappointments about it;[15] Susan Lee Johnson has made the case perhaps best. Gender remains the most invisible analytic category in Western Studies, as she puts it, more invisible even than race, for though race has often been represented in offensive ways, it nonetheless has been represented.[16]

How can literary sources help historians do Western gender studies? How can historians make use of literature for feminist ends? First, we should note that literary sources are less absent from feminist history than they are from the New Western History canon or the New Western History at large. White women's diaries and memoirs have played a central role in re-framing the story of Western settlement so that it is represented via a family, not a single man's, tale.[17] And the major "synthetic" works of women's history, *The Women's West*, and *Western Women: Their Land, Their Lives*, have included a few essays written by literary critics who use women's "high" literature to comment on violence in Western families, as well as to comment on the challenges that nineteenth-century domestic ideology underwent in a Western context.[18] Feminist uses of literary sources suggest, therefore, that far from being conservative of it, literature subverts dominant renderings of the West. But feminist historians have only scratched the surface. At the end of this essay I want to suggest that literature might shed light on issues women's history deems especially important, namely the problem of the "engendered region" itself. I also want to suggest, provocatively I'm sure, that mythic discourse sometimes even enables feminist thought, and I will focus on female imagined sexuality to make my case.

For now I want to turn to a far less obvious source for feminist history-making: literature by white men. I aim to show here that Western literature by men represents a hugely gendered fictive world, and that it can highlight questions of gender when one talks about *men*, men's history, and male engagement with the masculinism of the regional imaginary. Literary Westerns bring sustained critique to a masculine identity based on frontier aggression and masculine narcissism. The price of "progress" in the West, so literary Westerns by men of the 1920s–1960s argue, turns out to have been high indeed. I urge the New Western History to call upon that tradition more often as one area in which "Western business as usual" has been challenged. The discussion of the male literary canon which follows here suggests one discourse in which the construction and re-construction of masculinity has long been underway.

THE LITERARY MAN'S CRITIQUE OF WESTERN MASCULINITY

Consider the canonical writers of the literary West, at least as the dominant trend in Western criticism conceives them: Robinson Jeffers, Harvey Fergusson, A. B. Guthrie, Vardis Fisher, Walter Van Tilburg Clark, Wallace Stegner, Frank Waters. These are mostly white male writers whose "big works" come out roughly between 1930 and 1970. They are the writers through whom Western critics initially conceived a high-culture and incidentally, a "realist" tradition.[19] If we look at, say, Guthrie's *The Big Sky* (1947), or if we look at Stegner's *The Big Rock Candy Mountain* (1943), we see that the protagonists of these texts, Boone Caudill and Bo Mason, respectively, are just the kind of men that Patty Limerick often features in the "Empire of Innocence" section of *Legacy of Conquest*. Indeed, we begin to see the broad, enabling discursive context out of which a book like *Legacy of Conquest* ultimately emerges.

Let's focus on Stegner's Bo Mason first, for given the recent attention to Stegner by some historians, he is one of the most likely writers to be read. *The Big Rock Candy Mountain*'s story is one wherein young man and young woman go West, independently of one another, meet up, fall in love, marry, become lovers, have children, stay lovers, and forever thereafter search for "the big rock candy mountain." They're looking for that Western place where something can be gotten for nothing, that place that is America at its best, if you can just find it, if you're quick and clever enough to get there early, before the cream's been skimmed off, before the dream's gone bad. Bo Mason, the unquestioned head of this family, leads his wife and children on the search for Big Rock Candy Mountain, while Elsa Mason, though she consents to it, does not herself want, or need, what the search offers. At least she does not need it as much as does her husband. Elsa's desires center more around family stability and respectability, around her children's health and safety and the daily pleasures of domestic life.

Elsa and Bo Mason *are* quick and clever; they work hard, persevere, adapt. Their creativity in the face of new situations is of the best American kind. But the big rock candy mountain nonetheless eludes them. This family saga takes a bitter turn early on, and by the end, one young son has died; the surviving son openly hates his father. The father cheats on the wife he loves, and the mother wonders what has happened to her backbone, for she no longer stands her own ground.

This story is not an unusual one for anyone familiar with Western history. Bo Mason is charismatic, romantic, stylish, virile, a risk-taker. He's a bootlegger. For a time he plays professional baseball. That is, Bo's an all-American hero. He's a lover, a charmer, but, in the end, he's an abusive son of a bitch. He is cruel, narcissistic, and the demands of being a father and husband make him more so. When things don't go his way, which is usually, it's always someone else's fault. The children have held him back, the blasted weather has ruined his crops, the Klondike isn't what it was made out to be, all is against him. Bo Mason, as New Western historians will be quick to grasp, very much illustrates the general type Limerick describes as the "injured Western innocent." Though he is the unquestioned patriarch of the family, the center of power, he conceives himself its victim. An intense individualist, someone who deeply believes a man lives or dies by his own merits, he still curses the powers-that-be for not helping him enough, for not creating some kind of even playing field, for not making, in essence, the Big Rock Candy Mountain a sure thing. Of course few of these ironies dawn on Bo Mason; he is as entitled and guileless as a two-year-old. But the ironies dawn on Wallace Stegner. Indeed, the ironies are the point.

The important fact about *Big Rock Candy Mountain* is this. The burden of the text is critique. This is a story about the failures of Western men to live up to social and familial obligations, to curb their own dreams of grandeur when those dreams are exposed as unattainable, misguided, antisocial, destructive to others, or just plain juvenile. *Big*

Rock Candy Mountain does not celebrate Bo Mason; it empathizes with him enough so that it understands him, at times it is helplessly seduced by his considerable charisma, but it finally hates him, rages at him for the anguish his type of man causes his family and society at large.

Ponder the symbolic implication of Bo Mason's final moments: he murders his mistress and turns the gun on himself. Stegner's is a statement about the limits of Bo Mason's kind of masculinity for the future of the West. Published on the eve of the American Century in 1947, *Big Rock Candy Mountain* is a Joan Didion-like cautionary tale about the social ills Westerners must root out of "the Western imagination" if the West is to be a civilized post–World War II region. Or ponder Stegner's closing eulogy to Bo Mason:

> Bo Mason was a child and a man. Whatever he did, any time, he was a completely masculine being, and almost always he was a child, even in his rages. In an earlier time [frontier days], under other circumstances, he might have become something the nation would have elected to honor, but he would have been no different. He would always have been an undeveloped human being, an immature social animal, and the further the nation goes the less room there is for that kind of man. (562)

This eulogy is explicitly anti-mythic and anti-nostalgic, and herein one begins, I hope, to see its relevance to the New Western History. Like the canonical books of the New Western History, Stegner's novel is very much invested in debunking the myth of the "innocent injured" Western man. It shows repeatedly that Bo Mason's troubles are, as often as not, of his own making. His problems with money, with his sons, and with his beloved wife, start with *him* and his breed of masculine identity. This narrative's ethical frame judges Bo Mason's expectations of "something for nothing" as not just misguided or foolhardy or immature, but aggressively willful and self-serving. They are at the center of the West's problems.

Bo Mason—and the Western man he illustrates—is held accountable for his actions, he is judged and convicted. And the sentence for his crimes is to banish him from the ranks of "desirable" Western men. He should be no father figure whom a son would emulate as he grows into full manhood. On the occasion of Bo Mason's funeral, his son,

Bruce Mason, does not deny that his father was "talented," "versatile," "energetic," "the raw material for a notable man" (561–62). Still, the son can neither "honor" nor "respect" him (561–62). Stegner's adjudication of Bo Mason intervenes on the notion that the Old West was peopled by "men's men" and that the closing of that West is a tragedy for masculine subjectivity.

There are other points to make here. The first is that this text is representative of canonical literary Westerns in that it demonstrates a countercurrent to what many New Western historians often call "business as usual" or "Western history as usual." Nearly all major literary Westerns by men written between about 1910 and the late 1950s are heavily ironic in their representations of the West, Western masculinity, and Western race relations.[20] A. B. Guthrie's Boone Caudill, protagonist of *The Big Sky*, is a mountain man whose own selfish recklessness implicates him in the destruction of the frontier he so loves. Not only that, but it leads him to kill his best friend for mistaken reasons, and to cut himself off forever from his baby son and his cherished Blackfoot wife, Teal Eye. Walter Van Tilburg Clark's *Ox-Bow Incident* is a story about middle-aged has-been cowboys. Their town has gone from boom to about bust, and in response, they drink too much, talk too much, and sit around all day doing nothing. The old days when male competence and vigor were taken for granted are gone. Turn-of-the-century masculine identity is clearly at stake in this post-frontier town, and the way these men resolve it is through a kind of lynch mob orgy, which results in the hanging of three innocent men.[21] Or think of the moral take behind Frank Water's *The Man Who Killed the Deer*: that self-sufficiency and ego-driven behavior is at the root of the half-breed Martiniano's troubles with his fellow tribesmen.[22]

In all of the above cases, writers take to task what is supposed to be the most seductive feature of the Western imaginary—its individualistic definition of freedom. It isn't white women's arrival that ruins the good times, it isn't economic displacement and hardship, or the disappearance of the noble savage. What ruins the West is that its men do not know how to direct masculine desire toward constructive, sustainable ends. Or rather, the men who would direct masculinity toward those ends—literary men—are not the power-brokers, not the Teddy Roosevelts or Frederic Remingtons of Western history.

Now, having made a case here about the ways that western male writers self-consciously narrativize western masculinity, a self-consciousness I would urge on practitioners of the New Western History, let me be sure to emphasize that I am not saying that the male canon (or canon-makers) shows no love of, or nostalgia about, "the good old days." Of course it does. That's probably the bulk of what you get from it at first glance. Texts like *The Big Sky* or *The Way West* or *The Track of the Cat* or *The Big Rock Candy Mountain* all long intensely for the romance of the Old West, and for the "virgin land" that is so much a part of that pathos. With those longings goes every kind of racial and gender and class politic that contemporaries rightly object to. But, rather than pursue any of those legitimate, but rather obvious objections, I would speculate instead about a less common topic with sweeping implications for gender studies: the nostalgia for male homosociality one often feels in literary and popular Westerns.

For all of the skepticism about Western masculinity going on in literary Westerns, they also overflow with continual waves of male pleasure, desire, "authentic masculinity," and sensual gratification. To be sure, male ecstasy is sometimes tied to heterosexual love (which is also frequently interracial); it also is tied to the love of, and communion with, female-gendered nature. But just as often it is tied to moments in which men's love of men is uncomplicated and complete. Literary Westerns by men are, by and large, about men, the relationships between men, and the effort to articulate something like mature male desire. Even Stegner, whom critics talk a lot about as someone very interested in gender relations, is just as interested in men and manhood as he is in male/female love and lifelong companionship.

Indeed, it is when relationships between men go wrong, when the Virginian must hang Steve, when the son of Bo Mason cannot emulate his father, when Boone Caudill rashly kills Jim and abandons his infant son, when the lynch mob of *Ox-Bow Incident* martyrs three innocent men, it is here that the tragedy occurs. For what is lost when men's relationships go awry is the imaginative experience of male connection and primary love—the kind of love that Freudians reserve for mother and child, the kind that becomes taboo in the twentieth century as same-sex love is increasingly pathologized.

The canonical literary West is a kind of compromise fable. It captures and negotiates the turn-of-the-century transition from Victorian "manly" masculinity to Western "virile" masculinity by forwarding stories of male community in which "manly" ethical values prevail even as the "virile" manhood of male characters is upheld.[23] That is, canonical narratives bow to the new twentieth-century heterosexual imperative promoted by someone like Teddy Roosevelt but they simultaneously keep alive the commitment of "manly men" to right relations between men (or between men and women, for that matter). Since the prohibition against same-sex love polices the ways that "right relations" might be represented, the canonical West focuses less on "successful" or emotionally "realized" love between men, and instead tells stories of male love gone wrong. These stories satisfy readers by punishing men who victimize the less powerful men they love. We get a system of justice, then, internal to this discourse, that exposes and criticizes abusive men, and by so doing, acknowledges the wounds of those who have been hurt. Which is to say that the canonical West *limits* the power it allows "masculine men," and censures, even banishes, those men who push the boundaries of ethical manhood too far.

But a tremendous amount of longing for better bonds between men persists. Put differently, if a text like *The Virginian* consolidates the new twentieth-century heterosexual imperative, it also consolidates the struggle *against* that imperative. Though *The Virginian* would seem to mark the watershed moment from which a new, more entitled and aggressive breed of masculinity is stamped onto "things authentically Western," *The Virginian* also lingeringly preserves the bonds between the Virginian and Steve, and more deep and formative still, between the Virginian and the "tenderfoot" narrator. The point here is that contained within twentieth-century mythic discourse is both the justification for a new male power bloc as well as a longing for love and camaraderie between men, a love *not* defined (or less defined) against the backdrop of male power over women. Thus mythic discourse, though it can be deployed toward misogynist ends, is also potentially radical to male literary Westerns. It affords male writers and popular audiences an imaginative arena in which to claim and celebrate bonds between men, even as the "frontier" of male homosociality has closed.

When it comes to a critique of Western masculinity, then, New Western historians have more than fifty years of company. Literary men (including critics) have been in the midst of a serious and sustained effort to ask questions like: what does it mean to be an ethical man in a region that is synonymous with male prerogative? The male literary canon, and the canon-makers too, have been very much part of a general impulse to challenge "Western *men* as usual." Indeed, they have created the discursive context out of which the New Western History currently operates.

Historians will note, further, that this discourse about ethical western manhood reaches a denouement in the immediate post-war period, when America, now armed with the Bomb, ascends to unquestioned world dominance. Think not only of the literary West but also of supposedly "formula" Westerns like John Ford's *The Searchers* or Jack Schaefer's *Shane.*[24] That is, this nationalist discourse about the role of masculinity in national identity consolidation greets the beginning of the Cold War not with the yell of "charge!" but instead with a warning. There is a lesson to be learned from the West of the nineteenth century. And the lesson is, beware of cowboy diplomacy. Don't, for God's sake, let it govern the arms race. It brings heartache; in the end, it spoils the very hopes it nurtured.

Now having given the male literary West its due, I want to be clear that I do not hold up the canon (or canon-makers) as some kind of ideal of gender sensitivity when it comes to *women's* needs, thoughts, desires, experiences, hopes, daily lives, or politics. Clearly, in the geographic imaginary I have sketched above, there is limited room to imagine *female* desire. For that one must go to women's history, feminist criticism, or women's literature, because it is only there that men's stories are de-centered enough to get a word in edgewise.

Let me turn then to what I'm calling the "canon" in the women's studies wing of the New Western History, and consider both its representation of gendered subjectivity, as well as the ways that literary sources inform that representation. As I noted at the outset, feminist history is less conservative about narrative issues than is the New Western History at large. But feminist historians are not without their own anxieties about literature, especially, as we will see, "high literature." One of the ironic twists in recent historiography is that in order to rescue non-traditional writing from historical oblivion so that the goal of "people's history" might be served, feminist historians have relied to a fault on non-high literary narratives to conceptualize their female Wests. "High literature" of the nineteenth and twentieth centuries, thus, receives nearly no mention in the vast majority of feminist historical texts. Though feminist historians would seem to be less committed to the myth/reality divide, women's literature is not a source that historians claim as their own. This fact distances women's history from an embrace of "the imaginative" which, in the final analysis, shrinks the possible contexts from which historical narrative can be conceived.

EMBRACING "THE IMAGINATIVE" IN WESTERN WOMEN'S HISTORY

A "canon" of women's history texts? The very suggestion may offend. It may offend all the more because, since the late 1980s, western women's history has been so sensitized to the problems of racial domination—so aware that *white* women's history easily becomes a stand-in for "women's" history—that it refused, by the early 1990s, to put forward any "center" to its feminist project.[25]

Women's history might be better characterized, then, as a field in which at least two competing impulses are operative. The first grows out of the basic feminist insight that the master subject of historical narrative—the white man—is a gendered subject. This insight enabled feminist scholars in the late 1970s to dislodge the persistent equation of white men's history with Western history, and to thereby create new epistemological space in which feminists could imagine female-gendered histories.[26] John Mack Faragher's *Women and Men on the Overland Trail* is an enduring example, as is Joan Jensen and Darliss Miller's "The Gentle Tamers Revisted."[27]

The second impulse is the trend toward "intercultural analysis" which begins to be laid out in Elizabeth Jameson's "Toward a Multicultural History of Women in the Western United States," and culminates in Peggy Pascoe's very highly regarded *Relations of Rescue* (1990).[28] Confronted throughout the 1980s with the fact that the new space women's historians carved out for female historical subjects most often described *white* women's western experiences, the "intercultural analysis" branch of women's history attends to the multiple and simultaneous racial contexts that shape women's social relations and gendered identities.[29] To the degree that histories of women of color were associated with *any* school of Western history, versus say Chicana or Asian American history, they were associated with this one. The major classroom textbook of women's history comes from the "intercultural analysis" school—*The Women's West*, edited by Sue Armitage and Elizabeth Jameson (1988).[30]

The above list is one I would submit as a kind of "canon" of women's history. I would add two pieces from the 1990s. The first is Susan Lee Johnson's essay "A Memory Sweet to Soldiers" (1993), because it is widely read and presages new theoretical ground in women's history: namely its link to cultural studies and to masculinity studies.[31] I would also include one essay from a special issue of *Pacific Historical Review*: Antonia Castañeda's "Women of Color and the Rewriting of Western History," for it too has played a significant role in shaping the current women's history agenda.[32] The above list represents to my mind the broad trends and goals of Western women's history to date. Of course it is flawed, but I am less interested in defending this list than in using it as a kind of practical tool that lets me evaluate the degree to which "the imaginative" is a category in feminist historians' reconceptualizations of the West.

The first point to make, then, is that in the "canon" of women's history, women's literary writings are a sometimes-used historical source, especially when those writings are of the genre of "Westering diary," or "letters home," and (to a lesser extent) Western memoir. When it comes to "high literature," historians are less at ease, and they leave those texts to literary critics. *The Women's West* is a case in point. On the topic of literary critics, Susan Johnson is one of the few historians who uses critics' texts argumentatively, as part of her own conceptual apparatus. And no one is interested in the literary West by men, unless it is to point out the "gentle tamer" female stereotype represented say, in *The Virginian*'s Molly Stark. Here I should note that though I support the feminist historical project behind such a characterization, I nonetheless see Molly Stark in considerably more complex terms.

None of the above is, perhaps, so hard to understand. Disciplinary divides are quite hard to cross, and women's history has been very busy locating the basic, much less the more sophisticated, historical sources. But I would observe here that western women's history at the end of the 1980s was sincerely engaged in a discussion about the difficulties of investigating the lives of historical subjects who left behind no letters or diaries, who perhaps were illiterate, or did not speak or write English, or who were averse to the tradition of written narrative altogether. Informal discussions among feminist scholars centered on the need for new research methods that would enable access to these women's lives. Material culture seemed to provide one avenue. Oral histories, a women's studies tried-and-true methodology imported from anthropology, provided another. And, as critic Judy Nolte Temple pointed out with gentle tact in "Beyond the Intellectual Meridian: Transdisciplinary Studies of Women" (1992), cultural studies and literary criticism also provided enabling and sophisticated methodologies—discourse analysis being one that Temple noted was already in use in a few western women's history texts.[33] With the incorporation of literary narratives into historical narratives, Temple hoped, would come the more important transdisciplinary shift: the softening of the line between texts which offered "real" versus those which offered "fictive" narratives of the past.

If recent histories have indeed made use of new and creative methodologies, they also have stayed away from literature as a source for women's history. That is, the paradigmatic bias against especially "high" literature found in the women's history canon remains. The driving impulses of the field that I sketched above—the investment in the westering story as well as the investment in intercultural analysis—have become increasingly sophisticated and specialized in the 1990s. White women's history currently enjoys a real flowering of scholarly activity.[34] So does the history of women of color.[35] Researchers seem to be bending and stretching the "texts" they consider legitimate sources as often as possible in order to "get at" women's lives. The paradigms of American women's history and American Studies are increasingly visible in western women's history titles.[36] And some western titles with an old-fashioned frontier "feel" to them now appear in non-regional formats, like *American Quarterly*.[37] Reviewers make a similar point about the new "'90s approach" in reviews of one exemplary work: *What This Awl Means: Feminist Archeology at an Wahpeton Dakota Village* by Janet Spector.[38]

And yet in spite of what seems a real expansion of choices of methodologies, women writers remain on the outside of this massive feminist history project. From a feminist literary critic's perspective, this development is hard to understand. There are exceptions, yes, like Joan Jensen's *One Foot on the Rockies*, a book that is an admirable attempt to go after a topic as big as the relationships between postmodernism, the West, women, and creativity.[39] And a few cultural biographies have appeared that try to center "culture" more visibly within history.[40] But overall, literary sources and cultural studies-informed analysis are not big players in 1990s women's history.

It makes one wonder if feminist historians know how many western writers there are, or how widely read many of them were or are? Perhaps not. If not, a weighty chunk of responsibility must fall on feminist critics' shoulders, for feminist criticism has not, it would seem, shown the way. Certainly it has not been driven by, or blessed with, the same kind of dynamic outpouring of scholarly work as has feminist history. Feminist criticism is in a rather funny inverse position relative to feminist history, in fact, in that it needs a few synthetic works just so boundaries and/or periods are enough defined to make people fight about and revise them. The history of literary women, or of women as image-producers, is still very much incomplete. Critics have some sense of the early period (1830–1850); we have a lot of information on particular writers, and some sense of the cluster of modernist writers who lived and worked around Taos and throughout the Southwest.[41] My own forthcoming book tries to think broadly about the postmodern period, and writers' various engagements with postmodernism and post–Cold War nationalism.[42] But there are many, many conceptual gaps in feminist criticism that have yet to be filled in. Feminist history, actually, were it so inclined, is in a relatively strong position to enter this scholarly territory and pursue it.

What does women's literature and feminist criticism offer to women's history that women's history does not already know? One of the big and quite provocative claims of women's history is that the region of the West itself is gendered male. Katherine Morrissey would make this premise a point of departure for any study of the Western past.[43] Susan Armitage and Susan Lee Johnson embrace that claim, and proceed in their own works from it.[44] But women's history is far from understanding the various constituent processes by which the gendering of the region takes place. Women's literature and feminist criticism can help here. One of the central ways in which masculinist discourse claims the region for itself, both criticism and literature make clear, is to dominate the discourse of nature. One only needs to recall the trope of "virgin land" to remember the various uses—economic, psychosexual, and racialist—to which a gendered discourse about nature can be put.

Women's historians should *not* leave the study of nature to ecocritics or environmental historians alone for generally, they do not do gender analysis. They do not begin, as feminists will, from the assumption that discourses about nature are gendered, or that, indeed, it is hard to imagine a discourse more important to the ways in which Americans came to construct "the West," the nation, or to construct male and female subjects within both.

Annette Kolodny's *The Land Before Her* remains the trendsetting work here.[45] Kolodny demonstrates that white women's "promotional" literature (as she calls it) of the 1830s–1860s formulated an alternative discourse *about nature* through which women writers took their readers west. The writers she considers (some of which will be surprises as "westerners") are Caroline Kirkland, Mary Austin Holley, Eliza Farnham, Margaret Fuller, Alice Carey, Caroline Soule, E.D.E.N. Southworth, and Maria Susanna Cummins. In *their* fictive worlds, the land was "home" to a dream of hearth, garden, and community. They searched not for the Big Rock Candy Mountain. But theirs was not only an alternative discourse. It was a counter-discourse which broadly critiqued the idea that female-gendered nature was "there for the taking." This critique challenged white men's right to exploit both the land and women's bodies. It alerted women travelers to the trials that awaited them in Westering spaces, in the hopes that to be forewarned was to be forearmed. Finally, the critique implicitly sanctioned indigenous peoples' land claims. Not only, then, did women's production of a counter-discourse about nature give rise to an alternative nationalist program, this counter-discourse also was one of the "seeds" that kept alive white women's ambivalence about indigenous peoples' dispossession and extermination.

What I would have us consider here, and this is part of Kolodny's reason to take seriously the realm of "fantasy," is that literary narratives of this early expansion period actually "made history" to the extent that they profoundly influenced women's (and men's) self-perceptions, their sense of the new world around them, their attitudes toward the inhabitants of that new world, and the terms by which they would carry out their lives. Indeed, in the final analysis, these narratives may "make history" in much more immediate and efficacious ways than does historical narrative itself which, after all, makes history (literally constructs history) only retrospectively.

This alternative vision of the nation that Kolodny documents—written via a discourse about nature—will set the paradigmatic stage for many, many later women writers. A second period of enormous literary production by women began in the early 1880s with the works of Mary

Hallock Foote, Helen Hunt Jackson, Ina Coolbrith, Sarah Winnemucca Hopkins, and Amparo Ruiz de Burton. It continued through the 1890s, and by the end of the First World War it included Gertrude Atherton, B. M. Bower, Mary Austin, Willa Cather, Mabel Dodge Luhan, Sharlot Hall, Mary Corbin Henderson, Mrs. Lu Wheat, Sui Sin Far (Edith Eaton), and Zitkala Sa. Certainly this group of writers did not represent the West in any one, uniform way. Nor is this an exhaustive list. I have mentioned these writers, many of whom are associated with California literature in particular, because they are writers about whom critics know a fair amount.[46] I gather them together here to suggest that a viable counter-discourse was happening in and around the symbolic and literal site of California and California's "natural environment."

What was at issue, at this later historic moment, is again, the imperial uses to which the symbolism of "the West" will be put by a figure like Teddy Roosevelt. But more, this time, what is at issue is the sexualized character of Roosevelt's new nation.[47] We begin to see as early as the 1880s an overt discourse about female sexuality emerge from within western women's writings. It puts out its own vision of a sexualized nation to compete with that of Roosevelt. But in *it*, sexuality is not linked to an anti-modern version of the "authentic West," nor to Anglo-Saxon racial purity. Rather, female desire is linked to the broader project of modernity. And this alliance will enable western female discourse, throughout the twentieth century, to withstand and challenge some of the most anti-feminist parts of the western problematic.

Let me forward here, then, a broad thesis. Women writers, from the 1830s on, seem noticeably more invested in representing sexuality than are their male counterparts. There is something about Western "wilderness"—its association with a topography of desire, I believe—that has tempted, even finally required, women writers to locate within it their own fantasied pleasures.[48] Because the trope of "wild landscape" is a symbolic trajectory emplotted by European and later American male desire and prerogative, women must first expose it, if they are to avoid being its victim. But then to go further, and survive with any kind of female subjectivity intact, they must re-emplot it.

This discourse about female sexuality thus accomplishes several critical goals. It reveals the pivotal role that sexual discourse plays in the process by which the region is gendered and racialized; it rejects a masculinist sexual discourse in which men's pleasure is the only pleasure that counts; and it represents *female* visions of desire. In the twentieth century, women's fantasies include those that Kolodny argues are so much a part of settler women's writings: a worry that environmental exploitation is foolhardy and a desire for permanent homes and communities. But fantasy, for twentieth-century women, is expressed increasingly in erotic, not domestic, terms. It is increasingly linked, too, to visions of a just State. Even in feminism's "quiet years"—during the "doldrums" between the Vote and the 1960s, years when public sexual expressiveness for women risked severe social censure—western women writers wrote extensively about female sexuality.[49]

Consider Mary Hallock Foote, whose gentlewomanly propriety forbade her to write publicly about childbirth in the wilds, birth control, or sexual identity, but who nonetheless was driven by her Western experience to write at great length in personal correspondence about these topics to her long-time female friend.[50] Or Mabel Dodge Luhan, who loved both women and men, wrote of fondling women's breasts, was also married four times, and the last, to an American Indian man.[51] Or think of Willa Cather's eroticized landscapes, like those in *Song of the Lark*, which link creativity to representations of the female body, and which express something of Cather's frustrated lesbianism.[52] Or consider any number of Mary Austin's works—but especially *Cactus Thorn*, which though written in 1927 was not published until the 1980s, in part because of its explicit sexual materials and the grittiness of its understanding of the gender politics of heterosexual sex.[53] How about Edith Summers Kelley, not a writer conventionally considered "western," but one who nonetheless writes a western book, *The Devil's Hand* (1925)? This is a book about two female farmers in Southern California, the less "manly" of whom feels a new libido out West, which she explores explicitly with her male Hindu neighbor, and implicitly, with her female homesteading partner.

Let us pause for a moment on Kelley's *The Devil's Hand*, which, like Mary Austin's *Cactus Thorn*, also was unpublished until recently in 1972. I want to make a claim here *not* for the novel's ability to influence the course of western history. The novel was not in circulation until the 1970s, and thus it did not have the opportunity to shape the actions, both individual and collective, that comprise "history." Thus, I'm not making a case here, as I have throughout this essay, for the very active role that literature plays in the making of history. Rather, I'm interested in this novel as one example of the ways in which mythologies about the West—especially the notion of the West as land of taboo desire—shape a female story in very unanticipated ways. This discussion is certainly speculative, but I hope suggestive nonetheless.

The editor of *The Devil's Hand* reasons that the novel was not published earlier because it is not Kelley's best work.[54] And while this observation seems justifiable, for *The Devil's Hand* is a half-try at a proletarian novel (and proletarian novels are rarely judged "good" by critical standards), one imagines that the love affairs the protagonist engages in, both explicitly and implicitly, didn't help its chances. Else why would the novel, like Austin's *Cactus Thorn*, appear fifty years later when aesthetic standards have changed less than have public attitudes about female sexuality?

What we have in *The Devil's Hand* is a sexual coming of age story that raises the possibility of lesbian love, does not overtly investigate it, and leaves it intact at story's end. The plot is thus: two women go west in the 1920s to make a go of a farm. One the narrator calls "mannish." Her name is Kate and she is singularly unlikeable. She is hardworking, strong, courageous, but also bossy, crude, uncompanionable. The other, Rhonda, is compliant, bossed, a women with an under-nurtured intellectual side. Theirs is an early study in butch/femme roles in women's relationships. A huge silence in this book revolves around, as the neighbors might whisperingly wonder, what these two women are doing out on their farm, all alone, night after night, without any men around. But the reader is left to wonder, for on this topic, the novel is all suspended tension, no release.

No release until we begin to see Rhonda, the protagonist, become, as the narrator puts it, "freer." After three months of ranch life, we are told:

> [Rhonda] walked with a springy step and sometimes broke into a run and raced with a young collie that hung at her heels. Her khaki shirt, open at the throat and rolled to the elbow, showed neck and arms browned to a pale tobacco color and healthy glow showed through the tan of her cheeks. . . . In this elastic girl who looked not more than twenty five there was little resemblance to the rather pinched woman in a decent tailored suit over a respectable corset. (39)

This description of a "freer" Rhonda, we should first note, is linked to "natural elements" like sunshine and clean air and the great western outdoors. That is, "nature" is a symbolic template through which is narrated this woman's psychic evolution. But Rhonda's is a very specific evolution. Her new freedom and energy come from her new capacity for passionate abandon. She leaves behind the corseted Victorianism and the schoolteacherly "decent suit-edness" of her former female self. In its place develops a more exposed, even "masculinized" female self, willing to reveal her body to the natural elements and revel in its previously unknown capacities. Not only is Rhonda a "freer" woman, moreover, she is a *browner* woman. We see here a quite specific example of the ways that nature negotiates not only psychic development, but an emergent multiply gendered sexual identity, which is also multiply racialized.

Rhonda's new sense of freedom encourages her to take her Hindu neighbor as lover. She is immensely thrilled by this affair, and pursues it with unconcealed eagerness. Part of what attracts her to this man is that he represents an exocitized "other" to her. She remarks on his "dark, sensuous, full lips." But, in my reading, she is not as much interested in re-inventing his otherness, in reinscribing racial difference, as she is in exploring taboo sexuality. One has the feeling that any (male) partner would have sufficed; this one was handy enough to live next door. Rhonda does not, interestingly, confide in Kate about the affair. When the Hindu's farm goes under and he must leave town, she regrets that much of the thrill has left her life, but she does not miss this man, for she did not love him. When the book's union organizer hero comes to town and meets up with the newly lonely Rhonda, she develops feelings for him, part of which are generated by his intelligence and political convictions. But he is passionate only about the unionist cause, and their relationship remains disappointingly platonic.

Here I would like to point out the degree to which the "genre" issues (proletarianism) mentioned by the book's editor overlap with and complicate Kelley's engagement with California as a regional imaginary. Kelley was, for a time, both assistant to Upton Sinclair as he finished *The Jungle*, and even engaged to him before she broke it off to marry someone else. Kelley circulated among New York City's radical literati, and was very much interested in and committed to radical trade unionism. Her first book, *Weeds*, set on a Kentucky farm, showed something of this influence. It also showed her feminist leanings, for *Weeds* is a very complex and often troubling portrait of the strains that farm life puts on farm women.[55] But this new book she had on her hands, set not in Hamlin Garland country but in dreamy Southern California, presented her, I am speculating, with some rather novel problems. It would not quite adhere to the proletarian formula, though Kelley tried hard to make it adhere. *The Devil's Hand* shows Kelley's very heavy-handed social message: those who work the land should unite, unionize, and resist the unjust relations which keep the white affluent townspeople on top of the economic hierarchy.

The fictional situation Kelley created, however, overwhelmed the proletarian line. First of all, the peoples working the land in her novel—the independent farmers like Kelley's female protagonists, their neighbors the Hindus, the Mexican migrant workers, and the Japanese tenant farmers—occupied very different places in the agricultural hierarchy and economy. Even if people's racial or gendered differences could be novelistically overcome, which they could not, they were not a cohesive class of workers who could be organized into a unionist narrative to begin with.

But even more of a challenge was the fact that by setting her book in Southern California, Kelley inherited certain "tendencies" that came with that regional imaginary. Most important, she engaged a particular tradition of landscape representation which supports the notion that nature is not over-powering (as it is in the Hamlin Garland tradition) but em-powering. And part of what nature empowers is sexual experience. Thus, sexual narratives always "lurk," if you will, in western and California narratives. Kelley not only found the sexual narrative hard to discipline; in the end she did *not* discipline it. That is, she kept the proletarian story and proletarian politics, even as she deconstructed it all the while. But she framed the proletarian story, at beginning and end, within a bigger story about two women, who live and work together in a sexually charged topography associated with taboo love. Kelley has reframed what constitutes a "political story" here, and the political story she is struggling to tell (and which she only finally suggests) is about female sexuality which does not center on men.

The editor of this novel reads its ending—wherein Rhonda is courted by one of the white townsmen who tar and feather the union hero—as prelude to a desperation marriage. I am not so sure. For Rhonda is not "desperate." On the contrary, the novel is committed to showing Rhonda's increasing vitality as well as her willingness to take risks that ultimately satisfy her. It represents, too, a range of relational possibilities. But most of all, in the beginning and in the end, there is the relationship between the two women. Though there remains a lack of sympathy between them, what also remains is a huge silence about what keeps them together. Is theirs a Boston marriage? What are we to make of a repeatedly frustrated romance plot in which the female heroine seems nonetheless to grow and deepen? Perhaps what we are to make of it is that the romance plot, or for that matter the proletarian plot, does not work if the featured protagonists are two women. The one narrative that seems to glue the other two narratives together, however, is western narrative. Because it is a narrative already steeped in associations of taboo male desire, western narrative offers women writers, too, a chance to narrate taboo topics. Edith Summer Kelley's *The Devil's Hand* does just this, for what is more taboo than female sexuality where men play no sure role?

By putting forward Kelley as exemplar of a developing discourse about female sexuality, I do not mean to say that women writers' representations of Western space always empower women or female sexuality. Jean Stafford's *The Mountain Lion* (1947) is one of the more chilling demonstrations of the masculinism of the Western sexual imaginary. Its protagonist, the precocious and artistic Molly, is killed off by her brother at precisely the moment when she is about to come of sexual age: puberty. This is Stafford's grim take on the West as an imaginative arena for women.[56] Equally chilling is Joan Didion's *Run River* (1963), a book that may well be one of the most sexual books of Western literature to appear before the Sexual Revolution. If Jean Stafford satirizes the West, Joan Didion narrates it as a more tragic enterprise. Didion's western women are as dissipated as her men, and more sexually indiscriminate. But the consequences of sexual activity, it turns out, are most tragic for women: namely, unwanted pregnancy, and sometimes, coerced abortion. The imaginative space provided by western mythic discourse enables Didion to represent yet another taboo female topic, abortion. And this representation comes a full decade before *Roe v. Wade*.

What I have hoped to show in this discussion about female sexuality is that mythic discourse does not always constrain, restrain, oppress, and impoverish; indeed through it, twentieth-century women writers have fantasied a good bit about what women want, and how exactly they want it. Importantly, part of what they want has nothing to do, per se, with sexuality, and everything to do with the conditions under which sexual activity takes place. The discussion of sexuality is thus also an implicit discussion of female independence, economic autonomy, or female bodily safety. That is, this discussion ultimately links the discourse of female sexuality to various discourses of the nation. Issues of citizenship, reproductive rights, female education, and economic security—different components of female civil rights—are issues entirely relevant to female sexuality.

Women writers, for much of the twentieth century, have been forwarding a broad historical education program in which female sexuality dovetails with broader national discourses about civilization. But it dovetails by way of critique and disagreement. It represents a counter-discourse to the discourse of "masculine manhood" that had produced, at century's turn, the vision of virile nationhood that Roosevelt so cherished. Women writers looked at the vision of virile nationhood with chagrin and dread, for that kind of nation, they knew, is not generally compatible with secure, female pleasure.

CONCLUSION

The literary West has paved the way for the New Western History's critique of, and re-representation of, the Western past. As long as the literary West plays no role in renderings of the Western past, however, historians mis-represent, by *not* representing, the *discursive* context that has created and facilitated their own emergence as a public history discourse. More is at stake here than setting the scholarly record straight, though, namely, the pressing need for political coalition among Western Studies intellectuals. The absence of literary narratives in the New Western History robs the New Western History of many resources that would forward and deepen its own varied intellectual projects. In an era in which Proposition #187 and the so-called California Civil Rights Initiative #209 await appeal, in which the Hopwood Decision is now the law of the Fifth District, leftists who don't join forces risk losing further ground to the massively organized and well-financed anti-civil rights Right.[57] One place we can stand ground—and the New Right is so aware of this that it has modeled its own offensives after those of the left—is on the battlefield of culture.[58] The relative conservatism of Ken Burns' recent PBS documentary, "The West," a public history project in which New Western Historians had a complex and considerably agonized role, shows that the cultural playing field is shifting in ever more rightist directions.[59] This is no time, therefore, to squander political allies.[60] Making sense of culture, as well as mobilizing its political contours, should be a priority for any scholarly movement in the humanities dedicated to progressive politics.

I have focused here on gender studies within the New Western History because what is at issue in *this* historical moment's culture wars is the displacement of the white man as Western history's star protagonist. This is precisely the political project that so many New Right anti-affirmative action projects want to overturn, and that progressives must defend. One defense is to re-insert both gender analysis and women back into civil rights discussions and anti-affirmative action debates.[61]

I have hoped to show that Western literary discourse is a very gender-sensitive discourse that has long been committed to an alternative vision of Western manhood. I used the work of Wallace Stegner, in particular, to argue for the compatibility of the male literary canon with feminist cultural politics. I generalized more broadly that the male literary West not only supports the anti-romantic project of the New Western History, but it affirms the basic building block of feminist philosophy, that men are gendered subjects. I urge historians, including feminists, therefore, to claim, study, and teach the male literary West. It is a discourse consistently self-conscious about gendered difference—it "knows" that the male and female Wests were dissimilar. There's little quarrel about that fact, even if there is plenty of quarreling between men and women about whose West is going to dominate the nation's or the family's plans for the future.

In the women's history section of this essay, I have hoped, by laying out different versions of the major periods of female literary production, to show the various ways that literary works have "made history" and created alternative historical sensibilities that then do battle with the dominant powers that be. Women's alternative visions of the nation, for example, have promoted, and continue to promote today, an economic philosophy that is more socialist and communitarian than profit-driven. That philosophy, as it is applied to environmental issues, is more concerned with the long-term health and survival of the natural environment than it is with short-term profitable use of it. Thus restraint is this discourse's unspoken impulse when it comes to decisions about urban development, natural resource use, and the impact of human civilization upon non-human nature. This is a political vision, obviously, at complete odds with the aggressive pride, the sense of global mission, the simple and bold *machismo* that one sees in a hegemonic text like Teddy Roosevelt's *The Winning of the West* (1889).

To make the above claims is not to say that women's early "promotional" literature, in particular, was not implicated in the dream and consolidation of empire. Unquestionably, it was. White women's voices dominate the early discourse; and their views about indigenous people sometimes dominated public policy in disastrous ways (e.g., Helen Hunt Jackson and the Dawes Act). And yet, female discourse is also entirely self-doubting about the ultimate righteousness of Manifest Destiny. This doubt has produced a huge opening in twentieth-century discourse, which has made it receptive (imperfectly, to be sure) to the interventions of women of color.

I have wanted to spend time, too, to show that women writers have claimed, in western spaces, a site for the exploration and representation of female sexuality. I have suggested that western spaces are themselves always already sexualized spaces, emplotted with European male desire. Women writers, in order to survive this kind of imaginative realm, have therefore taken up and re-worked sexual narratives in ways that do not violate female integrity. But, of course, female integrity can only be assured if this ostensibly "personal" matter of sexuality is linked to the State. This premise has important implications for the ways that we understand the relationship of the West to the general project of modernity—for it would suggest that though the West is generally associated with anti-modern rhetoric, a *female* West is very invested in modernity, because with it comes female civil rights.

The real challenge for any of us who study literature and culture is not simply to recover writers as opinion-makers in Western intellectual, cultural, or political history. That is done relatively easily enough. The harder and much messier task is to make sense of the ways that cultural works themselves shape, influence, and prevail upon history. In my call to rethink the status of "the imaginative" and its relationship to historical narratives, I have tried to point out that "mythic" discourse does not always signal political regressiveness, nor does "realist" discourse inevitably liberate. It is the possibility of taboo desire emplotted upon Western lands, and contained in Western mythology, that sometimes enables women to imagine their own versions of female pleasure. That same emplotment provides contemporary men with the experience of a world in which men connect with each other. What kind of defended edge would soften if non-competitive, non-misogynistic bonds between men were claimed as part of the western past? Perhaps McMurtry would get some of the energy that he and so many others need from symbols of western-ness. And that energy could be gotten without resorting to narratives about the "winning of the West," or the winning of the west's women.

Rice University

NOTES

Many readers have given their time and thoughts to this project, in particular Forrest Robinson and José F. Aranda, Jr. I am also grateful to Laura Santigian and Dorothee Kocks.

1. See "Westward Ho Hum: What the New Historians Have Done to the Old West," *The New Republic*, Oct. 1990, 32–38.

2. Well-known discussions of narrative organization include Hayden V. White, *The Content of the Form: Narrative Discourse and Historical Representation* (Baltimore: Johns Hopkins University Press, 1987); or Homi K. Bhabha, *The Location of Culture* (New York: Routledge, 1994).

3. William Cronon is the most notable exception, for he takes up narrative tropes directly. See "A Place for Stories: Nature, History, and Narrative," *Journal of American History* 78 (1992): 1347–76. For a relevant additional discussion see Cronon, ed. "Introduction," and "The Trouble with Wilderness, Or, Getting Back to the Wrong Kind of Nature," in *Uncommon Ground: Toward Reinventing Nature* (New York: Norton, 1995) 23–68, 69–90. On somewhat different grounds see Donald Worster, "Nature and the Disorder of History," *Environmental History Review* 18:2 (1994): 1–15. Richard White has taken up another, but relevant, theoretical avenue when he pursues the relationship of theoretical geography to classic Marxist materialism. See Richard White, "The Made and Unmade Worlds: Labor and Western Spaces," paper presented at Western History Association, Albuquerque, N.M., 1994. Taken together, these combined meditations suggest that some of the most prominent of the New Western historians may take the field in a more liberal direction when it comes to narrative issues.

4. This topic is taken up at length by Forrest Robinson in *Having It Both Ways: Self-Subversion in Western Popular Classics* (Albuquerque: University of New Mexico Press, 1994).

5. Walter Nugent, "Where Is the American West: Report on a Survey," *Montana, The Magazine of Western History* 42.3 (1992): 1–24.

6. Nugent 7.

7. July, 1992.

8. Limerick has made the "realist" case at both the conferences noted here, held in Lincoln, Nebraska. She made a similar case in her address, "The Realization of the American West," to The New Regionalism Conference, University of Mississippi, Oct. 1993.

9. For the connection between minority subjectivity and postmodern form, see Philip Brian Harper, *Framing the Margins: The Social Logic of Postmodern Culture* (New York: Oxford University Press, 1994).

10. See my forthcoming book, *Women Writers, the New West, and the Politics of Landscape* (Durham: University of North Carolina Press).

11. Susan Lee Johnson, "'A Memory Sweet to Soldiers': The Significance of Gender in the History of the 'American West'," *Western Historical Quarterly* 24.4 (1993): 495–518.

12. The "canon" includes Patricia Nelson Limerick's *The Legacy of Conquest: The Unbroken Past of the American West* (New York: Norton, 1987); Richard White's *"It's Your Own Misfortune and None of My Own": A New History of the American West* (Norman: University of Oklahoma Press, 1993); William Cronon, George Miles, Jay Gitlin, eds., *Under an Open Sky: Rethinking America's Western Past* (New York: Norton, 1992); and Donald Worster, *Rivers of Empire: Water, Aridity, and the Growth of the American West* (New York: Pantheon Books, 1985).

13. On the relationship between 1980s neoconservative politics and white racialism, see Michael Omi and Howard Winant, *Racial Formation in the United States: From the 1960s to the 1980s* (New York: Routledge, 1986, revised 1994) 113–37.

14. Cronon's work includes Katherine Morrissey's "Engendering the West." White tries harder to incorporate women's history into his text, and offers gender analysis of men at times. And yet neither text incorporates women or gender analysis into the center of their historical projects.

15. See, for example, Glenda Riley's review of *It's Your Misfortune*, *Western History Quarterly* 23 (May 1992): 223–25.

16. Johnson 499.

17. Lillian Schlissel, *Women's Diaries of the Westward Journey* (New York: Schocken Books, 1982); Joanna L. Stratton, *Pioneer Women: Voices from the Kansas Frontier* (New York: Simon and Schuster, 1981).

18. See Susan Armitage, *The Women's West* (Norman: University of Oklahoma Press, 1987); Lillian Schlissel, Vicki L Ruíz, and Janice Monk, eds., *Western Women: Their Land, Their Lives* (Albuquerque: University of New Mexico Press, 1988).

19. For a survey of the major critical books which taken together form what I call "the tradition," see James K. Folsom, *The Western American Novel* (New Haven: Yale University Press, 1966); Robert Edson Lee, *From West to East: Studies of the Literature of the American West* (Urbana: Illinois University Press, 1966); John

R. Milton, *The Novel of the American West* (Lincoln: University of Nebraska Press, 1980); *Critical Essays on the Western American Novel,* William T. Pilkington, ed. (Boston: G. K. Hall, 1980); Harold P. Simonson, *Writers, Western Regionalism, and A Sense of Place* (Fort Worth: Texas Christian University Press, 1989) and *A Literary History of the American West,* George Day, gen. ed. (Fort Worth: Texas Christian University Press, 1987).

20. Critics have written at length about the ironic bent to Western literature, its implicit critique of a progressive view of history, and of modernity. See essays by Mark Busby and David Mogen in *The Frontier Experience and the American Dream: Essays on American Literature* (College Station: Texas A&M University Press, 1989) 15–30, 95–106, respectively; Jay Gurian, *Western American Writing: Tradition and Promise* (Delano, Fla.: Everett/Edwards, 1975); for a fine and very recent commentary see Thomas J. Lyon, "Revisionist Western Classics," in *Rending the West: New Essays on the Literature of the American West,* Michael Kowalewski, ed. (New York: Cambridge University Press, 1996) 144–56.

21. For a keen summary of Clark's work which lends itself to issues of masculinity, see Max Westbrook, "Walter Van Tilburg Clark and the American Dream," in *A Literary History of the American West* 989–99.

22. Here I rely on Thomas J. Lyon, "Revisionist Western Classics."

23. I draw these categories and the later notion of "virile nationhood" from Gail Bederman, *Manliness and Civilization: A Cultural History of Gender and Race in the United States, 1880–1917* (Chicago: University of Chicago Press, 1995). Susan Johnson also attends to this transition in "A Memory Sweet to Soldiers."

24. These examples were suggested to me by Forrest Robinson, who also noted the novel's description of Shane: "He was the symbol of all the dim, formless imaginings of danger and terror in the untested realm of human potentialities beyond my understanding. The impact of the menace that marked him was like a physical blow" (qtd. in Bantam edition, p. 105) 1983. Many other examples come to mind, among them, the final moments of *Dr. Strangelove,* when Slim Pickens rides the H-Bomb—like a bucking bronco—down to its ironic doom.

25. One sees this explicitly in the editors' introduction to *Western Women: Their Land, Their Lives.* "This is not a book that presents any synthetic vision. It is too early for that" (8).

26. It begins with Dee Brown's *The Gentle Tamers: Women of the Old Wild West* (Lincoln: University of Nebraska Press, 1958), and opens up in the 1970s to include Julie Roy Jeffrey, *Frontier Women: The Transmississippi West, 1840–1880* (New York: Hill and Wang, 1979). By the 1980s, something of an internal revision is afoot. Nonetheless, an interest in the "westering experience" as it is more classically defined but now with a female twist, continues in the works of Sandra Myers, *Westering Women and the Frontier Experience, 1800–1950* (Albuquerque: University of New Mexico Press, 1982), and Glenda Riley, *The Female Frontier: A Comparative View of Women on the Prairie and the Plains* (Lawrence: University Press of Kansas, 1988).

27. John Mack Faragher, *Women and Men on the Overland Trail* (New Haven:

Yale University Press, 1979); Joan M. Jensen and Darliss A. Miller, "The Gentle Tamers Revisited: New Approaches to the History of Women in the American West," *Pacific Historical Review*, XLIX (1980): 173–213.

28. Elizabeth Jameson, "Toward a Multicultural History of Women in the Western United States," *Signs: Journal of Women in Culture and Society* 13.4 (1988): 761–91; Peggy Pascoe, *Relations of Rescue*.

29. Evidence of this mounting trend during the 1980s include Sylvia Van Kirk, *"Many Tender Ties": Women in Fur Trade Society in Western Canada, 1670–1870* (Winnipeg: Watson & Dwyer, 1980); Sarah Deutsch, *No Separate Refuge: Culture, Class, and Gender on an Anglo-Hispanic Frontier in the American Southwest, 1880–1940* (New York: Oxford University Press, 1987); Susan Armitage and Elizabeth Jameson's *The Women's West* (1988); and Lillian Schlissel et al., ed., *Western Women: Their Land, Their Lives* (1989). Two labor histories written in dialogue with this paradigm include Vicki Ruíz, *Cannery Women, Cannery Lives: Mexican Women, Unionization, and the California Food Processing Industry, 1930–1950* (Albuquerque: University of New Mexico Press, 1987) and Evelyn Nakano Glenn, *Issei, Nisei, War Bride: Three Generations of Japanese American Women in Domestic Service* (Philadelphia: Temple University Press, 1986).

30. Some scholars find *Western Women: Their Land, Their Lives* the more useful classroom text, because of the essay/response format. I prefer *The Women's West* for its interdisciplinarity.

31. Johnson, "A Memory Sweet to Soldiers." Other recent masculinity studies and/or gender studies include Blake Allmendinger, *The Cowboy: Representations of Labor in an American Work Culture* (New York: Oxford University Press, 1992); Ramon Gutierrez, *When Jesus Came the Corn Mothers Went Away: Marriage, Sexuality, and Power in New Mexico, 1500–1846* (Stanford: Stanford University Press, 1991); and *Becoming Brave: The Path to Native American Manhood*, Laine Thom, comp. (San Francisco: Chronicle Books, 1992).

32. This issue, 61.4 (1992), is not the only one devoted to evaluating the state of Western women's history. Also see *Frontiers: A Journal of Women's Studies* 12:1 (1991); and *Montana: The Magazine of Western History* 41:2 (1991): 57–73.

33. Temple cites Peggy Pascoe's *Relations of Rescue* and Susan Lee Johnson's "Sharing Bed and Board," in *The Women's West*, as examples. See Temple, "Beyond the Intellectual Meridian: Transdisciplinary Studies of Women," *Pacific Historical Review* 61.4 (1992): 463–80.

34. Any number of studies in white women's history have appeared which take up very well-known public figures like Jessie Benton Fremont, Narcissa Whitman, Elizabeth Bacon Custer, and Annie Oakley. At the same time, "ordinary white women" are the subjects of studies focused on subjects as varied as the Texas cattle industry, the Mormon Church, Colorado homesteads, prison reform, and the Seattle labor movement, see Glenda Riley, *The Life and Legend of Annie Oakley* (Norman: University of Oklahoma Press, 1994); Shirley Leckie, *Elizabeth Bacon Custer and the Making of a Myth* (Norman: University of Oklahoma Press, 1992); *The Letters of Jessie Benton Fremont*, Pamela Herr and Mary Lee Spence, eds. (Champaign:

University of Illinois Press, 1993); Julie Roy Jeffrey, *Converting the West: A Biography of Narcissa Whitman* (Norman: University of Oklahoma Press, 1991). Also see Elizabeth Maret, *Women of the Range: Women's Roles in the Texas Beef Cattle Industry* (College Station: Texas A&M University Press, 1993); Julie Jones Eddy, *Homesteading Women: An Oral History of Colorado, 1890–1950* (New York: Twayne, 1992); Anne M. Butler, "Women's Work in Prisons of the American West, 1865–1920," *Western Legal History* 7 (1994); Dana Frank, *Purchasing Power: Consumer Organizing, Gender, and the Seattle Labor Movement, 1919–1929* (New York: Cambridge University Press, 1994).

35. See Beth Bailey and David Farber, *The First Strange Place: The Alchemy of Race and Sex in World War II Hawaii* (New York: Free Press, 1992); Devon A. Mihesuah, *Cultivating the Rosebuds: The Education of Women at the Cherokee Female Seminary, 1851–1909* (Urbana: University Press of Illinois, 1993); Karen Isaksen Leonard, *Making Ethnic Choices: California's Punjabi Mexican Americans* (Philadelphia: Temple University Press, 1992): Ruth McDonald and Narcissus Duffy Gayton, *Apache Mothers and Daughters: Four Generations of a Family* (Norman: University of Oklahoma Press, 1992); Patricia Preciado Martin, *Songs My Mother Sang to Me: An Oral History of Mexican-American Women* (Tucson: University of Arizona Press, 1992): Valerie Matsumoto, *Farming the Home Place: A Japanese American Community in California, 1919–1982* (Ithaca: Cornell University Press, 1993); Judy Yung, *Unbound Feet: A Social History of Chinese Women in San Francisco* (Berkeley: University of California Press, 1995).

36. See Dana Frank, *Purchasing Power*; Katherine Jellison, *Entitled to Power: Farm Women and Technology, 1913–1963* (Chapel Hill: University of North Carolina Press, 1993); Joanne Passet, *Cultural Crusaders: Women Librarians in the American West, 1900–1917* (Albuquerque: University of New Mexico Press, 1995); Sandra Schackel, *Social Housekeepers: Women Shaping Public Policy in New Mexico, 1920–1940* (Albuquerque: University of New Mexico Press, 1992).

37. Mary Murphy, "Bootlegging Mothers and Drinking Daughters: Gender and Prohibition in Butte, Montana," *American Quarterly* 46 (June 1994): 174–94.

38. Barbara Little, "Review," *Journal of American History* 81 (1994): 682–83. See also Jan Zita Grover, "Disturbing History," *Women's Review of Books* 11:2 (1993): 2, 5–6.

39. *One Foot on the Rockies: Women and Creativity in the Making of the American West* (Albuquerque: University of New Mexico Press, 1995).

40. Other exceptions include Nancy Warren Ferrell, *Barret Willoughby: Alaska's Forgotten Lady* (Fairbanks: University Press of Alaska, 1995); Emily Leider, *California's Daughters: Gertrude Atherton and Her Times* (Stanford: Stanford University Press, 1991); John Miller, *Laura Ingalls Wilder's Little Town: Where History and Literature Meet* (Lawrence: University Press of Kansas, 1994); June Namais, *White Captives: Gender and Ethnicity on the American Frontier* (Chapel Hill: University of North Carolina Press, 1993).

41. On the modernist period and the Southwest, see *The Desert Is No Lady: Southwestern Landscapes in Women's Writing and Art*, Janice Monk and Vera Norwood, eds. (New Haven: Yale University Press, 1987). On turn-of-the-century and

modernist writers, see Melody Graulich, "'O Beautiful for Spacious Guys': An Essay on 'the Legitimate Inclinations of the Sexes,'" *The Frontier Experience and the American Dream*, David Mogen, Mark Busby, and Paul Bryant, eds. (College Station: Texas A&M University Press, 1987) 186–204. For a feminist reading of popular westerns at the turn of the century, see Jane Tompkins, *West of Everything: The Inner Life of Popular Westerns* (New York: Oxford University Press, 1992).

42. *Women Writers, The New West, and the Politics of Landscape* (forthcoming).

43. See "Engendering the West" in Cronon et al., *Under an Open Sky*.

44. See Susan Armitage and Elizabeth Jameson, "Editors' Introduction," *The Women's West* 3–6; also Johnson, "Memory Sweet to Soldiers."

45. Annette Kolodny, *The Land Before Her: Fantasy and Experience on the American Frontier, 1690–1860* (Chapel Hill: University of North Carolina Press, 1984).

46. For a "sampler" of some of these writers, see Ida Rae Egli, *No Rooms of Their Own: Women Writers of Early California* (Berkeley: Heydey Books, 1992).

47. See Bederman, *Manliness and Civilization*.

48. For an original discussion of desire in western contexts, see Zeese Papanikolas, *Trickster in the Land of Dreams* (Lincoln: University of Nebraska Press, 1995).

49. Leila J. Rupp, *Survival in the Doldrums: The American Women's Rights Movement, 1945–1960s* (New York: Oxford University Press, 1987).

50. Graulich, "O Beautiful for Spacious Guys" 192.

51. Lesbian erotica is featured in Jonathan Katz, *Gay American History: Lesbians and Gay Men in the USA* (New York: Peter Lang, 1993). Also see, Mabel Dodge Luhan, *Intimate Memories*, 1933–1937 (New York: Harcourt, Brace, 1937). Rudnick's biography addresses some of these issues; see *Mabel Dodge Luhan* (Albuquerque: University of New Mexico Press, 1984).

52. See especially Frances Kaye, *Isolation and Masquerade: Willa Cather's Women* (New York: Peter Lang, 1993); Sharon O'Brien, *Willa Cather: The Emerging Voice* (New York: Oxford University Press, 1987); and Mary Loeffelholz, *Experimental Lives: Women and Literature* (New York: Twayne, 1995) 109–14. Also Judith Fryer, "Desert, Rock, Shelter, Legend," in *The Desert Is No Lady* 26–46.

53. On the landscape as sexual partner for Austin and Luhan, see Lois Rudnick, "Re-Naming the Land: Anglo Expatriate Women in the Southwest," in *The Desert Is No Lady* 10–26.

54. Edith Summers Kelley, *The Devil's Hand*, "Afterword" by Michael J. Bruccoli (Carbondale: Southern Illinois University Press, 1974) 291–98. Also see Michael Bruccoli, "Afterword," to *Weeds: A Novel* (Carbondale: Southern Illinois University Press, 1972) 335–43.

55. Edith Summers Kelley, *Weeds* (Carbondale: Southern Illinois University Press, 1972. Original publication 1923).

56. For a discussion of satire and Jean Stafford, see Melody Graulich "O Beautiful for Spacious Guys." Also see Susan J. Rosowski, "Jean Stafford Rewrites the Western," in *Reading the West* 157–76.

57. On the internal organization and finances of the New Right, see Ellen Messer-Davidow, "Manufacturing the Attack on Liberalized Higher Education," *Social Text* (1993): 40–80.

58. For a very provocative reading of the importance of culture to the New Right, see Messer-Davidow, "Manufacturing the Attack on Liberalized Higher Education," *Social Text* (Fall 1993): 40–80. For a consideration of the ways that New Right political strategy is modeled on that of radical civil rights rhetoric, see Omi and Winant, *Racial Formation*, especially Part III, but also Epilogue.

59. The recent WHA conference in Lincoln, Nebraska, featured a session on the making of this documentary, which revealed the degree to which the cultural milieu has changed. Out of specific fear of "West as America" and "Enola Gay" reprisals, the recent PBS series stayed more to a center political line.

60. For a hard look at the alliances that progressives should form in the 1990s, see Michael Berube, *Public Access: Literary Theory and American Cultural Politics* (London: Verso, 1994).

61. On the importance of gender to affirmative action discussions, see Zillah R. Eisenstein, *The Color of Gender: Reimaging Democracy* (Berkeley: University of California Press, 1994).

CARL GUTIÉRREZ-JONES

Haunting Presences and the New Western History: Reading Repetition, Negotiating Trauma

As a principal contributor to, and spokesperson for, the New Western History, Patricia Limerick has engaged critical problems that speak not only to the grounding assumptions of U.S. Western history, but also to ideas about what constitutes proper historiography more generally. From the outset, the New Western historians have attempted to negotiate a thick ideological context in which Western history writing has, according to them, too often served highly charged political purposes. The hallmark, synthesizing pluralism that one finds in New Western History (NWH) texts thus constitutes a strategic response to previous historiographic trends, trends which presumably failed in large measure because of their contribution to imperialistic nostalgia and other uncritical modes of nationalistic celebration. In turn, a logic of inclusiveness is a central component of the New Western History's intervention. However, the multicultural, feminist and environmental thematics which have been both praised and vilified by reviewers of the movement are not, for the most part, understood by these New Western historians to be expressions of special interests or particularly focused political interventions. These more obvious engagements of ideological issues are instead posed as part of a larger program with significant methodological implications.

One of the most explicit statements in this regard may be found in an essay by Patricia Limerick, "Turnerians All: The Dream of a Helpful History in an Intelligible World" (1995). Most obviously, this essay struggles against numerous "misreadings" of the NWH, including errors directed at Limerick's own highly influential contribution to the movement, *Legacy of Conquest: The Unbroken Past of the American West* (1987). At the same time, the essay's purpose extends beyond a defense of Limerick's particular project, or for that matter the ostensibly regional concerns of her fellow New Western historians. As controversial as the NWH's "revisionist" efforts have been, the response to the movement's reception that Limerick crafts in "Turnerians All" raises the stakes by arguing that the movement is defining a crucial "cutting edge" for the historical profession as a whole.

As the New Western historians themselves frame the issue, the most pressing methodological question has become: how should historiography change in response to the inclusion of experiences that have heretofore constituted our "blind spots," spots created when "elements of our social identity . . . limit our vision as sternly as racial assumptions limited Frederick Jackson Turner's vision" ("Turnerians All" 715)? Turner's exemplary failure is a central one for Limerick, as she "revisits" the NWH to date, because of a responsibility she acknowledges that would require her simultaneously to distance herself from, and to posit a proximity to, his work. Most explicitly, this complicating of Limerick's relation to Turner signals a response to critics, as well as to popularizers of the NWH, who would read the movement as a "trashing" of Turner's frontier thesis—in a very real sense the thesis upon which the study of U.S. Western history was founded. For those who have followed the booming rise of the NWH, the effort is bound to spark curiosity, if only because Turner has been treated with, at the very least, a great deal of ambivalence by the revisionists. While Limerick herself goes to great lengths in *Legacy of Conquest* to posit historical continuities where Turner would posit a radical break with the closing of the frontier, a number of Limerick's compatriots virtually refuse to acknowledge Turner's existence at all. Given this situation, one can easily understand why the popular media in particular has read the NWH's offerings as most importantly a dismissal of Turner.

Intervening in this situation, Limerick uses the "Turnerians All" essay to explore the different, and at times contradictory, strands of thought about the frontier in Turner's writing. Most importantly, according to Limerick, Turner had sufficient evidence to deeply challenge his frontier thesis and yet he refused the task. Despite changing ideas about agrarianism, and the rise of the factory, Turner apparently chose not to revise his thesis, a decision Limerick ties to his fear of jeopardizing his professional standing, built as it was around what must have seemed an increasingly compromised notion. In some of the more searching moments of "Turnerians All," Limerick also frames this failure in terms of Turner's commitment to a method of "presentism," a notion that the present could be made virtually transparent as the historian followed patterns identified in the study of the past, in turn applying them to problems in the contemporary setting. Such a distinguishing of consequential from inconsequential events presumably leaves the writing of history a relatively clear and linear matter, a tracing of movement from past to present as though one were following a railroad track, to use Limerick's typification ("Turnerians All" 704). That Turner should refuse to adhere to this principle and thereby revise his thesis when the railroad track so clearly curved leaves Limerick deeply impressed, especially because her own formation as a historian was shaped by the adoption of a similar methodology. In fact, this formation helps contextualize important aspects of her style, including her extensive engagement of contemporary media coverage in *Legacy of Conquest*. Ultimately, such aspects of Limerick's project reveal a strong identification with Turner's notion of the historian as a public servant—a scholar speaking to, and of, the present in politically significant ways.

At the same time that Limerick rethinks her relationship with Turner, she also documents an "ironic" twist to the enduring error that lies at the heart of the frontier thesis. Initially, the framing of this irony is fairly simple; hence, at the beginning of the essay, Limerick notes that the more New Western historians have worked to discredit the frontier thesis and the historical break it posits, the more forcefully the thesis appears to have rejuvenated itself via renewed attentions gained in the media. On a more subtle level, twists coded as ironic echo at key moments throughout the essay, setting a pattern that suggests that something more than a conventional understanding of the ironic is at play. This pattern is contextualized when Turner's thesis is said to exist in a "bewitched historiographic space" where critique *consistently* leaves the model unscathed, if not renewed. Limerick, in turn, builds on valences of the ironic while she explores the ways Turner's work actually incorporates its own best critique. Finally, Limerick's complicated identification with Turner is cast with a humorous, if biting, acknowledgment of his "haunting presence" for the field as a whole. In fact, it is this haunting quality which literally defines Turner in the essay.

These instances of "irony" have a special resonance that calls out for speculation particularly because the ironic's presentation here and elsewhere in Limerick's writings brings to mind something very much like the psychoanalytic concept of the uncanny. Although Freud's development of the topic in "Das Unheimliche" (1919) is complex and notably incomplete, the numerous rethinkings of the concept by other scholars have been united by a principle that is summed up with a phrase Freud borrows from Schelling: "the uncanny is the name for everything that ought to have remained . . . secret and hidden, but has come to light" ("Uncanny" 225). Building on Schelling's notion, and on the etymological slippages that exist between the terms "canny" and "uncanny," Freud suggests that the experience in question "is in reality nothing new or alien, but something which is familiar and old-established in the mind and which has become alienated from it only through the process of repression" ("Uncanny" 241). While subsequent critics have frequently modified or replaced the motors for such repression that were assumed by Freud, the larger model, describing a specific kind of disquieting "rememory," has continued to draw a good deal of critical interest.[1]

While a mining of the uncanny is not announced in Limerick's works—which for the most part avoid the explicit elaboration of theoretical concerns—the "Turnerians All" piece may be read as a more theoretically-invested extension of Limerick's focus on the play of continuities and discontinuities in Western history, a problematic intimately tied to the frontier thesis. Implicitly mapping her present as an uncanny repetition of Turner's efforts, Limerick argues that most of her generation of Western historians have worked themselves into the same corners regarding Turner that she has (714). A primary symptom of this repetition is a faith in reform, a hopefulness that understands the historian as a guide to "more benevolent action in our own time" (714).

Although for both Turner and Limerick this hope remains purely secular, there exists in both contexts a displaced drive toward redemptive plots of a religious order, a drive that Limerick blames for leading both writers to overestimate the historian's ability to establish the causal linkage of "progress-oriented" events (711–14). The recognition by Limerick of her own participation in this error subsequently leads her into speculation about the ways in which members of her profession might better understand relationships between past and present.

In the process, Limerick charts a disillusionment with her earlier "presentist" self in a highly personalized and virtually confessional passage. At issue is her belief that it would be possible with *Legacy of Conquest* to trace "a direct, clear line between past and present"—an action that she later credits with inadvertently fostering an "unhealthy fatalism" (710). The form of this self-critique is at least as important as the ostensible point, inasmuch as one of Limerick's trademarks as a historian is her willingness to assume an interpretive and quasi-literary stance not always celebrated by others in her profession.[2] Whatever the limits of this approach, it does have the virtue of registering key questions about the potentially transferential relationship that may exist between the historian and her object of study. As used here, the notion of a transferential relationship would designate a potentially unselfconscious, insufficiently critical, replication by the historian of problematics imbedded in the object of study.[3] Although not moving in a similar psychoanalytic register, the best of the work performed by Limerick's essay points toward self-understanding as precisely this kind of negotiation with one's object of study. Unfortunately, the essay truncates such issues by concluding with a fairly shallow listing of the everyday, often bureaucratic, practices that constitute the historical profession in the academy. While the "cotton wool" of these daily practices may well contribute to an avoidance of the issues Limerick sets in motion, the blanket citing of this everyday chaos actually obscures the specific responsibilities that fall upon historians negotiating transferential dynamics in their research.

One of the most striking opportunities to address such problems directly occurs in "Turnerians All" as Limerick considers an example of the present's power to bewilder "established" historical assumptions. Turning to recent events in the former Soviet Union, she notes that,

> While historians might disagree in their interpretations of the historical process that brought us to the present, until 1989 the outcome that historians sought to explain was not in dispute.

> But with the collapse of Soviet control over Eastern Europe, and then with the end of Russian communism itself, the narrative of history took a wild and unexpected turn. Surely, the past was still connected to the present, but the connections followed paths that were unexplored and unfamiliar, paths that would lead historians through terrain they had barely noticed in their previous efforts to explain a different, much more intelligible present. (713)

Putting aside the overhasty "end" attributed to Russian communism (the influence and effects of which continue to be pertinent), this passage and the historical event it draws upon imply much more than Limerick's specific line of argument allows. More than a betrayal of historical narratives by a chaotic present, this passage points toward a conception of historical understanding as a complicated process of repetition and change, a process in which historians must come to terms with their own responsibilities for the paths "unexplored and unfamiliar," the "paths that would lead historians through terrain they had barely noticed in their previous efforts" (713). Instead, Limerick offers the Russian example as proof of the way the present escapes us, and presumably escaped Turner as well. Of course the example does little to address the bewitching persistence of Turner's thesis that frames the essay.

In response, we may ask if "Turnerians All" ever really moves beyond the assumptions imbedded in presentism. Put another way, we might ask if the terms of Turner's self-understanding significantly affect the range of alternative methods entertained by Limerick as she reviews her own hermeneutic processes. Taking up her previous attempt to offer a redemptive ending to Western history in *Legacy of Conquest*, Limerick recounts,

> When I contemplated my failure to figure out the present, I began to wonder how I had ever fallen into the belief that such an achievement was within my reach, or within my job description. And happily, as disorientation with the present increased, enthusiasm for studying the past grew proportionately. Compared to the inscrutable present, the past was an open book. . . . History became correspondingly more interesting as it became more chaotic. (710)

In an essay that appears otherwise so invested in exploring the "uncanny" repetitions that obtain to Western historiography, this effort to formulate the process of historical understanding as a tension between presentist-oriented fatalism and presentist-oriented chaos is awkward at best. As much as the essay plays invitingly with the uncanny repetitions which have affected Limerick's earlier work, it is not hard to come away from the piece with the sense that the explorations of the uncanny have been staged in a kind of acting out of anxieties regarding the "newness" of the New Western History. And, of course, the NWH distinguishes itself, its newness, precisely by emphasizing *continuities* between past and present struggles as defined by conquest and exploitation. While play with the uncanny presumably highlights historical continuity, Limerick's essay also sets Turner's control over the past against a potentially sublime fascination with the chaos of history, a move that would strategically check the critically imprisoning qualities that can accompany such a strong emphasis on elements consistent through time. Unfortunately, a relationship between these different points of fascination—between continuity and contemporary chaos—is not articulated. As a result, the uncritical traffic between these points displaces the development of a truly alternative notion of how past and present interact. Finally, inasmuch as "patterns of clarity" are associated with Turner's fatalism, one might rightfully wonder what method of historical inquiry is still viable for Limerick after she has posed this methodological paradox (710).

"Turnerians All" is perhaps best read as a stage in an evolving process wherein the NWH is learning to grapple self-consciously with highly charged issues that have often been subject to processes of repression. In this sense, one might read the untheorized play with the uncanny in Limerick's essay as the tip of an iceberg, the body of which is constituted by the great diversity of conflicts precariously tapped as the NWH attempts to be strategically inclusive, especially where the stories of history's "marginal" players or losers are involved. Responding to a very significant aspect of the NWH's agenda, the reception of particular works has at times been very intolerant of the movement's consequent "bleak outlook." Here, the engagement of difficult episodes of trauma take center stage, most notably events which have adversely affected minority populations, women, and, in an extension of conventional notions of trauma, nature. Key texts of the NWH, including *Relations of Rescue*, *It's Your Misfortune and None of My Own*, *Rivers of Empire*, and of course *Legacy of Conquest*, all pursue a similar tactic.

Certainly, the tendency to focus on traumatic events or their representations, particularly in myth-making, is not "new" in Western history writing. Richard Slotkin's *Regeneration through Violence*, Henry Nash Smith's *Virgin Land*, and even Turner's frontier thesis itself build in crucial ways on some central notion of trauma or loss. However, it does appear that, as a movement, the NWH has developed the study of certain kinds of trauma in a unique and systematic fashion—though a fashion not explicitly informed by the theoretical treatments of trauma and historiography that have taken off in the last decade, especially around studies of the holocaust.[4] Trauma, as explored by the New Western historians, entails at least a double wounding, involving some form of initial victimization, as well as a repression within the historical record of the experience of suffering. When NWH writers like Limerick argue that processes of denial are at the core of western history (*Legacy* 96–97), the psychoanalytic force of the claim is grounded in this idea of a double wounding that is fed on a network of practices.

As Richard White has described the NWH's response to trauma, the goal is to produce "a relational history" in which western violence is dislodged from its conventional home as a theme of American mythology. White and his fellows would rethink such violence as a result of social struggles that continue into the present. For the most part, however, the principal works of the NWH do not explore specific history texts in which violent events have been politically and ethically repressed, or, as in the case of much American myth study, displaced to a more aesthetically distanced realm of experience. In this sense, the NWH tends to be much more invested in preaching through practice than in engaging polemical debates with predecessors in the field.

The fact remains that the "relational history" pursued by the NWH cadre takes on a political and cultural work that is strikingly at odds with the perspective established by Turner's speech in 1893, even though specific reference to Turner is often avoided. Given that this relational history embraces an inclusivity that must address not simply repressed historical material, but also the means by which historical representations have carried out the work of repression, or the doubled wounding, essays like "Turnerians All" mark a fundamentally important step for the NWH. Some of the best critical reviews of the NWH have also concentrated on the need for further methodological elaboration, leading one to suspect that the lack of polemical engagement manifested in the NWH comes with an important price.[5] In order to map out and contextualize this problematic, the remainder of this essay will turn to Limerick's *Legacy of Conquest* as a case study. The selection of Limerick's text is motivated by several factors, including: first, Limerick's relative willingness to engage larger historiographic questions (her focus on history as a process of repetition and change is key in this regard); second, her explicit treatment of victimization; and third, her tendency to be more explicitly polemical than her peers in the NWH.

Limerick's *Legacy of Conquest* begins with an extended exploration of the forms of denial which have allowed Americans benefiting from aggressive policies of conquest to legitimate their actions. Of these forms, one of the most predominant included settlers imagining themselves as uniquely innocent victims of the hardships almost necessarily befalling them as they tried to live out an individualistically-oriented escape from the past with the move west. As an antidote for this legacy, Limerick offers a method built around an ethic of pluralistic witnessing, a method which draws heavily on anecdotal material provided by memoirs and similar sources. On the most explicit front, such multiplicity provides an inclusion of varied castes and social positions as Limerick rethinks the history of the West.

However, such anecdotal material also documents the complex texture of everyday psychology, complementing and even correcting impressions drawn from official documents and policies. To her credit, Limerick is careful not to be overly critical regarding the study of such policies. Instead, she calls for more caution in how we place this work in relation to evidence we have regarding everyday lives. Here, Limerick echoes Richard White's desire to worry (and not to ignore) Western mythologies as they manifest in policy as well as history writing. Within *Legacy of Conquest*, the frontier thesis is the target of choice, and as such readers might view Limerick's fascination with repressed historical continuities as a reaction to Turner's—and not the West's—legacy. All the same, what gives this book much of its critical force is its ability to present Turner as one highly visible practitioner of a much broader cultural logic which effectively displaced ethical problems tied to a legacy of social and political conflict. Limerick accomplishes this by mining various historical contexts in order to rethink the optimism associated with Jeffersonian agrarian ideals and to pose this optimism as a crucial aspect of Western denial. Further, Limerick suggests that Turner's positioning of a historical break was in fact a means of reconstituting the agrarian fantasy as a form of "imperialistic nostalgia."[6]

The stress on historical continuities and denials that ostensibly defines *Legacy of Conquest* leads quite naturally to the methodological implications that inform "Turnerians All." Historical repetitions—not continuities proper—are really Limerick's focus in both works, and these gain an interpretive force to the extent that they demonstrate the denial she associates with the Old Western History throughout her writings. Read in this light, Limerick's "Turnerians All" looks to be more of a re-elaboration of *Legacy of Conquest* than a critical revision of the NWH. In both cases, the repetitions Limerick mines are almost always emotionally, politically and ethically charged by virtue of their association with traumatic losses, losses that have been subject to a crucial underdevelopment in the historical record.

Mapping out the process of denial in *Legacy of Conquest*, Limerick argues that migrants from the East were driven by a desire to break with a troubling past which they nonetheless carried with themselves in myriad ways, despite their best efforts. Notions of independent life in the West were maintained against the realities of the mining industry and other forms of labor relations within the migrant communities. In this context, the legitimation of colonial exploitation within and without migrant communities depended from the outset on the manufacture of an "innocence" that could level the field of social responsibility at the same time that victimhood virtually became a democratic right.

In a more contemporary instance, Limerick explores the ways such innocence can become embattled. Here, the focus is the government's attempt to wrestle with compensation for victims of radiation poisoning, a compensation which would have required the atomic energy commission to acknowledge its own part in the "callous" development of resources, replaying the worst of the West's boom mentalities. Glossing the event, Limerick asserts that the controversy presents a perfect example of how the "western past (repeatedly) refuses burial." It makes a certain sense that such a critically significant moment of the uncanny should focus on issues of inexhaustible byproducts that might be buried but refuse finally to "go away"; Limerick's drive toward inclusivity is, after all, at least partially propelled by an awareness of how Western U.S. life and its histories have been shaped by various repressions which nonetheless make themselves felt in the great variety of unselfconscious, unintended repetitions which she charts.

As with almost every other description of such "returns," Limerick overtly emphasizes an element of surprise that ultimately reframes an apparent lack of self-consciousness and intention. Boom bust mentalities crop up everywhere, as do natives and insects grown tolerant of pesticides. Even Manifest Destiny breathes new life, although in the less glorious body of the Aryan Nation. In terms of tone, the rhetorical effect of these gestures invites the reader to share the uncanny sense associated with the reapproach to repressed material. However, for all the richness that is implied by this mining of repression and the questions that might accompany it, Limerick distances herself from further methodological inquiry as the book develops and racial issues move to the forefront. In a fairly conventional critique of identity politics, her argument folds into an attack on stereotypes and categorization more generally.

Limerick's sense, while examining minority historians like Rudolfo Acuña, is that racially-focused histories have become too invested in legitimating their own displaced voices by positing a hierarchy of victimization. As problematic as such identity politics may be, Limerick's answer, a "pluralizing" of history, moves too quickly toward an erasure of crucial social and cultural distinctions. For example, in an effort to create a non-hierarchical playing field of victimization in the West, Limerick posits Mormons, Asian Americans and Latinos as ethnic groups with comparable traumatic experiences. The slippage between differences historically coded as racial and differences coded as ethnic is troubling, particularly in the quick shift Limerick makes between the Japanese American internment and the Mormon persecutions. My point lies not with who suffered more, but rather with questions about how particular instances of suffering were brought about and legitimated—in other words, with the mechanics (social, cultural, political) that were at play in these distinct episodes. Any blanket condemnation of categorical difference like that evoked by Limerick threatens to foreclose study of these distinct processes.

When readers come to *Legacy of Conquest*'s final pages, then, and find themselves asked to shed the racial and ethnic categories which have kept them strangers, more than a little skepticism is likely to take hold, but not for the reasons Limerick herself alludes to in "Turnerians All." For whatever problems presentism may contribute, it is not the linchpin here. Instead, *Legacy of Conquest*'s concluding critical moves fail because they enact an unfortunate shifting of methodological focus, turning the argument into an essentially formalist affair. As an alternative, Limerick might have capitalized more on the various historiographic displacements that she documents, displacements that are consistently associated with repression. While her book announces itself as an argument for continuity in the face of traditionally assumed historical breaks, Turner's most obviously, the deeper contribution of the study is actually its testimony to this complex process of displacements which has typified understandings of the American West.

Because the incorporation of multicultural issues has been so important for the New Western historians as they have defined their "newness," Limerick's formalist, category-phobic displacement of race itself merits a closer look. Midway through *Legacy*, Limerick hits one of her most polemical strides as she undertakes a disavowal of her "ethnocentric predecessors" in the historical profession (219). This distancing takes place as Limerick addresses the nagging "persistence of natives" in the West, a persistence that necessarily betrays the "vanishing Indian" trope she would critique. Expanding on this polemic, Limerick claims that complicit historians have posited this premature burial as a way of securing the record of the West as a "white" property (*Legacy* 220). Such a moment could provide an important opportunity for reflection regarding the NWH's own synthesis of material from minority historians, historians who frequently do not share the critical agendas of the NWH movement. Instead, a detour occurs wherein the property issue is reprocessed by Limerick as an ontological battle, a battle in which the goal is assumed to be the pluralistic incorporation of Native American, and other, forms of subjectivity. In the move to create a relational history, then, a form of corporate relativism appears to blur the ethical distinctions as the argument moves too quickly toward a "speaking out for the human dignity of all parties" (*Legacy* 221). With this displacement, Limerick sacrifices both an opportunity for self-reflection, and a fuller engagement of the minority historical projects which she acknowledges have been subject to complicated processes of denial and upon which the NWH draws heavily.

The costs of this displacement are readily apparent as Limerick takes up Southwestern border dynamics. Here, Limerick valorizes a critical notion of *mestisaje* in a chapter that consistently resolves the extended struggles over nomenclature in Mexican-descent populations by imposing the term "Hispanic." The choice is a highly problematic one, given the term's inherent elision of racial mixing. As much as this and similar chapters acknowledge racially-defined traumas which too frequently have been ignored or devalued by previous historical efforts, the ethical problems posed by the engagement of these traumas have not been worked through, and, at its most distressing, *Legacy of Conquest* actually manages to "unthink" racial problems yet again. One measure of such difficulties can be found in the way the concept of *mestisaje* is itself essentialized into a blurring of distinctions—a turn of events which appears to be linked in Limerick's account to a frustration with identity politics and racially-oriented studies in comparative sinning (257).

In a subsequent chapter, "Racialism on the Run," readers may begin to wonder if Limerick's target is actually race-conscious analysis itself, given the deep suspicions of racial categories that are announced. This distrust, combined with Limerick's earlier gloss of *mestisaje*, accentuates the sense that an evacuation is taking place of critical possibilities and ethical distinctions. The suspicions are compounded when Limerick starts to fashion an alternative form of analysis. According to Limerick:

> Minorities and majority in the American West occupied common ground—literally. A conquest for control of the land, for the labor applied to the land, and for the resulting profit set the terms of their meeting. Sharing turf, contesting turf, surrendering turf, Western groups, for all their difficulties, took part in the same story. Each group may well have had its own, self-defined story, but in the contest for property and profit, those stories meet. (291–92)

The turn to the dynamics of property and profit is certainly of interest. Yet readers should wonder why Limerick devalues racial dynamics. Most importantly, it seems that she has weakened her study—including its ability to yield insight regarding the complicated displacements at work in Western history—in order to purify the routes of critical departure. Putting the problem in the form of a question, one might ask why such an astute writer about the West would hold at bay all the evidence for the ways racism has moved in a non-utilitarian, fiscally destructive fashion, undeniably violating economic rationales. By way of just one example, readers might consider 1932 repatriation drives in Los Angeles which were openly protested by the Chamber of Commerce.

Given the tendency of other New Western historians to follow this path, it will be important to speculate further about the conditions that make this displacement onto the economic appear almost self-evidently appropriate. To be clear, my concern does not rest with demonizing Patricia Limerick and her engagement of the "embarrassment of riches" she associates with minority studies. Instead, I'd like to think more broadly about the range of rhetorical gestures that inform this Western history, and others like it, Old and New.

In this context, I would consider the way *Legacy of Conquest* presents an evolution in its own defining metaphors, an evolution that both reveals and conceals the implications of the uncanny returns situated throughout the text. In the first instance, Limerick opens her book by comparing the historian's task to the experience of someone walking over Colorado mine fields, a situation that could easily plunge the historian "unexpectedly into the legacy of Western history" (18).

Perhaps somewhat predictably, this ability for the past to return with surprising force is presumably mastered at that juncture in the book when Limerick supplants racial analysis with an economic focus. Here she offers a new notion of how the past might be negotiated by turning to

> a thoroughly un-Western metaphor for a complicated phenomenon—a subway system. Every station in the system is a center of sorts—trains and passengers converge on it; in both departure and arrival, the station is the pivot. But get on a train, and you are soon (with any luck) at another station, equally a center and a pivot. Every station is at the center of a particular world, yet that does not leave the observer of the system conceptually muddled, unable to decide which station represents the true point of view from which the entire system should be viewed. (292)

The surprise of the mine shaft is replaced here with a map and a token, but to hearken back to James Baldwin, we may want to ask "what is the price of the ticket"? If the "underground" in the first metaphor is understood to represent the complex workings of denial, a point Limerick stresses early on in her study, could any ticket be purchased that would simplify the historian's life in the manner suggested by the subway concept? Herein lies the particularly discursive and professional, as opposed to merely biographical, problem, in large part because Limerick finds herself far more within the expectations of history-as-a-discipline at the end of the book than at the outset. Acknowledging the exceptions posed by scholars who engage in more "experimental" forms of historiography, I am working from the notion that the field is still largely committed to the outlook that historians participate in a craft, and that this craft is best pursued when the writer assumes the stance of a detached, and ultimately "ironic" observer. In other words, the stance associated with the subway commuter, map in hand.

Considered in this context, readers might thus approach *Legacy of Conquest* with an eye for the contradictory pulls it evidences between an implicitly psychoanalytic interpretive framework that would play with the uncanny and a craftsman's framework that would map the West from a securely distanced vantage point. Perhaps no linguistic aspect of this tension is more readily felt than the consistent manner in which Limerick explicitly redefines surprising returns of real or displaced traumas as instances of the ironic in her writings. Like the shift to the subway metaphor, this evocation of the ironic tends to flatten out otherwise historically deep scenarios, writing them into an essentially atemporal rhetoric of simple, if shocking, juxtaposition and repetition based in a formal understanding of genre.

If such ironic recoding is itself a sign of displacement—a sign of the NWH's inability to sufficiently work through racial traumas in particular—it may be that there is a certain logic guiding Limerick and her NWH peers to settle upon profit as a "common ground," especially as they negotiate a synthesis of multicultural histories in the potential sunset of affirmative action. Inasmuch as a general appeal to functionality follows with the turn to economic interests, this particular interpretive dimension may actually foreclose self-critical avenues while also adding an apparent manageability to the troubling race issues which have acted as one important motor for the movement. Coming to terms with its own participation in uncanny dynamics, the most pressing question for the NWH may be bound once again to race, namely: can the record of racial dynamics in the West ground an analysis beyond identity politics, an analysis which would integrate different spheres of life in the West rather than presume a choice between economic and race issues?

University of California, Santa Barbara

NOTES

1. Samuel Weber has produced a Derridean reading that links Freud's theories about castration to post-structuralist explorations of difference per se; Helene Cixous has considered Freud's uncanny in terms of the ambivalences it expresses regarding women, especially as played out in textual and literary fashion; and Lloyd-Smith attempts to build on the feminist analysis by further historicizing Freud's thinking about women.

2. Limerick herself meditates on these stylistic points and their response in a recent essay entitled, "What Raymond Chandler Knew and Western Historians Forgot."

3. Dominick LaCapra has written extensively on these dynamics; for a general introduction, readers may examine the chapter "History and Psychoanalysis," in *Soundings in Critical Theory*. For a more detailed application, see LaCapra's *Representing the Holocaust*.

4. Some central texts in this growing field include Caruth's *Trauma*, Felman and Laub's *Testimony*, and LaCapra's *Representing the Holocaust*.

5. Donald Pisani makes a similar point when he notes of other NWH efforts that "social historians have not been notably successful in finding 'a new narrative form more appropriate to a pluralistic concept of history'" (170); Ostler and Johnson offer a more in-depth critique that is very suspicious of the NWH's incorporation of minority and women's issues, arguing that these end up being pushed aside for economic issues.

6. Renato Rosaldo has written a fascinating essay which offers an initial definition of such (post)colonial nostalgia.

WORKS CITED

Acuña, Rudolfo. *Occupied America: A History of Chicanos*. New York: Harper and Row, 1988.

Caruth, Cathy, ed. *Trauma: Explorations in Memory*. Baltimore: Johns Hopkins University Press, 1995.

Cixous, Hélène. "Fiction and its Phantoms." *New Literary History* 7 (1975): 525–48.

Felman, Shoshana and Dori Laub, M.D. *Testimony: Crises of Witnessing in Literature, Psychoanalysis and History*. New York: Routledge, 1992.

Freud, Sigmund. *The Standard Edition of the Complete Psychological Works of Sigmund Freud.* Vol. 17. Trans. James Strachey. London: Hogarth Press, 1955.

Guillory, John. "Canonical and Non-Canonical: A Critique of the Current Debate." *ELH* 54 (1987): 483–527.

Johnson, Robert and Jeffery Ostler. "The Politics and Antipolitics of Western History." Delivered Western Historical Conference, Denver, 1995.

LaCapra, Dominick. *Representing the Holocaust: History, Theory, Trauma.* Ithaca: Cornell University Press, 1994.

———. *Soundings in Critical Theory.* Ithaca: Cornell University Press, 1989.

Limerick, Patricia. *The Legacy of Conquest: The Unbroken Past of the American West.* New York: Norton, 1987.

———. "Turnerians All: The Dream of a Helpful History in an Intelligible World." *American Historical Review* 100 (1995): 697–716.

———. "What Raymond Chandler Knew and Western Historians Forgot." *Old West—New West: Centennial Essays.* Ed. Barbara Howard Meldrum. Moscow: University of Idaho Press, 1993. 28–42.

Lloyd-Smith, Allan. *Uncanny American Fiction: Medusa's Face.* London: MacMillan Press, 1989.

Pascoe, Peggy. *Relations of Rescue: The Search for Female Moral Authority in the American West, 1874–1939.* New York: Oxford University Press, 1990.

Pisani, Donald. "The 'New Western History' Comes of Age." *Reviews in American History* 21 (1993): 166–71.

Turner, Frederick Jackson. *The Frontier in American History.* New York: Holt Rinehart and Winston, 1920.

Rosaldo, Renato. "Imperialist Nostalgia." *Representations* 26 (1989): 107-22.

Weber, Samuel. "The Sideshow, or: Remarks on a Canny Moment." *Modern Language Notes* 88 (1973): 1102–133.

White, Richard. *"It's Your Misfortune and None of My Own": A New History of the American West.* Norman: University of Oklahoma Press, 1991.

STEPHEN TATUM

The Problem of the "Popular" in the New Western History

> To see this commercialized vision of the Old Frontier in concrete, three-dimensional form, the best place to go is Disneyland in Anaheim, California. When they enter Frontierland, visitors might ask Disneyland employees for directions, but they do not have to ask for a definition of the frontier. The frontier, every tourist knows, was the edge of Anglo-American settlement, the place where white Americans struggled to master the continent. This frontier, as everything in Frontierland confirms, was populated by a colorful and romantic cast of characters—mountain men, cowboys, prospectors, pioneer wives, saloon girls, sheriffs, and outlaws. . . . These images are very well understood. Tourists do not need any assistance in defining Frontierland.
>
> Patricia Nelson Limerick, "The Adventures of the Frontier in the Twentieth Century" (1994)

> My West is the *American* West: that fabled land where the restless pioneer moves ever forward, settling one frontier after another; where the American character becomes self-reliant, democratic, and endlessly eager for the new; where we strip off the garments of civilization and don a rude buckskin shirt; where millions of dejected immigrants gather from around the world to be rejuvenated as Americans, sounding together a manly, wild, barbaric yawp of freedom. That is my West: precisely that and nothing more. "Oh," my colleague [in Chinese studies] ventures, more perplexed now than cantankerous, "you mean 'the West'—the frontier, Indians, Clint Eastwood?" I nod vaguely and sidle off. It is all so hard to convey over a single, polite glass of academic sherry.
>
> Donald Worster, *Under Western Skies* (1992)

IN ONE OF THE EARLY CHAPTERS in his *We Pointed Them North: Recollections of a Cowpuncher*, E. C. "Teddy Blue" Abbott describes his adventures in 1880 while he worked for the CY Ranch out of Wyoming. Teddy Blue was born in England and grew up in the Lincoln, Nebraska, area where, as a young man being pressured to take up the life of a farmer, he routinely saw Texas cowpunchers and Texas cattle moving north to Wyoming and Montana, following the open range. Unlike his fathers and brothers before him, who did become farmers, and unlike one brother who in Teddy's words "ended up the worst of the lot—a sheepman and a Republican" (29), Teddy Blue left home at the age of eighteen to learn the cowboy way. In the summer of 1880, the then twenty-year-old Teddy Blue was supposed to rendezvous in Cheyenne with a few other cowpunchers and travel to Oregon so as to bring cattle back to stock the CY Ranch. But while waiting for the others to arrive, Teddy Blue met a man who had just come back from Oregon and who complained mightily about the rainy weather that plagued everyday work and travel on the trail.

Hearing this news, Teddy Blue and one comrade "quit the layout and went south" (41), heading for New Mexico to work on ranches there after a brief stop in Denver to see the sights. The "sights" for Teddy Blue invariably means saloons and brothels, and on this particular occasion he recalls getting "well lit up" and attending a "hot show" on Blake Street with some other cowpunchers (46). The show they saw was entitled "Poor Nell," a melodrama which featured a scene of a burglar beating his wife to death. One of the drunk cowpunchers, Teddy Blue recalls, had passed out during the performance, but was awakened by noise made by the actor playing the burglar, who would stamp his foot on the floor as he shook his co-star's head, so that it sounded like her head was hitting the floor. Upon being awakened by the noise and seeing the scene before him, this drunk, chivalrous cowpuncher jumped "onto the stage and busted the fellow on the head with his six-gun before he remembered where he was. The woman got up and began to cuss him, all hell broke loose, somebody pulled Bill off the stage, they called for the police, the boys shot out the lights, and everybody broke their necks getting away from there" (46–47).

"There" of course is figured as the interior, somewhat feminized space of culture, not nature, where entanglements with the social order erupt in ways that threaten masculine mobility and, hence, independence. This scene, as well as the overall narrative trajectory of *We Pointed Them North*—its periodic interruption of a predominant travel narrative by brief rest stops in towns such as Denver—points us toward Donald Worster's characterization of the "old mythology" of the West as a "retreat from the human community and all its conflicts" ("Beyond" 18). Moreoever, scenes such as this one in Teddy Blue's narrative usefully remind us why New Western historians interested particularly in women's history have been relatively indifferent to myths of male adventure which invariably include violence against women and animals. Patricia Nelson Limerick, in her distinctively witty way, has likened the role of the New Western historian to that of the person left behind to clean up such a mess created by Teddy Blue and his rowdy male friends, rather than being released to track the escapades of a variety of male adventurers and entrepreneurs whose regeneration is grounded on the conquest of physical and human resources. Limerick's metaphor implicitly criticizes the Old Western History for seeing darkly through gendered glasses in so far as it defined any scholarly attention to the tragic or ironic consequences of masculine conquest as women's domestic work. But in addition to asking us to think about the disciplinary positioning of historians like herself, Limerick's metaphor neatly reminds us that there is indeed a "mess" which cannot be cleaned up and forgotten but should be confronted seriously and responsibly by historians. Facing the mess of environmental degradation, racism, and class oppression left by over a century's worth of capitalistic development, New Western historians, as Worster has written, "could not pretend that the only story that mattered in the West was one of stagecoach lines, treasure hunts, cattle brands, and wildcatters, nor for that matter aircraft plants, opera companies, bank deposits, or middle-class whites learning how to ski. What was missing was a frank, hard look at the violent imperialistic process by which the West was wrested from its original owners and the violence by which it had been secured against the continuing claims of minorities, women, and the forces of nature" ("Beyond" 15–16).

Both Worster and Limerick deploy metaphors of surveillance—viewing, gazing, and seeing—to define and distinguish the New Western History's methodological approach to the field of historical events and actors comprising the American West. Certain critics of the New Western History to date have debated of course whether in fact the previous historiography of the West did not see the "winning of the West" as a "violent imperialistic process." What interests me here, as I think over

Worster's quote with the life and narration of Teddy Blue in mind, is how the issue of proper seeing and, hence, naming and interpreting what one has seen, ultimately becomes a matter of ethics. Because Worster in his "Beyond the Agrarian Myth" essay explicitly contrasts "frank looking" with "pretending," the ethical issue of having the courage to see, not to deny, rather than the issue simply of ignorance or blindness, emerges as a paramount concern. We can no longer afford to ignore, by extension of this logic, Teddy Blue's status as, say, a working-class laborer in the service of an emerging corporate economy. We can no longer afford to ignore the social and economic function performed by the numerous prostitutes Teddy Blue chronicles as greeting the cowpunchers when they return to that place that they are usually wanting to be getting away from. We can no longer ignore real and imagined violence against women, whether on the Denver stage or in factories and on farms in the West.

Now in its benign form, denial for the New Western historians is a matter of not seeing the real itself and not understanding the truths about reality because of the persuasive power of wishes and dreams, which is to say precisely because between humans and an external reality there always exists desire. Limerick for one seems inclined to define "a net of denial" woven by Westerners as a matter of *bad faith*, since she posits that humans "have a well-established capacity to meet facts of life with disbelief" (*Legacy* 96). In its more sinister or pessimistic form, however, pretending or what I'm now, following Limerick's lead, calling "denial" occurs because the ideological interests associated with the forces of capital are so successfully transmitted by popular cultural representations of western American history that people cannot truly recognize their manipulation and subordination. Denial in this more sinister or pessimistic form looks to be a matter of *false consciousness*. With this distinction between bad faith and false consciousness in mind, we can perhaps better understand Worster's seemingly gratuitous, albeit humorous, reference to "middle-class whites learning how to ski." It's not just that this reference condenses for us the New Western historians' brief against the monovocal nature of the Old Western historians' repetitive focus on Anglo-European bourgeois fortunes in the western United States. Worster's image also asks his readers, regardless of their own class and ethnic positions, to identify with his rhetorical "we," constructed here as a no-nonsense, populist collective whose work ethic seemingly inoculates them (or should it be "us") against the culture of tourism and recreation—a culture which represents in a shorthand way the intensified culture of consumption which Worster loathes. For those bourgeois readers of western American history who do find it humorous to contemplate the spectacle of yuppies *learning* how to ski while environmental disasters are occurring all around them, Worster would point out that a "frank, hard look" at such a recreational mode of consumption would lead such readers to see how leisure time is organized and marketed precisely for the benefit of a multinational corporate economy. To invert the order of clauses in a Worster statement, "as we face unblinkingly the fact that from its earliest days the fate of the western region has been one of furnishing raw materials for industrialism's development," "truth is breaking in, driving out myth and self-deception" ("Beyond" 19).

"Unblinkingly"; "truth" breaking in like sunlight where once there was darkness and confusion; "myth and self-deception"—this perspective on surveillance, mystification, and denial introduces us to the territory of "ideology" and the "ideological." This territory of beliefs, values, and meanings mediates between humans and reality, and for representative New Western historians this territory's contours occlude insights and foster blindness. In the accumulating discourse of the New Western historians this territory of ideological self-deception is dominated by the landmarks of "myth," "old mythic thinking," "the old mythology," variously specified as the agrarian myth, the myth of progress, the myth of the frontier, or the myth of rugged individualism. (Limerick updates that list by referring to the grail-like allure of the more recent "hi-tech myth" driving political and economic decisions in the West as various locales model themselves after northern California's Silicon Valley [*Legacy* 150].) In the narrative being fashioned by various New Western historians for the past decade, the "old mythology" of the West was produced by a modernizing industrial culture in the form of paintings, photographs, novels, movies, theme parks, carnivals, and television shows for popular consumption by the masses desiring leisure-time entertainment. Moreover, this cultural mythology, whose permutations through time basically wring variations on a core American myth of rugged individualism (see Worster, *Wealth* 117–18), was also fostered and disseminated by the Old Western History, whose own origins are traced to Frederick Jackson Turner's frontier thesis as it was formulated in his various essays in the 1890s and early-1900s which were published in such widely-distributed and read magazines as the *Atlantic Monthly*.

For the most part, New Western historians define the "popular" and "popular culture" straightforwardly as either synonymous with mass culture or as signifying what the masses of people enjoy. General references are made in their writings to such things as "the popular imagination" and the "popular mind," and these generic, holistic concepts indicate their interest in making observations about the *content* of those works produced for and consumed by the people, not, it should be emphasized, in the complicated production and reception history of those works. On the one hand, the status of the "popular" would seem to be of utmost importance for the project of the New Western History, since two of its leading practitioners (Worster and Limerick) self-consciously aspire to being "public intellectuals."[1] The status of the "popular" would also seem to be important since, as Richard White has particularly recognized in his work, the transition from agrarian capitalism to industrial capitalism in this country occurred precisely at the moment when the West as a region and the Western as a popular genre were gaining cultural prominence in this country. During this transitional moment, there was, to use Stuart Hall's words from a theoretical essay on the meaning of "the popular," "a more or less continuous struggle over the culture of the working people, the labouring classes and the poor" (455) on the part of the dominant classes in order to train and educate working people to take their positions in the emerging industrial workplace.

What Allan Trachtenberg has called "the incorporation of America" during Turner's era reveals itself in such developments as the standardization of time zones, clothing sizes, and machine parts, and in the development of linked transportation routes and of the hub-and-spoke system for the manufacturing and distributing of goods. We can document the incorporation of America during this period not only by studying the number of cattle brought to market in a given year as a result of trail drives north from Texas. We can also consider how Teddy Blue's reference to the various stage plays and light operas produced in cow towns throughout the plains states suggests a developing transportation system which linked metropolitan centers with outlying areas in the distribution of cultural capital. This struggle by the forces of capital over the culture of subordinate groups is particularly evident also in the rise of a popular commercial press—dime novels, newspapers, inexpensive illustrated magazines which were intensely interested in things western—funded by the forces of capital but putatively representing and speaking for "the people." Limerick for one recognizes the potential importance of this cultural material, for she describes one aspect of her education as a historian as being "off to the literary wars, off to the trenches to reread Cooper's Leatherstocking Tales and to keep track of the plots of dime novels. This topic seemed to me, in other words, to give marching orders that directed me to the periphery, away from the daylight zone of political, economic, and social behavior and off to the twilight zone of myth and symbol" ("Making" 169).

Limerick's contrast between the "daylight zone" of actual behavior and the "twilight zone" of myth and symbol condenses for us the "problem of the popular" for historians of the American West. The "popular" constitutes a problem since in the realm of popular culture, and particularly at the point of the people's consumption of commodities, the various myths, stereotypes, idylls, and romances conspire to obscure the truths of some putatively "real" history. Consider these representative comments, in addition to Worster's phrase quoted earlier regarding how at last "the truth is breaking in, driving out myth and self-deception": "old clouds of myth and romance" (Worster, *Under* 5); "an important truth obscured by the old mythology" (Worster, *Under* 13); "borderlands scholars have shown little interest in the grand national mythologies associated with a 'westward movement'" (Robbins 195); or, as Richard White puts it, in phrasing that repeats imagery of sight and links Old Western historians with Turner's frontier thesis, "New Western Historians have abandoned frontier blinders that restricted their [Old Western historians] view" (*Trails* 31); "removing western history from the domain of myth and symbol and restoring it to actuality" (Limerick, *Legacy* 52). Not surprisingly, Hollywood film and television productions, Wild West Shows, and Disney's Frontierland frequently are referenced by New Western historians as illustrating the worst features of popular culture mythologizing of the "real" West. According to Donald Worster, for example, "That traditional faith in the region's natural healing power endures even now in the popular mind, which tends to think of the 'real West' as a place without industry or cities, as an idyll starring Robert Redford in the role of lonely trapper wandering through an awesomely beautiful wilderness" (*Under* 13). The overall point is, as Limerick writes in her essay "The Adventures of the Frontier in the Twentieth Century," that "whatever meanings historians give the term, in popular culture it [the "frontier"] carries a persistently happy affect, a tone of adventure, heroism, and even fun very much in contrast with the tough, complicated, and sometimes bloody and brutal realities of conquest" (75).

What I find intriguing here is how the discourse of the New Western History in its more didactic, polemical moments seemingly grounds itself on binary oppositions just as steadfastly as do, say, the old myths of western movies and novels supposedly depend upon fateful contests between savagery and civilization, cowboys and Indians, and the good guys in white and the bad guys in black. Though I honor Limerick's claim that "human experience" cannot be simply divided "between the light and the dark, the positive and the negative" ("Trail" 74), the discourse of the New Western history defines a border in human experience between, on the one hand, an ethnocentric, exceptionalist, and fundamentally "smiling" mythos of adventure, this surrounded by images of clouds, smoke, haze, veils, and darkness—these tropes suggesting the concealment of external truths and both the bad faith and the false consciousness fostered by our elemental human desire for heroes and heroines. And on the other hand, standing free of "the twilight zone of myth and symbol," there exists the daylight zone of "tough, complicated, and sometimes bloody and brutal realities of conquest," the zone of the actual and the factual brought to light by the work of the New Western historians. Such work has helped the West "become a more thoughtful and self-aware community than it has been, a community that no longer insists on its special innocence but accepts the fact that it is inextricably part of a flawed world" (*Under* 18). Thus as a result of the "unblinking," "frank and hard look" at the past done by the New Western historians, who unlike their forbears have removed the blinders of the frontier thesis, "innocence"—with its connotations of the infantile or the adolescent—is being transformed into maturity, naïve comedy into tragic complexity, Teddy Blue's straight line north with the herd spatialized instead as travel into mazes and box canyons, and academic insularity into being at one with the people who themselves have endured the travails and disappointments attendant upon western American history.

Thus, in either its benign or pessimistic form, pretending not to see, or what I've been calling denial, defines the problem of the "popular" for the New Western History essentially as one of *presence and absence*:

that is, the presence of myths, symbols, and romances associated with narratives of adventure in the popular culture means a space for critical reflection is absent; absent a space of critical distance, one becomes the prey of the ideological construction of reality promoted by the dominant class, who controls both the economic and symbolic means of production; the powerful presence of the dominant class' ideological version of reality means the presence of a partial version of experience and the absence of a true grasp of the complex, multicultural history of the American West. The Teddy Blue description of what happened at the melodrama in Denver thus illustrates not only the pull of adventure and the perennial flight from community typical of the "twilight zone" of Cooper, dime novels, and Hollywood movies. The cowpuncher who jumps on the stage and begins beating on one of the male actors allegorizes for us the loss of critical distance from entertaining cultural commodities and the dangers attendant upon blurring of the boundaries between cultural representation and actuality. This loss of critical distance, this inability to stand apart from and evaluate and judge the cultural products disseminated by "the powers that be" (*Trails* 22), results in tragic consequences, since in the narrative fashioned by New Western historians—most prominently by the overarching plot Limerick constructs in her *The Legacy of Conquest*—"the most dramatic and sustained case of high expectations and naïveté meet[s] a frustrating and intractable reality" (*Legacy* 29).

This observation leads me to say that Richard White is entirely accurate in describing the narratives of the New Western History as plotted typically in either tragic or ironic modes (*Trails* 33). But I would add to his insight that in their position papers and more polemical statements, such as in the *Trails* collection of essays, the texture of New Western historians' texts weaves together just such a tragic or ironic plot about the course of western history with an implied romance kind of plot about the activities of the New Western historian as an archetypal "deliverer" figure—the wise parent or savvy older brother or sister—who doesn't blink in the hard light of day, who promotes frank appraisals concerning the continuity of conquest and exploitation between past and present, and whose perspective redeems the community from the thrall of myth and symbol. Consider, for instance, in this context how Limerick refers occasionally in her work to the resurrection of a moribund field of study as a result of the New Western historians' scholarship or how Worster defines the work of "critical intellectuals" as *mastering* rather than becoming "prisoners of ideology" ("Beyond" 23).

The myth of the frontier promoted in the popular culture and by historians in league with Chamber of Commerce types constitutes a pernicious kind of contagious magic because the New Western historians find the function of such a mythology to be that of escape into fantasy or daydream, a kind of wish-fulfillment or compensation for misfortunes in the present. Limerick suggests that mythic adventures on the frontier not only "have no bearing on the complex realities of twentieth-century America," but also that their promotion of stereotypes are valued by the popular imagination "precisely because they offered an escape from modern troubles" (*Legacy* 19).[2] All told, then, the problem of the "popular" for the New Western historians is this: as much as popular mythologies do important cultural work in providing the ideological duct tape which binds us together and defines who "we" are, a point noted throughout the discourse of the New Western historians, such mythologies both obscure the *real* and, considering the binary of innocence and experience that pervades the polemical register of the New Western historians' discourse, such mythologies arrest our development toward greater self-understanding of ourselves, our past, and our present.

The additional "problem of the popular," as Limerick points out in her 1994 essay "The Adventures of the Frontier in the Twentieth Century," is that the intense and sometimes vitriolic academic debates about the meaning of the western American experience waged by professional historians do not amount to a hill of beans for audiences outside the academy: "If professional Western American historians find themselves conceptually without anchor when they visit [Disney's] Frontierland, the reason is clear: with the possible exception of the suggestion that environmental carelessness produced the settler's cabin fire, the work of academic historians has had virtually no impact either on Disneyland's vision of the frontier or on the thinking of Disneyland's visitors" (72). For New Western historians, the "popular" becomes synonymous with seductive and spectacular cultural entertainment for the masses, and the terrain of the "popular" is demarcated as something different from "the people" on the one hand, and "professional Western American historians" on the other. Hence, Limerick's particular strategy, which at times is paralleled by Worster's rhetorical tactics in his occasional essays, becomes that of identifying various real "people" whom she knows or has known, people who are to be distinguished from "tourists," people whose personal histories of living in the West are a testament to the enduring and damaging boundary between real life experiences and the culture industry's propagation of escapist fantasy.

II

I do not want here to dispute either Limerick's claim that humankind weaves nets of denial or Worster's charge that the people suffer from the organization of leisure time by the forces of capital. And I agree with New Western historians that tragic consequences can and often do occur when our actions and identities are unduly influenced by mythic representations or when, as Limerick points out when discussing a statement by Reagan's Secretary of the Interior, James Watt, ideology "overrule[s] an understanding of history" (*Legacy* 336). Nevertheless, significant problems with the problem of "the popular" in the New Western History remain. Given the specific plot of the *Jeremiah Johnson* film from 1972 starring Robert Redford, for instance, a plot which dramatizes graphically at some length the "tough, complicated, and sometimes bloody and brutal realities of conquest," and given the series of revisionist western films produced particularly during the 1960s and 1970s which explicitly question the consequences of Manifest Destiny, I am hard pressed to understand the reductiveness of certain summary comments by New Western historians who seem unwilling to accord popular culture art forms and to their reception to their own evolving *history*. Turner's narratives about the course of western history at the beginning of this century often stand as synecdoches for an entire popular culture and a paradigmatic historiographical tradition of telling the story about the West. In this context, consider how Limerick claims that "in the popular imagination, the frontier froze as a biracial confrontation between 'whites' and 'Indians'" (*Legacy* 259). Whether this claim is true or not, it would at least seem to warrant further elaboration since "the popular imagination" is not only overly vague and holistic as a covering label, but also depends upon a stereotypical view of the content of this imagination's thought.

Although I believe Limerick is right to point out how the multicultural West has often been ignored or repressed by popular representations, I would nevertheless argue that "the popular" has itself been as frozen by New Western historians as some so-called popular imagination has frozen racial conflict in the West between whites and Indians. My claim, which this essay will begin to develop, is basically two-fold: (1) that the history of popular western texts—if studied and accepted as an evolving rather than frozen one—is everywhere invested in dramatizing struggles for cultural dominance, complex issues of morality, and contests for property and propriety; and (2) that the objectives of New Western History—in Limerick's unobjectionable words to make a "responsible and thorough assessment of our common past" so as to live "responsibly" in the present American West ("What" 87); in Worster's words "to stand apart from power and think critically about it, as it is to think critically about western society as a whole, about its ideals and drives, about the contradictions it has created, about its prospects for new identities, goals, and values ("Beyond" 22)—that these objectives can move even further toward fulfillment if New Western historians would cease demonizing the popular and begin considering how at times in even the most seemingly retrograde popular texts critical thinking about ideals, drives, contradictions, and prospects can and does occur.

Finally, I want to begin developing this claim because it is also unclear to me how one can stand apart from one's culture, let alone from the forces of "power" within which academics and universities are enmeshed. It is unclear to me how in putting off the frontier blinders that restricted the vision of Old Western historians, for instance, one can avoid putting on another sort of blinder; it is unclear to me, however much we might desire it to be the case, how one can at some point become a "master" of ideology or get "beyond" the mythic West. New Western History theorizing in certain instances recapitulates the hotly-contested debate in American Studies scholarship over whether "cultural texts are unable [or able] to engage in processes of reflection on the values that generate them without at the same time being subsumed by those values" (Gunn 11). Suffice it to say that in certain instances what New Western historians assume to be the case—that critical distance and reflection is possible; that myth and symbol are divorced from reality—is in fact under debate, not a done deal.

We can begin to approach the problems arising from what I'm calling the "problem of the popular" in the New Western History by noticing, first, that just prior to the above quotation in Limerick's essay she briefly discusses the "curious politics" of the shooting gallery entrance to Disney's Frontierland ("Adventures" 71). Limerick astutely raises the issue of identity formation, or what I'll call here "the politics of audience identification," when she notices the proclivity of visitors taking a fake firearm in hand and shooting at "a railroad train, winding its way through a sculpted landscape . . ." (71):

> If you are firing on the train, then you seem to be either a hostile Indian or a murderous and larcenous outlaw. What is going on here? Is the visitor receiving an invitation to play with point of view, to reconsider the whole question of the identity and interests of good guys and bad guys, champions of progress and opponents of progress? Or is this casting of the railroad as target simply the product of Disneyland's designers working under the mandate to create a scene chock-full of the shapes and forms that will say 'frontier,' with the assumption that any visitor so stimulated visually will fall into step with the mythic patterns of frontier life, pick up a gun, and blast away at whatever is in sight? (71–72)

Limerick does not specifically answer any of the questions she raises here—although we should note that in other moments in the essay her point is precisely that visitors have been so stimulated by images of the Wild West that they will "fall into step with the mythic patterns of frontier life, pick up a gun, and blast away at whatever is in sight." Her rhetorical strategy here seems to be that there is no simple or pat answer to "what is going on here" questions, that in fact what is going on here at the shooting gallery can't be analytically anchored either in the consumer's playing with point of view or in the producer's (the design team) stimulating and manipulating the consumer. The indeterminacy of meaning circulating in this event highlights the problem that Disneyland's version of history is basically indifferent to the work of academic historians who for some time now have been critiquing "the mythic patterns of frontier life" that Disney transparently updates and promotes for the gullible consumer in Frontierland.

What I find most interesting about Limerick's lament, however, is its provisional staging of a more complex notion of how popular culture works than is typically found in the discourse of the New Western historians, and, subsequently, its moving toward a conclusion that neither follows upon its observational evidence nor picks up on the interpretive possibilities about the popular which it has inaugurated. If it is fair to say that the New Western historians have "sought to restore to memory all those unsmiling aspects that Turner wanted to leave out" (*Under* 12), have critiqued "Happy Face History, Have a Nice Day History, because it was so firmly centered on Anglo-Americans, and because it seemed to end so well, with white people in charge of the continent, and with a lot of natural resources converted into cash in white people's pockets" (Limerick, "Progress" 46), then the possibility that in the Frontierland shooting gallery visitors are reconsidering "the whole question of the identity and interests of good guys and bad guys, champions of progress and opponents of progress," suggests, contrary to Limerick's concluding complaint, two important insights about tourists who come to Frontierland—*tourists whose consumer experience is in fact rhetorically figured as a synecdoche for all of us who negotiate representations of frontier history in the United States' industrial popular culture.* First, tourists who reconsider what "progress" means when they blast away at the railroad may in fact be disclosing how they have in fact internalized revisionist notions of Western history as these have been circulated by academic historians in print, on radio, on television, in public lectures, and in the classroom. Secondly, if we recall that in the iconography of dime novels, the popular Western novel, and Hollywood Westerns both railroads and banks have long symbolized a corrupt, anti-democratic modernizing process, then Limerick's example implicitly begins to recognize how a critique of the grand old myths of progress and Manifest Destiny associated with frontier conquest can conceivably be advanced not only by certain academic historians who are not in league with the Chamber of Commerce, but also by the productions of the culture industry and those who consume them.

Limerick's basic point is that in American culture such theme parks as Disneyland, whose Frontierland essentially promotes the same mythologies as the Wild West shows of the last century, constitute difficult terrain because they keep us "conceptually without anchor," force us "to stumble in the uncertain turf along the border between the imagined and the actual" (72, 70). Her particular lament is not just that the popular culture is indifferent to academic history, but that academic historians have themselves partly to blame for not reaching audiences who are so visually stimulated by cultural commodities that they accept mythic stories and stereotypes which run against the grain of the hard facts of their own experiences.[3] My point—using Limerick's same evidence about the fluidity of audience identification when in the presence of popular culture texts (i.e., an audience's potential ability to identify with outlaws as well as agents of civilization), and her phrasing about the border between the imagined and actual—unfolds in two directions. In the first place, just what the visitors to Disneyland are thinking constitutes a complex problem, regardless of the jocular connotations of "tourists." The visitors' potential questioning of just what is and is not "progress" suggests how industrial popular culture should not be reduced to some kind of pleasure machine whose function is simply to reproduce the dominant culture's ideology and to foster false consciousness in its consumers. As Richard Slotkin has noted in his discussion of the fluid interaction of myth, ideology, and history at the point of audience reception, "the response of a given audience to myth tends to reflect that group's ambivalence toward its own ideology: The genteel reader may, in his dismay with modern society, identify simultaneously with the primitive Indian of an idealized past and with the elite agents of modernity; the proletarian reader may identify his own suppressed rage with that of the defeated Red Man in certain moods, while in others his aspiration to power and respectability will be paradoxically invested in the conquering white man" ("Myth" 85–86).

In the second place, a populist critique of the smiling myths of progressive development is as entirely evident in the history of popular culture westerns in print and on film (consider, for starters, the cult of the outlaw that has grown up around Jesse James and Billy the Kid) as it is in the work of the New Western historians. Since mythologies themselves ought to be regarded as "stories drawn from a society's history that have acquired through persistent usage the power of symbolizing that society's ideology and of dramatizing its moral consciousness" (Slotkin, *Gunfighter* 5), then it becomes entirely unclear how one would locate that "border" between that imagined Frontierland and some "actual" West. This boundary—between the daylight zone and the twilight zone, between myth and reality, between fantasy and actuality, between a "Happy Face" version of history and a more reasoned view of history's tragic events—is a permeable, volatile one which has been relentlessly explored by popular culture texts themselves from Buffalo Bill Cody's "Wild West Show," through director John Ford's

The Man Who Shot Liberty Valence (1962) and on to director Clint Eastwood's more recent Academy Award–winning film *Unforgiven* (1992). Indeed, boundary or border is not the right word at all to use in this context. As cultural theorists in the past few decades have argued, rather than "popular culture" being regarded as a monolithic, fixed entity either identical with mass culture or in opposition to all that is considered high culture, popular culture can be more accurately regarded as a kind of *borderland*, as a *terrain of negotiation* in which, as Stuart Hall argues, "there is a continuous and necessarily uneven and unequal struggle, by the dominant culture, constantly to disorganize and reorganize popular culture; to enclose and confine its definitions and forms within a more inclusive range of dominant forms" (455).

Hall's language, emphasizing here a "continuous and necessarily uneven and unequal struggle" between a dominant class and a subordinate class over the content and meaning of "the popular," discloses how any important intellectual work in cultural history must come to terms with power relations and with the fact that the dominant class' hegemony over subordinate groups is never established once and for all, but must be continuously created and renewed through cultural forms. Worster and Limerick, as well as other historians of women and labor in the West, have on the one hand impressively re-inserted the issue of power relations into discussions of western American history (See Worster, "Beyond" 21; Limerick, *Legacy* 292). But their attention to the continuous creation and renewal of a dominant class' power to define the "normal," the "natural," and the "tradition" has been sporadic at best, perhaps in large part because their discourse assumes culture to be an epiphenomenon of more central political and economic issues. If we understand what everyday experience as well as what theorists and critics writing under the sign of Foucault have been telling us about the workings of "power"—that it is not necessarily hierarchical in a top-down mode but rather dispersed throughout the culture (hence imagery of culture as negotiation, this spatialized via imagery of terrains, crossroads, intersections, and fields)—then we should be alert to how popular representations of western American history are not seamless texts promoting one political perspective. Ambivalences and ambiguities about, and counter statements to, dominant class beliefs and meanings circulate at the level both of the production and reception of popular culture representations.

Understanding the dominant culture's process of a continuous territorializing and de-territorializing the "space" of the popular in industrialized nation-states is in large part based on post-Marxist thinking, particularly the Italian Antonio Gramsci's theorizing of the concept of hegemony in his *Prison Notebooks* from the 1920s and 1930s. This revisionist thinking by scholars about definitions of "the popular" argues that the forces of capital are not monovocal and singular, but rather appear, particularly in the multinational corporate economy which has grown up in this century, through an array of cultural commodities which dramatically "speak" capitalism in a variety of ways for a variety of subjects living in a variety of locations. Despite the powerfully homogenizing force of the dominant culture's constant effort to enclose and confine the popular in accordance with its own values and needs, then, subordinate groups under capitalism's sway have yet retained and developed a remarkable diversity of social identities. The point is that in industrial popular cultures there are a multiplicity of points or locations at which one can gauge both accommodation to and resistance against a dominant patriarchal bourgeois ideology—which for the New Western historians is manifestly expressed by the Old Western historiography "booster" mentality. With these observations in mind, I believe the problem associated with "the problem of the popular" as it is defined in the discourse of both the Old and the New Western History centers on 1) its discourse's rigid separation, both thematically and formally, of popular myth and historical reality, a separation at odds with both the course of history and the history of popular western texts both thematically and formally; on 2) its reduction of the variety of voices speaking in cultural texts such as Hollywood films and dime novels to one monolithic voice of power; and 3) on its relative inattention to the shifting points of resistance and accommodation on the part of consumers due to its positing of some holistic, monolithic entity such as "the popular mind."

This statement of the problem with the problem of the popular in the New Western history is influenced by various methodological critiques of ideological analysis as it has been worked out in academic criticism of the 1970s and 1980s, largely under the sign of the Frankfurt School critique of the culture industry (Worster, for one, cites two of the leading members of the Frankfurt School—Theodor Adorno and Max Horkheimer—in his work). That is, in this perspective—which is not dissimilar to that advanced by other New Western historians besides Worster—the "popular" is commonly associated with what the people enjoy and consume, and the people are seen as encapsulated or manipulated by the dominant ideology, which is imposed on them from "outside," whether by members of a Disneyland design team, or producers of Hollywood Westerns, or Eastern artists and writers. For the historian in particular, the issues of historical memory and the definition of national tradition are key sites for the dominant culture to fashion or interpellate ("hail") concrete individuals as subjects of the nation-state, both in the sense of a subject who has agency and a subject who is subjected to a larger power. According to this view, the critic is positioned either beyond ideology, to quote Worster, or in the sphere of the ideologically correct due to his or her difference and distance from the ideological mystifications promoted by the culture industry. Because of this definition of the critic's task, the critic of culture should recover heretofore silent voices in the past or retrieve forgotten or suppressed episodes and construct alternative interpretations to the dominant paradigm that justifies the present *status quo* as a legitimate and natural continuation of "tradition" originating in the past, a tradition which has attracted to itself more recently the epithets "racist," "imperialist," "sexist," and "homophobic."

The problem with this view is neither that it has necessarily named the tradition linking past and present wrongly, though that charge is in fact what the more conservative-minded defenders of Turner's legacy have found problematic with the New Western History's project, nor that its alternative interpretations and its giving "voice" to heretofore silenced voices have not been compelling. Rather, as several theorists have observed in different disciplines, the problem is that while we must recognize both the effort by the culture industry to manipulate audiences for profit and the moments of willing consent to cultural commodities by the people, we must also recognize that popular audiences are neither willing dupes of the culture industry all the time nor critical and creative all the time in their responses to cultural texts. As Michael Schudson has written, "The fact that an anthropologist or literary critic can read an evening meal or a fast food advertisement or the names of athletic teams or the design of Disneyland as a commentary or meta-commentary on culture does not mean that participant natives also read the texts that way" (490). As Christine Gledhill has also argued, "meaning is neither imposed, nor passively imbibed, but arises out of a struggle or negotiation between competing frames of reference, motivation and experience" (244). This struggle or negotiation to make meaning with a found or constructed popular culture text about western history is precisely what Limerick observes happening in Frontierland's shooting gallery. But the opportunity to develop this point, and to emerge with a more nuanced sense of what popular culture is and how it works is missed, in large part because of a hermeneutic of suspicion grounded on the rigid binary opposition of history and fiction, myth and fantasy.

III

This dialectical sense of the production and reception of popular texts has led cultural critics to re-think the problem of the popular in at least three important new directions. In a new way of thinking about the point of production, critics working with more sophisticated notions of textuality have been examining how so-called mainstream popular culture books, films, and television shows both reveal textual ideologies not fully identical with or expressive of a patriarchal/bourgeois ideology and raise utopian possibilities to the foreground as part of their audience appeal. In another direction, this dialectical sense of reception of popular texts has fostered a rethinking of the function of pleasurable escape and its relation to social reality and to political change. Finally, another direction for rethinking the work of popular culture texts at the point of reception centers on how consumers take what is produced for them by the forces of capital and re-appropriate such commodities for their own ends in ways not only not intended by producers but also not foreseen by them either. Taken together, such revisionist thinking about popular culture production and reception reminds us, contrary to the older ideological analysis favored by New Western historians who employ the "popular" as a straw dog or scapegoat, that the domain of popular culture is highly complex, that popular culture fantasies are not simply escapes from some putative reality, and that consumers have conflicted and vexed relations to popular culture texts.

At the point of thinking about popular Westerns as themselves constituting a complex terrain of negotiation or stage for "competing frames of reference, motivation, and experience," let us consider Zane

Grey's 1912 novel *Riders of the Purple Sage*, perhaps the best known novel by this fabulously successful writer, an Eastern dude who toured the West prior to World War I. In his *Under Western Skies* collection of essays, Worster refers to Zane Grey's writings as a way of discussing the dominance, until recently, of "our drama of technological conquest over nature" (242):

> Americans in the West were the best of the good and the strongest of the strong. They wore leather, even the women, and packed guns. They fought to the last man. Pick up any Zane Grey novel and the names of its characters still resonate with command: Wade Holden from *Shadow on the Trail*, the lone man Lassiter from *Riders of the Purple Sage*, Jim Cleve from *The Border Legion*. . . . But always, regardless of the individuals involved, the common end must be one of gaining control over the land in the name of a higher morality. No other outcome was conceivable. (243)

Worster argues that this "traditional story of the West" represented famously in Grey's novels has as its "classic distillation" a phrase from Frederick Jackson Turner's "The Significance of the Frontier in American History" essay ("Little by little he transforms the wilderness"), and that this thematic struggle between an untamed nature and a male frontiersman defines the *essence* of "that old, simplified story of 'the Conquest'" (243) dramatized in popular Western fiction from Owen Wister's *The Virginian* through the novels of Louis L'Amour. Surely Worster is right in seeing Grey's novels assay a link between control of the land and a higher morality—but is it any less simple to reduce the cultural work of his novels, and by extension those of Wister and L'Amour, to always already forwarding the story of conquest, of gaining control over the land? The fact is that Grey's higher morality in certain novels forwards a kind of stewardship ethos regarding the land which is different by degree, if not also by kind, from the possessive, rapacious attitudes toward the land disclosed by these novels' villains. And is it any less simplistic not to recognize that Grey's novels, rather than being about the history of conquest, display as material objects themselves how they are inscribed by history, are that history, and as a result might differ in certain key respects from Turner's story of the West?

Consider how a little over half-way through *Riders of the Purple Sage*, in the "Solitude and Storm" chapter, Grey portrays Bern Venters and Bess Oldring wandering in a secluded retreat named Surprise Valley, exploring in particular the caves, houses, and kivas of the long-departed Anasazi. As they bring out from the dust and darkness of the cliff dwellers' earthen floors various flints, curved sticks, frayed hemp ropes, and pottery, Venters realizes that "bits of whitish stone which crushed to powder at a touch and seemed to vanish in the air" (151) were all that remained of the bones of an Anasazi. The "gray ashes in Venters's hand" shock this sagebrush Adam and Eve out of their dreamy, fanciful play and into an awareness of the imprint of time, the course of human history, the inevitability of death, and—as a consequence—the need to consider their own destinies. "What's the meaning of it all—of us?" (152) Bess asks Bern, who at first tentatively remarks that it's an open question as to whether the passing of time has meant present-day humans have progressed beyond the cliff-dwellers in terms of intelligence. More surely, he adds that modern humans "can't be any higher in the things for which life is lived at all," which he defines in response to her query as "relationship, friendship—love" (152).

The dash Grey uses to render Venters's thoughts after the word "friendship" indicates the three "things" do not exactly form a series of equal entities, but that "love" encompasses and contains whatever "relationship" and "friendship" might connote. Whether one is a cliff-dweller living a thousand years ago or a modern American man and woman, for Venters "the nature, the meaning, the best of life itself" is epitomized by the "love of man for woman—love of woman for man" (152). As the chapter concludes, Grey depicts a raging thunderstorm blanketing Surprise Valley. The pair huddle together against the elements, and Venters—the outcast who has "longed for the sound of a voice, the touch of a hand" (39)—discovers, "with the touch of clinging hands and the throbbing bosom" of Bess Oldring pressed against him, the parallel, inward storm of "real love" (158). Later, as the plot sequence dramatizing this couple's newly-forged relationship in Surprise Valley nears its conclusion, Venters proposes marriage to Bess, his "real love," his "love of man for woman" defined finally as that of a husband for a wife, not merely that of a man for a friend or relative.

In this sagebrush scene of instruction Venters assumes the role of authoritative interpreter of signs, divining here the significance of powdery ash as just earlier he had "divined the significance" (86) of the precariously-balanced boulder that guards the entrance to Surprise Valley. Contemplating briefly the potential meaninglessness of human history (that it makes no sense, that no progress has occurred)—precipitates his articulating a fundamental truth. As the imagery of touching hands, throbbing bosoms, and lightning-struck and wind-lashed trees suggests, any "real love" between man and woman will be incarnated, manifested by physical bodies acting in accord with spiritual ideals. Seen finally as a word made flesh, Venters' abstract concept of "love" can truly represent "the nature, the meaning, the best of life itself" precisely because it connotes for him the possibility of both spiritual regeneration and physical or biological generation. And this redemptive possibility mitigates his awareness of death's presence in the form of the gray ash, the "knell" tolled by Bess' outlaw father, and Jane Withersteen's catalogue in the novel of the bloody chronicle authored by history's male "blood-spillers" (273).

In this chapter at the novel's center, Venters literally and symbolically finds an abode, a home in both nature and history, and from this perspective his reading of the signs left behind by the cliff-dwellers allegorizes the basic desire of a novel reader in modernizing societies, which, in Walter Benjamin's words, is "the hope of warming his shivering life with a death he reads about" (101). In the context of the entire novel, Venters' finding a home or a center identifies for us a dimension to Grey's writing that is ignored or subordinated in recent discussion of his novel by historians and literary critics. In Jane Tompkins' recent influential discussions of the western genre and of Grey's novel, the western hero, particularly as personified by Grey's hero Lassiter in *Riders of the Purple Sage*, stands for "secularism, individual rights, retributive justice, and the ultimate reality of matter and physical force," an ideology of beliefs and actions which spawns "our own era," which symbolically gives birth to "the twentieth century" (xx). Tompkins' provocative focus on ho v Lassiter's values insinuate themselves into Jane Withersteen's consciousness crystallizes her notion of the work performed by this cultural text, which is to reaffirm the dominant culture's class and gender hegemony, to accommodate audiences via an adventure story's mythos to the social and cultural transformations occurring in a modernizing United States economic and social order. Certainly Venters' discoveries in the Surprise Valley sequence and his belief in the possibility of spiritual and social redemption amidst a magnificent and secluded natural backdrop, one somehow analogous to Turner's notion of the frontier as a "crucible," support the notion that this popular Western affirms an eroticized myth of progress by means of an escapist return to nature.

Grey constructs the novel's "middle" as a series of chapters alternating between, on the one hand, scenes depicting the growing intimacy of Bern and Bess in Surprise Valley and, on the other, scenes depicting the developing Jane Withersteen-Lassiter relationship in the town of Cottonwoods and its environs. As the sequence in Surprise Valley makes clear, true love, marriage, and friendship ideally represent what Howard Horwitz, in critiquing anxieties over representation in Frank Norris' novel *The Pit*, has described as a kind of Aristotelian economy in which fundamental *value* emerges as a consequence of the proper regard, care, and handling of objects (see Horwitz). This value emerges not only as a result of balanced exchange, a sense of mutual obligations between persons, but also as one is able to look beyond, behind, or through surface externals—such as Bess' disguise and her violent reputation as Oldring's "Masked Rider"—in order to discern reality, that hidden realm of "character" rather than the public realm of "personality." Value is thus determined properly to be intrinsic, inherent in objects, not at bottom indefinite, not determined by the shifting process of valuation associated with marketplace attitudes but as fixed and determinate as the value of gold—the base metal whose discovery will enable Bern and Bess to leave Utah near novel's end.

Though the end ultimately desired by the participants in the two separate sequences is the same—love of man for woman and woman for man—in the Surprise Valley sequence a disguise or surface representation is shed, while in the Cottonwoods sequence a disguise in the form of Jane's feminine flirtation is adopted. In self-adornment, in "the artifices that she knew were unworthy of her, but which she deliberately chose to employ," in the oscillating moods "wherein a girl might be more desirable," Jane is described by the narrator as employing the methods "of an inexperienced though natural flirt" (122) in order to keep Lassiter from his vengeance killings of Mormon men. In her duplicity, in the discrepancy between the letter of her actions and words and the true intentions in her head, Jane threatens the certainty of self-possession that the Surprise Valley sequence finds necessary to true love and marriage. In Surprise Valley, where a person's exterior is homologous with his or her interior, where eyes and language communicate the soul's yearnings, Bern and Bess discover eternal values; in Cottonwoods, where "Things ain't what they seem" (225), the difficulty of telling, much less retrieving "absolute truth" indicates how value is putative and insubstantial.

As a model of human relations, Jane's coquetry with Lassiter resembles a risk-taking investment of her physical capital toward a future gain, a form of commodity speculation which is radically opposed to the balanced exchange in the true love realized by Bern and Bess. The flirtatious mode in Cottonwoods recapitulates Edward Bellamy's critique of the logic of a credit economy in his utopian novel from the late-nineteenth century, *Looking Backward*: "once people 'accepted promises for money,' they 'ceased to look at all behind the representative for the thing represented'" (Horwitz 228). Now when external representations or physical signifiers of gesture and words are, like credit, merely signs of signs, then one looks for the truth of signified and discovers only another sign, which happens to Jane at one point when she doesn't see Lassiter so much when he stands before her with his big guns but rather sees the Samson and Delilah story. Or one searches but cannot trace or verify the causes determining an action, a fate endured not only by Lassiter but also by Jane—who of course is the object of desire prompting the mysterious workings of the Mormon patriarchy. The visible hands touching each other in Surprise Valley contrast with "The Invisible Hand" (the chapter twelve title) of the Mormon patriarchy intent on making Jane take the bit and halter and become subservient not to women's law but to Mormon law (10, 146).

Though the novel's plot proceeds due to the dynamic opposition of Jane to the desires of the Mormon patriarchy, we should recognize how the characteristics used to describe the dark, nefarious deeds of the patriarchy—for example, "masked feeling" and "strange secretiveness" (211)—can equally describe Jane's flirtatious mode with Lassiter. I bring together a structural similarity between Jane's flirtatious mode and the patriarchy's dark (72), unseen (37) "secret oppression" (145) mainly to suggest, via our consideration of the difference between the market economy of human relations in Surprise Valley and the credit economy of relations in Cottonwoods, the grounds for considering Grey's Mormon patriarchy as something in addition to an anachronistic feudal economy the text explicitly identifies (7, 29). The conventional reading of the evil represented by the Mormon patriarchs Tull and Dyer focuses on Grey's use of the word "empire" and, after locating this character coding in the traditional Western plot dramatizing the triumph of civilization over savagery, identifies the Mormon elders as representing frontier borderland savagery, as a feudal despotism that will, as a result of Lassiter's and Jane's actions, fall before the nascent egalitarian and entrepreneurial civilization. Thus, as Tompkins has observed, Lassiter's triumph is that of the twentieth century and its modernizing process over backward regional despots.

But if we consider Grey's characterization of the "invisible hand" motif in the context of then-contemporary concerns over the corporate form of ownership evolving in the era's finance capitalism based on industrial technology, another directly oppositional reading emerges. Though on one level "The Invisible Hand" chapter title and imagery no doubt glosses Adam Smith's economic theories, Grey's characterization of a soulless Mormon patriarchy working in the dark to fulfill a cold, inscrutable policy reducing individuals to atoms recapitulates the critique of modern corporate ownership present in American culture at the turn of the century—present both in the iconography of the dime novels which precede Grey's career and present potentially in that moment in Disney's Frontierland when tourists bang away at the passing railroad cars. In 1911, the year before *Riders of the Purple Sage* appeared, Arthur Machen in legal discourse defined the corporation as "a fictitious, artificial person," existing only "in contemplation of law, invisible, soulless, immortal" (qtd. in Michaels 204). We also can consider, during the previous decade's discursive attention to the Populist crusade, James H. "Cyclone" Davis' 1894 diatribe against the corporation as an artificial entity—illimitable, insatiable, infinite—without human sympathy, moved by greed, and that makes automatons out of individuals by depriving them of moral "sympathy" and by reducing men to mere things. As Alan Trachtenberg has summarized the social and cultural ramifications of the transformation from a market to a corporate economy, "with the corporate device as its chief instrument, business grew increasingly arcane and mysterious . . . the entire apparatus of twentieth-century corporate life was developed in these years and clouded the public perception of the typical acts of business" (84).

If Jane's flirtatious mode in Cottonwoods metaphorically resembles a credit economy model of human relations, and if the characterization of the Mormon patriarchy's "work" disseminates in allegorical fashion the descriptive iconography deployed to describe fears about the modern corporation, and if Surprise Valley locates a natural realm where humans actualize an ideal model of social relations, then *Riders of the Purple Sage* poses Lassiter and Venters not as the bringers of the twentieth century but as anti-modernist warriors resisting what looks to be a modern corporate era in which fluctuating market values, mysterious market forces, and the commodification of desire threaten personal autonomy and the personal ideal of sincerity. The novel's end, when Lassiter's very visible hands dislodge the Balanced Rock down upon Tull and his "invisible hand" ethos, indicates its official project is not so much to accommodate readers, via their identification with Jane Withersteen, to the birth of the modern era, but rather to dramatize the survival of the residual values associated with the individualist phases of the market economy from an earlier moment in the nineteenth century. The text's ideology, in this light, centers on a critique of the modern era which threatened domesticity, bourgeois individualism, traditional masculinity, and Christian piety. The opposition between visible and invisible hands throughout the novel suggests a conflict in Grey's cultural moment between sense as a physical shape and image of the world or body and sense as a non-physical, mystifyingly plastic shape. The moment of this novel, perhaps the moment of all popular Westerns born in this century in which, to quote Marx, "things that are solid melt into air," seems to stage a visionary recovery of true meaning and value as incarnated in the bodies of humans and nature and as resistant to the assaults of an impoverished modern present. In *Riders of the Purple Sage*, Lassiter rolls the stone at novel's end, sealing off himself and Jane Withersteen, as well as Surprise Valley, from contamination by the hands of an anti-democratic corporate empire.

Riders of the Purple Sage, as a mainstream popular Western, employs both melodramatic and realist modes in achieving its resistance to and critique of modernization. Grey's multicultural cast of characters, sprawling landscape descriptions, and formal interweaving of plot sequences allow the text to attract readers by working on more than one level. The melodramatic framework focuses on a moral order built as a result of a struggle between good and evil, whose representatives are imaged in Manichean polar oppositions, and this framework allows the novel to work on a symbolic imaginary level. "At the same time," as Christine Gledhill has written about the formal arrangements of most mainstream popular genres, "such conflicts have power only on the premise of a recognizable, socially constructed world; the pressure towards realism and contemporaneity means that a popular text must also conform to ever-shifting criteria of relevance and credibility" (251). Gledhill's allusion to the "ever-shifting criteria of relevance and credibility" a popular text must exhibit in order to have meaning for an audience reminds us how popular texts are themselves in history and are facts of history, not in some twilight zone of myth and symbol divorced from a historical reality. Hence the vocabulary and images in Grey's novels illustrate then-contemporary concerns by the dominant class over immigration, over "white slavery," and the invisible, bodiless power of corporations to direct lives in an anti-democratic manner.

My reading of *Riders of the Purple Sage* is intended to illustrate the popular text instead as a force field of conflict where images and plotting motifs with lasting cultural resonance embody the contradictory pressures of and ambivalent responses to a compelling story of transformation and conquest which haltingly ushers in the modern world. With this reading in mind, it should be clear that one simply cannot deduce the "politics" of Grey's novels and other popular representations of the West by primarily focusing, as most New Western historians do when treating cultural texts, on plotted endings or static iconic images. My historicizing of Grey's novel with regard to how its models of human relations provide a coded *critique* of an emerging corporate order could, with more elaboration, also suggest how its antimodern impulse is distinctively grounded on rather conventional notions of gender, both masculine and feminine. Thus the "politics" of *Riders of the Purple Sage*, which might from a class perspective seem "progressive" due to its resistance to soulless corporate endeavors, can also seem from a gender perspective to promote "regressive" attitudes about women's roles and functions. In any case, my overall point is that Grey's novel, while perhaps not intending to move its readers much "beyond a primitive emotional need of heroes and heroines," to use Worster's words, does yet move us at moments, like the New Western History Worster sees being published in our present moment, "beyond any public role of justifying or legitimating what had happened" (*Under* 12) in a story often plotted heretofore as the winning of the West.

IV

One New Western historian whose work both attests to the complexity of popular culture (how its texts do not always legitimate the dominant culture's story of conquest and the ideology of bourgeois patriarchy) and also recognizes the difficulty of identifying that border line between the mythic and the actual is Richard White. As he says in the concluding chapter of his history textbook "*It's Your Misfortune and None of* My *Own*," "if myth, the imagined West, is a historical product, we must remember that history . . . is also the product of myth. . . . The mythic West imagined by Americans has shaped the West of history just as the West of history has helped create the West Americans have imagined. The two cannot be easily severed" (616). Moreover, White recognizes not only the dialectical relation, rather than binary opposition, between history and myth, but he also recognizes that there "is not and never has been a single myth, a single imagined West" (617). His lengthy essay "Frederick Jackson Turner and Buffalo Bill," which appears in the *Frontier in American Culture* volume containing Limerick's essay "The Adventures of the Frontier in the Twentieth Century," significantly puts into practice what his more general comments, drawn from the work of Richard Slotkin on the evolving mythologies of the American frontier, argue. White attends both to the similarities and differences in the popular representations of the course of western history in Turner's writing and Cody's Wild West Shows, interestingly and convincingly contextualizes how Turner's essays on frontier history resonated with audiences by tracing the iconography of "the log cabin in the clearing" that Turner draws on, and he illustrates the interaction of perspectives on the meaning of western history and the complexity of cultural texts by discussing how Lakota drawings of the fight with Custer at the Little Big Horn were "produced in a style that borrows elements from popular illustrations to depict a scene in a white man's play written to communicate the Indians' point of view" (43).

Perhaps this essay's most provocative comment occurs when White suggests that the "imaginative creation of a diverse and performative West, one with more roots in Buffalo Bill than in Turner, prepared the way for a new history that reexamined actual lived nineteenth-century experience in a West much more diverse than that of the Turnerian story" (54). Acknowledging, somewhat surprisingly, for a moment the indebtedness of the New Western histories produced during the past decade to the popular culture performances of Cody and his cast, White offers as a kind of aside a uniquely brilliant genealogy of influence. And yet a few sentences later, White defines the challenge confronting New Western historians as portraying "an experience more varied and complicated than Buffalo Bill or Turner or [Charles] Russell had provided" (54). What New Western historians must apparently achieve to be successful is here not really objectionable or original, since one could say that the challenge facing any historian with any subject matter is to portray a more varied and complicated experience than her predecessors, whether academicians or entertainers. Thus to my mind what White accomplishes in this essay is not just the trumping of Cody's and Turner's simplicity with New Western History's emergent complexity and multicultural emphasis. The essay provocatively restores to the foreground of our thinking about cultural history in the West the complexity of both Turner's and Cody's performative texts and the potentially varied interpretive responses to them through the years.[4]

White in this essay neither assumes bad faith on the part of Turner and Cody nor reduces human ambition to that of getting away from that "uncertain turf" between the imagined and actual West. His dialectical sense of the interaction of academic and popular discursive representations and of dominant and subordinate class interpretations suggests there is room for a more complicated view of how cultural mythologies are used for audiences enjoying popular entertainments. In other words, White's essay prompts us to think further about the relationship between popular pleasures and escapism, which as I've indicated above represents a second direction for thinking about the problem of the popular advanced by cultural critics during the past few decades. Since most New Western historians who do address cultural history in the American West are inclined to argue that cultural representations should have a *social* dimension, the problem with "escapist" popular pleasures has two aspects to it. In the first place, escapist fantasies about adventurous conquest seemingly confine consumers, usually male ones at that, to the personal or subjective dimension, imprison them in ephemeral, solipsistic pleasures—and so the social dimension is never realized. We fiddle and dance and sing while the western air and water are polluted and animal species are pushed to the brink of extinction by the spread of human habitats. But, in the second place, sometimes individuals do act on the fictions promoted by popular culture representations—so escapist fantasies at some point ultimately connect with the social and the political dimension as well as with privatized pleasures. In this instance, the problem for New Western historians is that, whether intended or not, dangerous and sometimes tragic consequences follow from such actions based on what are usually called myths and stereotypes. On the one hand, then, popular representations of the West are not important and should be ignored because they are fables and dreams divorced from contemporary issues and concerns, are hence *not real*. With this perspective uppermost, cultural history itself possesses or is accorded an inferior status in relationship to economic and political history. On the other hand, since people do occasionally fashion their identities and actions according to various fictive popular visions they consume, such visions should not be ignored or dismissed by historians because they are all *too dangerously real*. With this latter view in mind, cultural history seemingly is where the action is for historians, since how people make sense of their experience and how a "tradition" is defined in relation to, say, the concept of a "nation" must be understood before meaningful, progressive social change can occur.

My own thinking, as I hope this essay has made clear, inclines to the latter view. Moreover, I should again indicate that due to specific studies authored by various New Western historians about both women's and ethnic groups' histories in the West, and due to my own everyday experiences and my family's history, I do not want to underestimate the material consequences on human bodies and landscapes documented as a result of western expansion. But as the agenda for the New Western History continues to develop, I worry for a variety of reasons about the New Western historians' logical inconsistencies and theoretical simplicity at the point of popular pleasures. For one thing, the New Western History's suspicion of privatized escapist fantasy too conveniently ignores how fantasy, and particularly the fantasies involved with the myth of adventure as it has developed since Defoe's *Robinson Crusoe*, involve both an escape *from* something as well as an escape to something. Dismissing myths, symbols, romance, and idylls for being simply compensatory for the hard facts of everyday life avoids the important question of "why is escape necessary? what is being left behind?"

The fantasies and utopian longings in popular culture texts offer escapism, to be sure, but this escapism is not just a failure to come to terms with reality's daylight zone but itself constitutes an aestheticized—*but no less real for that*—version of the sociopolitical domain. As Angela McRobbie argues in her *Postmodernism and Popular Culture*, we should also understand that any desire for powerful resistance on the social and collective level of the kind most forcefully advocated, in the context of the New Western History, by Donald Worster's essays cannot operate effectively or even exist independently of the kind of interior, subjective resistance raised to the conscious level by the various utopian desires and dreams of popular westerns. In terms of popular culture versions of the western, the signal failing of the New Western History with regard to its problem with the popular appears to be that discourse's reluctance or refusal to engage, except at the point of White's scholarship, the deeply antimodernist critiques of conquest present even in the most retrograde written texts by a Remington, a Wister, a Zane Grey, or films such as *The Misfits* (1961) and *McCabe and Mrs. Miller* (1971); the complicated critiques of racism and ideologies of masculinity offered by such films as *The Searchers* (1956), *The Last Hunt* (1955), and *Bad Day at Black Rock* (1954); and visions of stewardship toward the land and the constitution of the family in *Shane* (1952), *The Far Country* (1954), and *The Outlaw Josie Wales* (1976).

But escapism is of course not only the provenance of the popular text. While the possibility of resistance to or ambivalence about the dominant story of redemptive conquest of a wild land and native peoples on the part of popular novels and films is, as I have argued using *Riders of the Purple Sage*, mostly missing in the New Western History, missing also is a recognition of the potentially positive value of pleasurable escape at the point of audience reception. Part of the argument here seems to be that the fantasies and compensatory wish-fulfillments promoted by popular westerns appeal to an audience's interior life. And even if audiences can identify with critiques of the *status quo* dramatized in popular texts, that identification has no power in the end because it never gets outside or beyond simple emotional gratification. As Angela McRobbie has argued, however, the origin of resistance to the status quo's arrangement of power and status can be traced not only to the actual, social experiences of subordination by cultural groups. The origins of resistance also can be located in the *sense* such groups make of their social experiences. In everyday lives, that is, experience itself cannot be easily separated from the meanings given it—experience is precisely what we make of it as we endure it. And what we make of it, of course, depends enormously on the emergent and accumulating perceptions, emotions, and feelings of the interior life. Indeed, this logic informing McRobbie's general argument I take to be one of the distinctive features of film director John Ford's *The Man Who Shot Liberty Valence.*

Fantasies in this view conceivably stand as marking out of an area of experience that cannot finally be colonized by those in power, as ethnographic research into women's readings groups and as Michael Denning's recent study of working class readers' responses to dime novels has documented. On the one hand, this insight could lead us into a larger discussion of the third direction recent studies of the popular have taken, and which should be part of the road taken by future work in New Western History: this is the process by which subordinate groups and certain class factions of the dominant social and economic group appropriate elements produced by the dominant culture and use them to advance their own interests and to solidify their own identities. Here we can consider, for instance, Blake Allmendinger's discussion of how working cowboys—through their songs, poems, and folktales—would subvert the rancher's notion of ownership by using brands to indicate their future religious salvation in heaven, not their economic subjection to the owner. This subversion of ownership occurs as the brand is transferred from the rancher to God, who marks the cowboy with a sign of religious distinction unavailable to the rancher (29–31). Here we should also consider how Teddy Blue describes his cowboy friends' appropriation of the moralistic warning against the vices of popular culture couched in "The Cowboy's Lament": "I always had to stop and laugh every time I sang the Laredo song, in spite of it being so sad. . . . 'I first took to drinking and then to card-playing'—and they'd all be drunk when they was singing it, most likely" (222–23; also see Tatum 67–70).

Worster, in discussing the contradictory appeals of Owen Wister's *The Virginian*, identifies what he calls "two dreams . . . tugging at our feelings: one of a life in nature, the other with machines; one of a life in the past, the other in the future," and "If the West has any spiritual claim to uniqueness, I believe it lies in its intensity of devotion to those opposing dreams" (*Under* 81). Worster calls this the "Western Paradox," this "difficulty in figuring out how it [the western region] can achieve material success and yet maintain the landscape of freedom" (86). Though he recognizes that both dreams have something attractive about them, "the West has hardly acknowledged that it has created any contradiction at all. It has simply built more dams, made more money, packed in as many people as it could, ignored the costs to the environment and society that had to be paid, and told itself all the while it was the freest place around." The problem is that now, due to such building and population growth, "it is clear that neither a simple-minded nature fantasy nor a simple-minded greed will give us a future worth living." To deal with this paradox, whose "dreams" have become characterized as "simple-minded nature fantasy" and "simple-minded greed," Worster suggests that we transcend it: we need to find "some new vision for this region that will, in a thoughtful way, incorporate what was most noble in its old visions, leaving out the base excesses. . . . An alternative vision ought to suggest how we might live free and live well for the longest period of time—all of us, men and women, white and nonwhite, natives and immigrants alike" (90).

Worster's own utopian impulse seemingly depends upon the transformation of agency from an impersonal, disembodied "West" which has overdeveloped the land at the behest of corporate capitalism to the "we" and "us" who will act to transcend the paradox by incorporating—by making visible and manifest—the best of agrarianism and technological development, and by melding together a sense of freedom with one of responsibility. I share his hope and his inclusive vision, and I want to believe in such prospects having some chance of realization. But any transcendence of the "Western paradox" constitutes, paradoxically, a transcendence of history itself. Since the late-nineteenth century the history of the American West has been, as Worster recognizes in his discussion of Wister, not only the story of conquest but also the story told simultaneously of "our affection for a precapitalist Eden even while we reaffirm our affiliation with the values and priorities of bourgeois society" (Slotkin 86). For Worster, any redemptive vision will likely emerge when people begin to care about their communities, to care for the land rather than abuse it, and to understand the consequences of an economics of scarcity. The continuing irony present in the New Western historians' ironic perspective on the heretofore predominant Turnerian story of conquest and progress is, I would argue, that Worster's utopian vision is variously present in any number of popular western novels and films produced during the past century in the wake of *The Virginian.*

The popular Westerns in this century at key points address, even as they seemingly "legitimate the values and priorities of bourgeois society," all the important themes disseminated by the New Western historians: the development of a multi-racial, cosmopolitan society; the concern over the uses of violence against minorities and the environment; and an interrogation of "concentrated power" hiding itself "behind beguiling masks" (*Under* 15). Moreover, the people who will comprise the "we" and the "us" developing an alternative vision to that of conquest and exploitation of human and physical resources are often the same people who have for over a century consumed popular culture texts and presumably will continue in some fashion to consume them in the future. What is now seemingly needed in order for the New Western History to continue forwarding its scholarly objectives is both a readiness to acknowledge, as Richard White does at the end of his essay on Turner and Cody, the indebtedness of the New Western History to popular western entertainments, and a willingness to consider the recent trajectories in scholarly thinking about the problem of the popular and the historical evolution of popular representations of the West. We can begin not only by rationally understanding but also by internalizing just how tricky this business is of drawing boundaries between interior and exterior, myth and reality, fantasy and the actual, the imaginative and the real. Our not-so-unique fate as humans is always to live in a present moment with its own constraints and opportunities. And to experience—whether consciously or unconsciously—what Limerick calls "selective amnesia" (*Legacy* 292) and the fact of *desire* in the way our perceptions are framed by and frame the world. As a result, in our history we are always already slogging through the "uncertain turf along the border between the imagined and the actual." Though some might bemoan and have bemoaned this condition where foundations and touchstones have eroded or constantly are shifting, what I'm here calling our shared "fate" means that there will always be work for historians and critics to accomplish with regard to articulating how historical memories and traditions are continuously being frozen and defrosted.

University of Utah

NOTES

I would like to thank the helpful critiques of earlier drafts of this essay given me by Forrest Robinson, Howard Horwitz, and Peggy Pascoe.

1. Worster argues that "The New Western History insists that scholars must perform deliberately and thoughtfully the role of cultural analyst, even to the point of presuming now and then to be a self-appointed moral conscience of their society" (*Trails* 23). In briefly summarizing public response to the "Trails" symposium, Limerick suggests that in the West "the public is eager to join in this discussion, giving western historians in the late-twentieth century the finest opportunity imaginable to revive the role of the western public intellectual" (*Trails* 77).

2. By contrast, Limerick argues, the concept of *la frontera* associated with the southwestern borderlands fosters "no illusion of vacancy, of triumphal conclusion, or of simplicity," and for Limerick if only the historical reality of *la frontera* were as well known in the popular culture of the United States as the myth of the frontier, "we would be well launched toward self-understanding, directed toward a *realistic* view of this nation's position in the hemisphere and the world" ("Adventure" 90, emphasis added).

3. Limerick's complaint is specifically directed against the jargon, specialization, and what she calls "the academic timidity" which together have "placed a canyon between public audiences and intellectuals" (*Trails* 76). If only western historians would become "public intellectuals" instead of only writing and talking to each other, then this canyon would be bridged for everyone's good. Though I do not find this goal problematic, we should consider this complaint in the context of the New Western History's larger concerns over bad faith and false consciousness, its discursive opposition of myth and history, and its hope that the historian can stand apart from her culture and the powers that be and get a privileged purchase on the truth of the matter. I say "privileged" because in this context the historian as a critical public intellectual must need be immune from the seductions of popular entertainments so as to inform consumers of popular pleasures of their mystification. Such immunity presumably occurs by rationally apprehending things and not succumbing to the lure of the senses and the body.

The inherent idealism in the New Western History—disclosed by its binary oppositions and its faith in critical rationality—suggests a suspicion of the imagination and of "pleasure" associated with the sense and the body. A familiar point by now is that in western European intellectual traditions the excesses of the imagination, the emotions, and the body have been deemed inferior to reason, and the former have been coded feminine. As this essay's concluding section suggests at one point, feminist theorists have been doing important work on reclaiming the value of, say, thinking through the body, and one aspect of this work has been to reconsider the potentially "progressive" aspects of popular pleasures. Such work could provide further productive ways of studying gender in the West to complement work already published by such historians as Peggy Pascoe, Vicki Ruiz, and Sarah Deutsch.

4. In this context, a problem that arises at the end of White's new history of the American West centers on his formal separation of the imagined from the actual West. Though White's textbook promotes a varied and complicated interpretation and overview of western American history, and though White himself argues about the importance of the imagined West to understanding events and behaviors in its history, the historiographical style of his book does not convey the sense of "cross-fertilization" and "cultural cross-dressing" ("Turner" 43, 53) which figures in his essay on Turner and Cody.

In this regard, I would add that Limerick's *Legacy of Conquest*, formally speaking, deserves further attention and credit not just because of its interpretative perspectives but also for innovative structural arrangement—its braid-like weaving together of anecdote, narrative elements, dramatic scenes, and quantitative evidence— and its varied tonal registers.

WORKS CITED

Abbott, E. C. "Teddy Blue" and Helena Huntington Smith. *We Pointed Them North: Recollections of a Cowpuncher*. 1939. Norman: University of Oklahoma Press, 1971.

Allmendinger, Blake. *The Cowboy: Representations of Labor in an American Work Culture*. New York: Oxford University Press, 1992.

Benjamin, Walter. "The Storyteller." In *Illuminations: Essays and Reflections*. Ed. Hannah Arendt. Trans. Harry Zohn. New York: Schocken, 1969.

Denning, Michael. *Mechanic Accents: Dime Novels and Working-Class Culture in America*. New York: Verso, 1987.

Gledhill, Christine. "Pleasurable Negotiations." In *Cultural Theory and Popular Culture*. Ed. John Storey. New York: Harvester Wheatsheaf, 1994. 241–54.

Gramsci, Antonio. *Selections From the Prison Notebooks*. Eds. and trans. Quintin Hoare and Geoffrey Nowell Smith. New York: International Publishers, 1971.

Grey, Zane. *Riders of the Purple Sage*. 1912. New York: Penguin, 1990.

Gunn, Giles. "Beyond Transcendence or Beyond Ideology: The New Problematics of Cultural Criticism in America." *American Literary History* 2 (1990): 1–18.

Hall, Stuart. "Notes on Deconstructing the 'Popular.'" In *Cultural Theory and Popular Culture*." Ed. John Storey. New York: Harvester Wheatsheaf, 1994. 455–66.

Horwitz, Howard. "'To Find the Value of X': *The Pit* as a Renunciation of Romance." In *American Realism: New Essays*. Ed. Eric J. Sundquist. Baltimore: Johns Hopkins University Press, 1982. 215–37.

Limerick, Patricia Nelson. "The Adventures of the Frontier in the Twentieth Century." In *The Frontier in American Culture*. Ed. James R. Grossman. Berkeley: University of California Press, 1994. 67–102.

———. *The Legacy of Conquest: The Unbroken Past of the American West.* New York: Norton, 1987.

———. "Making the Most of Words: Verbal Activity and Western America." In *Under an Open Sky: Rethinking America's Western Past.* Eds. William Cronon, George Miles, and Jay Gitlin. New York: Norton, 1992. 167–84.

———. "Progress or Decline? Judging the History of Western Expansion." In *A Society to Match the Scenery.* Eds. Gary Holthaus, Patricia Nelson Limerick, Charles F. Wilkinson, and Eve Stryder Munson. Boulder: University of Colorado Press, 1991. 43–51.

———. "The Trail to Santa Fe: The Unleashing of the Western Public Intellectual." In *Trails: Toward a New Western History.* Eds. Patricia Nelson Limerick et al. Lawrence: University Press of Kansas, 1991. 59–77.

———. "What on Earth is the New Western History." In *Trails: Toward a New Western History.* Eds. Patricia Nelson Limerick et al. Lawrence: University Press of Kansas, 1991. 81–88.

McRobbie, Angela. *Postmodernism and Popular Culture.* London: Routledge, 1994.

Michaels, Walter Benn. "Corporate Fiction." In *The Gold Standard and the Logic of Naturalism.* Berkeley: University of California Press, 1987. 181–214.

Schudson, Michael. "The New Validation of Popular Culture." In *Cultural Theory and Popular Culture.* Ed. John Storey. New York: Harvester Wheatsheaf, 1994. 486–94.

Robbins, William G. "Laying Siege to Western History: The Emergence of New Paradigms." In *Trails: Toward a New Western History.* Eds. Patricia Nelson Limerick et al. Lawrence: University Press of Kansas, 1991. 182–214.

Slotkin, Richard. *Gunfighter Nation: The Myth of the Frontier in Twentieth-Century America.* New York: HarperPerennial, 1993.

———. "Myth and the Production of History." In *Ideology and Classic American Literature.* Eds. Sacvan Bercovitch and Myra Jehlen. Cambridge: Cambridge University Press, 1986. 70–90.

Tatum, Stephen."The Heart of the Wise is in the House of Mourning." In *Eye on the Future: Popular Culture Scholarship into the Twenty-First Century in Honor of Ray B. Browne.* Eds. Marilyn F. Motz, John G. Nachbar, Michael T. Marsden, and Ronald J. Ambrosetti. Bowling Green: Bowling Green State University Popular Press, 1994. 57–72.

Tompkins, Jane. "Introduction." *Riders of the Purple Sage.* By Zane Grey. New York: Penguin Books, 1990. v–xxiv.

Trachtenberg, Alan. *The Incorporation of America: Culture and Society in the Gilded Age.* New York: Hill and Wang, 1982.

Trails: Toward a New Western History. Eds. Patricia Nelson Limerick, Clyde A. Milner II, and Charles E. Rankin. Lawrence: University Press of Kansas, 1991.

White, Richard. "Frederick Jackson Turner and Buffalo Bill." In *The Frontier in American Culture.* Ed. James R. Grossman. Berkeley: University of California Press, 1994. 7–66.

———. *"It's Your Misfortune and None of My Own": A New History of the American West.* Norman: University of Oklahoma Press, 1991.

Worster, Donald. "Beyond the Agrarian Myth." In *Trails: Toward a New Western History*. Eds. Patricia Nelson Limerick et al. Lawrence: University Press of Kansas, 1991. 3–25.

———. *Under Western Skies: Nature and History in the American West*. New York: Oxford University Press, 1992.

———. *The Wealth of Nature: Environmental History and the Ecological Imagination*. New York: Oxford University Press, 1993.

SALLY K. FAIRFAX AND LYNN HUNTSINGER

The New Western History: An Essay from the Woods (and Rangelands)

ASKED TO DISCUSS the "New Western History" (NWH) from the resource management perspective, our immediate thought was that one of the virtues of the New Western History is that historians and literary types feel the need to include folks like us, specialists in natural resource management. Academic barriers being what they are, we seldom get such invitations. We infrequently employ terms like "mimetic" and "trope," and we are confident that we do not have much to contribute to a discussion of either literary criticism or historical method. Although we are clearly a bit off-site, we came to this discussion to reflect upon what the New Western History says about the role of nature and the environment in human history. If not the principle distinguishing feature of New Western historians, their explicit engagement in telling a story about the western United States that includes the biophysical world, environmental science, management, and nature is certainly what we call in dendrology a "key spotter."

Although resource managers are increasingly inclined to view their tasks as biological or technical rather than social, we are not strangers to telling stories about nature. "Resource management" as a profession and research area is comprised traditionally of fields like forestry, rangeland management, and wildlife management. Born out of progressive era goals of implementing scientific management on the forests and rangelands of North America, professional resource managers are charged with designing and implementing programs to conserve natural resources and ecosystems while producing goods and amenities sought by the public. After a brief sortie into interdisciplinarity and self-awareness, our profession appears to be reverting to an earlier phase—"the science knows best" approach to issues and concerned citizens. Our concern with that backsliding shapes our response to the New Western History.

The essay proceeds in three sections. In the first, we start with our assigned topic—how the natural world is depicted in the New Western History. As the depiction and use of nature has everything to do with the analytic tools brought to bear, method is discussed in the second section, as it focuses on two tools of the New Western History, region and narrative. Discussing region, we are less concerned with the exceptionalism issue that seems to bother the New Western historians, and are more concerned with whether the West, as an analytic focus, is a good place to explore the issues of human diversity, human interaction with nature, and kindred recurring themes that seem of central concern to New Western History authors. As a preliminary matter, we think not.

Narrative is probably the resource manager's least respected or acknowledged means of dealing with information. Yet we use it all the time, frequently without even noting that we are doing so. It is in dealing with narrative that we believe resource managers have the most to learn. Therefore, our discussion of traditionally NWH narrative is aimed less at commenting on their use of it than at demonstrating our own profession's frequently disguised and misguided reliance on storytelling.

Emphasis on narrative as a way of sharing information and engaging people in thoughtful reflection on their place in nature is very closely related to the topic of our third section, an exploration of the concept of a public history. The New Western History's efforts to lead fellow citizens to use the past in constructing a meaningful—one is tempted to say sustainable—future makes the discussions of region more sensible. In this political (or as we would construct it, managerial) context, the NWH's choice of region becomes plausible, and narrative methods emerge as critical to public debate and professional interaction. In its activist mode, the NWH emphasis on diversity also makes more than decorative sense. New Western historians argue, we find, two things: first, that one must have a history to have a place at the table; second, that one must have a past if one is to act responsibly regarding the future. It would simply compound past omissions if we were to stop after fluffing up stories with a fuller range of faces and did not intend to change our present and future. It is its public-policy orientation that pulls together and makes sensible much of the New Western History we have encountered. It is also what makes it especially beguiling to practitioners of the eroding, interactive "art" (as opposed to science) of Resource Management. Our field has always been "public." If it is to remain so, it must deal with many of the issues presently embroiling NWH types. We wind up saying more about our own profession than that of Limerick, Worster, White, and Cronon. We find their commitment to what happens next enviable in the face of the collapse of interdisciplinary discourse in the management field.

Most of what follows is therefore either familiar or ought to be. We take our guide from Professor Limerick, who in *Legacy of Conquest* is careful to point out that her goals "to pull the pieces together, to combine two or three decades of thriving scholarship with a decade of thriving journalism. . . . Others have said much of what I say in this book; nonetheless, the importance of the message and a widespread reluctance to receive it justify the deployment of many messengers."[1] We believe that as the managers of nature slip back into the reductionist, disciplinary mode, often under the guise of a shift of emphasis from resource management to "conservation biology," it is worth a clarion call to the sloppy and unscientific art and story end of our undertaking. Paraphrasing Limerick, we note that the importance of the message and a widespread reluctance to receive it within the resource management professions perhaps justify the deployment of yet more messengers, this time ones bearing gifts from the New Western historians.[2]

I. NATURE IN THE NEW WESTERN HISTORY

Asked to examine nature in the New Western History, we were somewhat disconcerted to find that no distinct "canon" emerges from reading broadly in the area. True, New Western historians emphasize that nature is a social construct. But beyond that, there is considerable diversity in how nature is presented in the various tales. The New Western History has constructed a variety of natures to meet a variety of analytical and political priorities. We found five more or less discrete approaches to the natural world which we will catalogue, and one which we find extremely problematic, and more than likely misleading, which we shall explore at greater length.

As if to prove the point that nature is a social construct, New Western historians construct nature in a number of different ways, sometimes simplifying nature just as traditional history simplified the story of the West. Most frequently, in New Western histories we see the natural world as the shaper of human action, as much of human activity in the West is centered on responding to or dealing with the forces of nature.[3] This is a story, as Donald Worster puts it, "of people encountering difficult environments, of driving to overcome them through technological means, of creating the necessary social organization to do so, of leading on and on to indigenous bureaucracy and corporatism."[4] Frequently, this shaping of society comes as the natural world is treated as an object for which humans struggle: western history, we are frequently told, is in large part a tale of different groups fighting over who gets to possess, occupy, or utilize natural resources.[5]

Second, and also frequently, nature is the shapee—is transformed by human activity. Chicago and the Great Plains are altered in tandem to create a new ecological and economic system.[6] In *Rivers of Empire* nature and human history are described as having a dialectical relationship, a give and take that creates the community and its environment.[7] Richard White claims that for New Western historians "there is no sharp line between nature and culture."[8] Less frequently, but probably most emphatically, when nature does appear, it is not just shaped by human activity but a victim of it. Worster states: "Far from being a child of nature, the West was actually given birth by modern technology and bears all the scars of that fierce gestation, like a baby born of an addict."[9] White states, "Where Old Western Historians see nature, New Western Historians see the debris and consequences of human use."[10]

Third, perhaps more interesting, nature emerges as a source of complexity. In this it is little different from the human diversity which New Western historians are so justifiably famous for emphasizing. Nature, like human diversity, is messy, not easily encompassed in a simple story line, and it puts the lie to simple models—such as the "white male dominated" notion of the frontier. Nature's messiness challenges the simplistic notions of control. As Limerick describes it, shortly after the turn of the century, early land and resource management agencies launched into massive undertakings geared toward controlling and protecting nature. But nature, in all its complexity, trumped Pinchot's effort to control fire, as fire turned out to be an integral factor in a functioning ecosystem. The Park Service's approach to preserving nature has been undercut by the extensive and long ignored history of Native American management (among other complications to our understanding of what nature is) and wildlife has become a "mockery of management" as we bumble about with our primitive knowledge of wildlife dynamics.[11]

Fourth, nature becomes a challenge, a tester, and ultimately a judge. Nature gets even. Sometimes we are merely unhappy collaborators in natural disaster.[12] But in the morality play of the New West, at least in some versions of the story, we are also subject to reckoning—nature will tell us, ultimately, what is possible. As Worster puts it, "the dream of conquest itself has begun to go sour among the white conquerors. They are losing the very property they won to the forces of environmental deterioration. . . ."[13] Stegner laments the fragility of the West, saying that "it could easily, under the attacks of those who will not admit its limits, degenerate and deteriorate until not even massive engineering can keep it livable."[14]

Finally, and most simply, nature is encountered as a stage or as the background for important struggle—a more complex struggle than that described by Limerick when she complains about the use of the West as a backdrop for Anglo heroism—but nevertheless a backdrop, however challenging or besieged.[15] The vast, open horizon so often cherished in western writings becomes the ideal site for human activity or competition. Introducing a trend there, almost always a trend of environmental decline, does not suffice to make a history "environmental." It is this that we find most troubling and to which we shall return.

As professionals who are paid to manipulate the natural world to produce products desired by our fellow citizens, we have some experience with constructing nature ourselves. Our approach is, however, radically different from what we encountered on our New Western History pilgrimage. We have a few questions and comments about how the New Western History folks do so, all of which center on the issue of insisting, at some point, that—social interpretations and constructions notwithstanding—there are limits to how far the biophysical world can be manipulated to fit a story line. We also want to complain slightly about the dominant themes of the stories, specifically that nature is out

West because that is where the people and the cities are not, and the ambivalence we encountered as to whether humans are natural or not.

We reject the story line that runs through several set pieces: that what makes the West the West is that the West is where "man" meets nature. Even amended to include ethnically diverse women and children, as the New Western historians generally insist upon doing, the focus on nature as the grand drama of the West is a bit disquieting on two counts. First, nature is not just wide open spaces where men meet challenges and either triumph or die. There is a huge cost to our understanding of environmental issues, environmental management, and environmental history in the neo-Jeffersonian tones of nature's construction in the New Western History. Humans meet nature in New York City, and in Denver, and in Los Angeles, as well as in Death Valley, on Mt. Rainier, and in Yellowstone. More precisely, there is no separating the city from the hinterland. Spinning the yarn that nature is the rural West is an error, and a costly one.

Second, the role of human activities in shaping nature is probably overplayed, or at least oversimplified, in much of the New Western History. One gets the idea that nature exists in human minds and is defined by human and cultural processes—almost as if without the human mind to construct it, nature would disappear. The complexity of large ecosystems is accordingly poorly treated. We do not consistently get a sense that there have been frequent, major changes in the ecology of the West, and that these changes are part of processes ongoing for millennia.

New Ecology Meets New History

The part of the theory of social construction that we find most troubling is where nature appears in its most elementary role—simply as backdrop for human activity. This turns quickly into an easily readable measuring stick for human ethics vis-à-vis natural systems. Frequently in the material we read, nature, particularly the arid landscape, is treated as a place that can be held constant, or can be referred to as subject to continual degradation. New Western History is concerned with the diversity and complexity of American history, yet it seems that the biophysical characteristics of the West are often used as a "blank slate," or as a relatively homogenous "control environment," where diverse social processes can be examined. Worster talks about a place of "difficult environments" where the story begins and ends with water—seeming to simplify the environments of the West around a theme of aridity, a background against which the complexity of the human story can be revealed.[16]

This "nature as backdrop" notion, or even the commonly appearing theme of the West as in steady ecological decline, is particularly out of step with emerging thinking in ecology. As historians have been busy making social history increasingly complex, ecologists have been building an equally and increasingly complex and less predictable vision of nature. Traditionally, the emphasis has been on explanations of ecosystem structure and function that describe competitive interactions among species that left undisturbed result in a relatively stable "equilibria." Early in this century, Frederic Clements observed that Great Plains grassland communities followed certain temporal patterns when recolonizing a site. A great body of ecological theory has flowed from this observation, centering on the idea that there is a predictable pattern of ecosystem development that eventually gives way to equilibrium. As Worster points out, for Eugene Odum ecology was the study of the structure and function of nature. The process of ecosystem development was orderly, reasonably directional, and predictable, and it culminated in stability, or what Odum called "maturity."[17] Ecosystem change had only two categories: "developmental stages" and "mature stages."[18] Even Darwin described evolution as change that leads somewhere, with a discernible direction, conventionally called progress.[19]

Much of resource management turns on this theoretical basis for understanding the response of ecosytems to human action and human use. Successional stages have traditionally been used as a way to judge management. Good management practices, according to this story, push a system towards equilibrium or maintain it. Improper management causes regression to earlier, less stable, stages in ecosystem development. Evaluation of the health of rangelands, for example, has until recently been entirely based on the "successional stage" of the vegetation.[20]

In recent decades, ecologists have noted that, most particularly in the arid environments of interest to the New Western historians, so much disturbance (mainly drought and fire) occurs so often that equilibrium or stability in nature makes no sense. Indeed, the competitive interactions that are the core of Clementian ecology often play a relatively small part in shaping the characteristics of these arid environments, and systems may never reach any semblance of a stable equilibrium. Of more relevance than inter-species competition in much of the arid West is how long it has been since the last wildfire, or the length of the last dry period. These environments are therefore called "disequilibrium systems" by some.[21] Western ecosystems are not a stable backdrop against which human actions can be highlighted; nor is it easy to judge the relative impact of human and natural forces on the landscape. Western ecosystems do not "decline," or "degrade," in a predictable fashion, and it is not always easy to determine when degradation has taken place or, more challenging still, why. Ecosystems, it seems, are as diverse and unpredictable as human society. Trying to describe a generalized western ecosystem may be more misleading than helpful.

If we accept that the primary story being told by the New Western historians is the social history, then "nature as backdrop" is perhaps a permissible literary device. It may do a disservice, though, to those who look to the New Western History for a better understanding of the ecological side of the story, and the interplay between human and ecological systems.

II. TOOLS

The Nature of the Region

Considering that the New Western History is primarily concerned with "the West," one might have anticipated that there would be considerably more coherence about the West as a region, than, say, about the meaning of nature. This would be an error. We observed no consistency regarding the definition of the region that the primary authors address. There is a serious and interesting debate within New Western History as to what constitutes the West as a region, and considerable lamentations about the legitimacy of focusing there at all.

This is, nevertheless, another area of imperfect kinship between resource managers and New Western historians. The resource management professions in fact share many characteristics with the West as defined by New Western historians: to some extent they are a regional phenomenon, derived in whole or part from the concentration of the public domain in the American West. Perhaps for that reason we do not anguish as much about region as do the New Western historians, and perhaps offer something to assuage their apparent discomfort.

The West itself, and the selection of the West as an analytic focus, ought, in our perception, to be a decision about the focus of analysis, which in turn suggests the appropriate scale. Is there a way of defining a West, or a region, that facilitates the story that New Western historians want to tell? Is the West a good place to tell the stories that the New Western historians want to emphasize? Which West will tell us most about human-nature interactions? Would any West be a good place to tell that story?

Here we will describe the array of definitions of the region that we encountered, beginning with Limerick's, in "The Unleashing of the Western Public Intellectual."[22] Needless to say, these many Wests overlap, contradict, and coincide with each other. The most pervasive assertion is that aridity is what unites the West as a region. However, this is not a ubiquitous feature, as residents of Portland, Seattle, and the Olympic peninsula could testify, although it is probably as close to a consensus factor as we have encountered. That definition would, however, have to draw significant portions of Canada and Mexico into closer view than the New Western historians seem inclined to admit, unless truncated by a political bounding that makes the topic the "American West."

Limerick notes that the West is characterized by Indian Reservations. This also has some merit, but seems overspecified—while it is true that the large reservations are in the western half of the country, experience dealing with Native Americans has colored every region of this country, Canada and Mexico. The extent of land in federal control is another contender for bounding the region, which has the apparently happy externality of keeping the West within the confines of the United States.[23] However, other than the bare fact of the federal presence, the ubiquitous federal lands do not appear to produce a region in terms of any discernible priorities that unite the West or distinguish it consistently from other regions.[24] It is true, however, that people may define themselves in relation to or in opposition to the federal presence—in fact, resource management was largely invented by the federal need to manage the public domain. We could set the boundaries historically, as Limerick suggests when she notes the West is a place settled after it was fairly clear that the United States was to succeed as a nation.[25]

Other theories of "the West" are in fact based on borders—the Pacific rim and the border with Mexico are unique to the Western region.

For this, one is (unfortunately) required to omit consideration of Canada. The West also perforce has a huge border with Canada, but off course, so does Maine, demonstrably down East. Similarly, one can take a more or less cartographic approach to defining the region, and many such lines appear in the New Western History. A line can be drawn across the North American continent, with everything to the west of it called the "West." Frequently, the 100th Meridian or the Mississippi River are used as such lines.[26] The New Western historians appear at different points to employ or acknowledge all of these delineations. We proffer our own suggestion: if we were interested in Western culture, we could define the region and sub-regions by such things as noting places where cowboy hats of certain styles are worn.

In ecology and management, the issue of "region" is tantamount to the issue of scale of analysis. Identifying the appropriate scale of analysis in large part defines the result. The goal, therefore, is to ask questions at the right scale to get useful answers. There is a relationship between the focus of the analysis and the boundaries and scale of the story. We have learned that spatial and temporal scale are crucial to examining the structure and function of ecosystems, and to determining the applicability of various models of how they might work. At the appropriate scale, we can make reasonable predictions for some periods of time for some things.

Inquiries can be addressed at small, intermediate, and large scales, and the processes that emerge as most important are in many ways scale-dependent. In the field of ecology, hierarchy theory seeks to explain the inter-relationships of different scales of action. More seriously, for both managers and for New Western historians, the scale must be appropriate to understanding the interactions of human and natural systems. This is true of both temporal and spatial scales of analysis. Is the appropriate scale for an environmental history to be defined by ecological or social parameters, or is it necessary to integrate the two in some as yet undefined way?

These issues, and not preoccupation with whether the West is a legitimate focus for study, ought to be primary in discussions of region in the New Western History. We have found little discussion that says that "this study focuses on human diversity, and therefore this particular time and place is the appropriate locale and scale for analysis." General defensiveness about the West is not, we suggest, an adequate justification for perusing particular topics at particular scales and with particular boundaries.

Moreover, we are not convinced that the tales of diversity, complexity, adaptation, and settlement are unique to the West. Just as all nature is not all in the West, and humans encounter nature everywhere, some of the most interesting material about human/nature interactions in this country are in fact written about the East.[27] Moreover, many of the forces and events that shaped the American West can be observed in Central and South America, Australia, and Africa as well. Exceptionalism is less of a problem than isolation.

We are less concerned with legitimating the West as a place with a history worth studying, and are more concerned with wondering whether the West, as an analytic focus, is a good place to explore the issues of human diversity, human interaction with nature, and kindred recurring themes that seem of central concern to the authors of New Western History. We are not persuaded that it is. We have some of the same concerns, in fact, about region as we do about the social construction of nature. There is too little conscious exploration of the process of creating boundaries in terms of the analysis at hand.

Narrative

The other tool of New Western History that immediately attracts our attention is the narrative. Although New Western historians discourse at length on the nature of the region and the nature of history, with exception of Cronon's piece,[28] they do not discuss the narrative much at all. We find this extraordinary. What to the NWH is obviously an acceptable means of presenting information is anathema to the resource manager. We do not, resource managers would emphasize if ever asked, "do" narrative. We do facts. When we tell stories, resource managers generally deny it, characterizing their narratives instead as "providing information."

The denial is learned. Resource managers are trained see themselves as scientists. The profession's tradition teaches them that what distinguishes them from others—for example, from self-interested politicians and locals who are trying to have a specifically illicit influence on management decisions—is that resource managers do experiments and talk about data. Resource managers are different because they can make decisions "objectively, based on science." Many of our colleagues believe that they lose power and respectability when they tell stories or even suggest that that is what they are doing.

In this, resource managers are responding to some of the same kinds of disciplinary pressures that Limerick discusses for post-modern historians in terms of presentism (the exercise of connecting the past to the present, which is "very bad indeed," as opposed to a "shifty, relativistic universe," in which hard, set facts waiting to be discovered is an "illusion").[29] We are allowed, encouraged, even required to be involved in using our minuscule collection of "facts" or data points to affect the present and the future. In doing so, we find ourselves framing our facts with stories, without acknowledging the process and the limitations of the data points we have collected. Using the data points to support the idea that the entire story must be true, we hold our stories to be distinguishable from and superior to everyone else's supposedly emotional input.[30]

We take some initial comfort from the fact that some New Western historians are willing to accept us, in part at least, as historians if not precisely as storytellers. Worster has observed that natural scientists have long been environmental historians.[31] Global warming, the creation of the Grand Canyon, rates of extinction, and the rise and fall of sea levels have all been framed as stories. Although resource management professionals and scientists often disdain narrative and proceed into public dialogue with considerable contempt for the public, we have some experience in the field in general. The New Western History underscores for us that there is a theory and a self-consciousness that accompanies telling stories well. We as managers are in need of better rules for better stories. We will demonstrate that by telling a few stories traditional in our field, and then by following Cronon's advice and telling some stories about those stories.[32]

Resource managers, despite abundant diversionary tactics to demonstrate the contrary, more often than not find themselves fitting their science into a narrative frame with a beginning and an end, with heroes and bad guys, and with a large cast of extras lurking in the wings. For example, the basic contours of Clementsian theories of succession and progression towards an equilibrium or in management lexicon, "climax," translate into a simple story which has guided management for much of this century.

The heroes of the piece are the climax plants and animals at one end, the bad guys are the weedy upstarts at the beginning of the path of succession—though one does have to admire the pluck and fortitude of these "pioneer species." As time goes on, however, the exploitative pioneers become a smaller and less important part of the community, with more stable, deeply rooted plant species taking over and determining the character of the community. There is a definite beginning and end to the pattern, with the community living happily ever after once climax has been achieved.

One of the advantages of looking at ecosystem development this way is that it provides a linear, progressive, road map to ecosystem "health," a crucial need of the manager. The predictability of the thing makes it easy to develop checklists of good characters and bad characters, up trends and downturns, that enable us to measure the impact of changes and of management. Disturbance, as it messes up this orderly progression, is a bad thing and to be avoided—another clear indicator of what we should be doing: reducing, preventing, eliminating disturbance from systems. Disturbance "sets us back."

Many have pointed out that we have long tended to look to orderly, progressive nature for a model of how society should work. Just as historians once called for a progressive western history, advancing the frontier of traditional western history, ecologists and resource managers once looked to the progressive model of ecosystem development. The stories of both have been built on these core paradigms.

The emerging ecological view, discussed above, that ecosystems are not necessarily trending toward a stable state, the conclusion of disequilibrium ecology, has made us rethink our assumptions about ecosystems today—and in fact, as Worster points out, our ideas of how ecosystems work have grown closer to our observations of how society works,[33] particularly the complex view of society held by the New Western historians. In fact, the shift toward a vision of a less stable, orderly, predictable or simple ecological scene parallels the way New Western History has emphasized the complexity, unpredictability, and heterogeneity of western social history.

Oversold Stories

Resource managers are, like the historians, stuck with the consequences of oversold stories. Professor Limerick has apparently folded her tents and abandoned her quest to expunge the notion of the frontier from the popular imagination.[34] Would that resource managers could do the same with their century long prevarication about fire as the unwelcome guest in a procession toward climax. Instead, the consequences of the "fire story" result in growing losses of life and homes each year.

In fact, one of the most publicly successful stories ever told by resource managers is that of Smokey Bear. Smokey is a personification of the Clementsian story that disturbance is bad; fire, one of the most common disturbances in the western U.S., is cast as a major bad guy in the story. Fire interrupts an orderly progression to climax or maturity; fire damages and destroys timber; fire destroys the beautiful forest and roasts small animals. This story, like those being created today, is based upon data points or facts, the "constraints" to nature as a social construction.

A corollary story to Smokey Bear is the "backward peasant" story, so ingrained in the resource manager's view of the world. "Educated experts" are needed to tell rural or indigenous residents how to manage natural resources.[35] Many Native American groups, ranchers, and farmers once used fire a lot, and the Forest Service and federal government took on the task of teaching them better after the turn of the century. As is now familiar to most of us, thanks largely to the works of Stephen Pyne[36] and John McPhee,[37] World War II and the threat of Japanese incendiary balloons gave Smokey Bear a kick-off that linked fighting fire with being a patriotic American: "careless matches aid the Axis" was a saying of the day.[38] As a result of this "oversold story," forests and rangelands are clogged with 50-year accumulations of dry, flammable plant material and are prone to wildfire and disease.

Now, it seems, the pendulum of expert opinion has swung the other way: With the disequilibrium ecology discussed above comes the acknowledgment that disturbance is okay, and fire is okay. Controlled fire is, in the eyes of many, a solution to the wildfire problem, a way of improving forest health, and a necessary part of maintaining the "natural" forest. In fact, burning to prescription appears to be taking on the character of a panacea among resource managers. Unfortunately, the public can be less than accepting of this new story, and resource managers are faced with the chronic problem of obtaining funding and public compliance for prescribed burning programs.

Perhaps "fire is good" is also doomed to become yet another oversold story. But there is apparently no end to the stories. Note our newest, increasingly ubiquitous tale—invading exotics. With loss of confidence in the Clementsian progression towards climax, resource managers have lost their successional or directional compass. For the manager, this is a serious problem: what now is the goal of management? Configuring nature even as explicitly as the NWH, we have hit upon protecting native species, a good fallback for providing clear standards for setting goals and evaluating management.

It is easy to rally behind the cause of removing "alien species" and protecting and enhancing the native ones. Often, because of the characteristics of invasive species, this also means protecting species diversity and the interlinkages with other native species. It is a measurable goal, one where we can create firm targets and arrive at clear results. The cast of characters is well-defined: natives are the heroes and non-natives are the bad guys. The story begins with the native ecosystem, comes to a crisis when it appears that the aliens will conquer, then fades out as the cavalry arrives and suppresses, eliminates, or heartily tortures the enemy. Our friends and neighbors spend the weekend in the headlands expunging exotics, Scotch Broom, German Ivy, even as we nervously await the arrival of Kudzu or African Killer Bees. The point is, resource managers both tell stories and, in addition, adapt their stories to their goals because they need to in order to get anything done.

Cronon, in his analysis of the role of stories, suggests that we need to tell stories about stories, in order to understand the function of stories and the affects they have.[39] We have taken that method to heart as a way to demonstrate the importance of telling stories well. We offer just one story about the non-native plant theme to indicate how effective it can be in correcting the assumptions and mis-directions of the first.

At U.C. Berkeley there is a program called the American Cultures Program, and as part of that we had seminars where we learned about how to teach about diversity and the experiences of other cultural groups. At one seminar, Eucalyptus trees and the controversy about a California State Parks program to remove them, because they are non-native, was being discussed. The chair of the Chicano studies program leaned back in his chair and asked, "Isn't that just another one of these anti-immigrant things?" Given the flavor of the day in political circles right now, is it coincidental that we find it so easy to rally around stamping out alien invaders as an ecological moral crusade? Does the story prove so compelling that we fail to consider the specificity of the particular problem we need to address? Or ignore other components of the ecosystem that may need additional or different courses of action?

Properly identifying the reason for the choice of a "region" or spatial scale is crucial for both the stories of resource management and New Western History. The more we understand about the past or nature, the messier and more "site specific" our stories become. The simple, heroic, stories we crave, and management bureaucracies crave, become overwhelmed by details we now realize we cannot ignore. The frontier becomes subsumed in a roil of social and environmental interactions; the stately progression to ecological equilibria takes an alternate route to an alternate destination almost every time. New characters, defined as much by the perspective of the storyteller as by advanced technique, keep jumping on stage and changing the plot. What does a good story have to offer us anymore, either as historians or resource managers?

III. PUBLIC HISTORY AND PUBLIC MANAGEMENT

While not particularly impressed with either the New Western historians' multiple configurations of nature nor their construction of a region, we suffer clearly from narrative envy. What makes their choices make sense, and renders our position tenable, is to recognize the political agenda of the NWH. What underlies the analytical choices and the stories is the goal of engaging a broad range of people in the stories told. They appear to want to involve not merely the history profession but average citizens in understanding their past and using it to actively shape their future.

Ultimately, it is the New Western History political agenda that justifies the choice of region. The New Western historians, even Worster, are careful to distance themselves from the notion, expressed by Stegner, that the West is "the New World's last chance to be something better, the only American society still malleable enough to be formed."[40] However, they also quote the phrase. A deep concern for home pervades both the formal and informal writings that we have traversed. At the foundation of the New Western History is the thought that history matters to the present. History is not of "mere historic interest," but informs how we as individuals and communities live.[41] In the struggle between objectivism and presentism, an activist engagement in the region, and with the people of the region is the clear choice of this group. To be responsible westerners, New Western historians tell us, we must understand how our past is linked to our present and our future. The West matters at last simply because home matters—and it matters to them that Limerick is from Banning, California, and Turner is from Portage, Wisconsin,[42] and that Worster grew up in the area of, but not in sight of, Cow Creek. For New Western historians, we must care about where we come from, and where we live, in order to understand the perspective of the storyteller.

At last, this ought to make enormous sense to resource managers. The resource management professions have considerable experience in "public involvement," having spent the better part of 30 years trying to get the public to sign off on or buy into their resource management decisions. The controversy that this engendered is probably responsible, in some part, for the retreat into disciplinary science lamented above. Where those involvement efforts have failed—and they have not entirely—it is probably in part because resource managers have insisted, fearing for their authority, that the public adapt themselves to the profession's terms. When confronted with stories different from their own, resource managers tend to dismiss the teller and the content as emotional input which does not carry much weight. Yet telling and listening to stories are essential elements of communicating with diverse groups of people about their own experience of the intersection of human culture and the natural world.

We believe that the best reason for telling better stories—explicitly sharing them and exploring them, and understanding their nature as stories—lies in the political agendas of public historians and public resource managers. It seems to us that the major justification for many individual and collective decisions in the New Western History field is the stated goal of stirring public involvement in local and regional decision making processes. It is this preoccupation that justifies not only the effort to integrate and improve by *frisson* our various professional tales, but also the choice of region.

The field of resource management is presently witnessing the emergence of local groups who are no longer willing to allow federal agencies or corporate "experts" make the decisions. Diverse groups of resource users and appreciators are converging to decide what is best for nature, life, and the economy in their region. These local consensus groups have emerged throughout the West and are transforming the dialogue about public and private resource management. Such activism has long appeared to us to have been spawned by frustration with planning processes that are insensitive to local needs. We now wonder if this emerging emphasis on the politics of place and the capacity to act as a community can in some part be linked to a shared sense of history.

CONCLUSIONS

We end feeling surprisingly closely allied with the New Western historians. Perhaps we are impressed with them because we are crabby about our own profession—for thirty years it appeared that the resource managers would create this multidisciplinary *abierto* into academic and more popular discourse about natural resources. Unfortunately, the resource management professions have turned from the interdisciplinary enthusiasms of the '60s and '70s and are more likely, in these fiscally constrained times, to return to a reliable counting of this and that than to integrating broad data and stories about humans and ecosystems. Yet, somewhere there is need for a coming together: a place, theme, or story that brings together the ecological and cultural. For now, we shall think of ourselves as New Western Resource Management historians.

University of California, Berkeley

NOTES

1. Patricia Nelson Limerick, *The Legacy Of Conquest: The Unbroken Past Of The American West*, 1st ed. (New York: Norton, 1987) 30–31.
2. Limerick, *Legacy* 30–31.
3. Donald Worster, *The Wealth of Nature: Environmental History and the Ecological Imaginaion* (New York: Oxford University Press, 1993) 18–20.
4. Donald Worster, *Rivers of Empire: Water, Aridity, and the Growth of the American West*, 1st ed. (New York: Pantheon Books, 1985) 11.
5. Richard White, *"It's Your Misfortune and None of My Own": A History of the American West*, 1st ed. (Norman: University of Oklahoma Press, 1991). See chapter 13.
6. William Cronon, *Nature's Metropolis: Chicago and the Great West*. 1st ed. (New York: Norton, 1991).
7. Worster, *Rivers* 22
8. Richard White, "Trashing the Trails," in *Trails: Toward A New Western History*, eds. Patricia Nelson Limerick, Clyde A. Milner II, and Charles E. Rankin (Lawrence: University Press of Kansas, 1991) 29.

9. Donald Worster, "Beyond the Agrarian Myth," in *Trails* 19.

10. White, "Trashing" 27.

11. Limerick, *Legacy* ch 9.

12. Limerick, *Legacy* 318.

13. Donald Worster, et al., "*Legacy of Conquest*, by Patricia Nelson Limerick: A Panel of Appraisal," *Western Historical Quarterly* 20.3 (1989): 305.

14. Wallace Stegner, "A Geography of Hope," in *A Society to Match the Scenery: Personal Visions of the Future of the American West*, eds. Gary Holthaus, Patricia Nelson Limerick, Charles F. Wildinson, and Eve Stryker Munson (Boulder: University Press of Colorado, 1991) 228.

15. Patricia Nelson Limerick, "The Unleashing of the Western Public Intellectual," in *Trails* 69.

16. Worster, *Rivers* 15

17. Eugene P. Odum, *Fundamentals of Ecology*, 3rd ed. (Philadelphia: Saunders Press, 1971).

18. See Donald Worster's "Nature and the Disorder of History." In *Reinventing Nature: Responses to Postmodern Deconstruction*, eds. M. E. Soule and G. Lease (Washington, D.C.: Island Press, 1996) 70.

19. Worster, "Nature" 69

20. Harold F. Heady, *Rangeland Management* (New York: McGraw-Hill, 1975).

21. Roy H. Behnke, Jr., Ian Scoones, and Carol Kerven, eds., *Range Ecology at Disequilibrium: New Models Of Natural Variability And Pastoral Adaptation In African Savannas* (London: Overseas Development Institute, 1993).

22. *Trails* 70–71.

23. Richard S. Kirkendall, *Social Scientists and Farm Politics in the Age of Roosevelt* (Ames: Iowa State University Press, 1982).

24. Sally Fairfax, "The Lands, Natural Resources, and Economy of the West," in *A Society to Match the Scenery: Personal Visions of the Future of the American West*, eds. Gary Holthaus, Patricia Nelson Limerick, Charles F. Wildinson, and Eve Stryker Munson (Boulder: University Press of Colorado) 196–205.

25. Limerick, "Unleashing" 71.

26. Wallace Stegner, *Beyond the Hundredth Meridian: John Wesley Powell and the Second Opening of the West* (Boston: Houghton, Mifflin, 1954).

27. For example, see Timothy Silver's *A New Face on the Countryside: Indians, Colonists, and Slaves in South Atlantic Forests, 1500–1800* (Cambridge; New York: Cambridge University Press, 1990), or William Cronon's *Changes in the Land: Indians, Colonists, and the Ecology of New England*, 1st ed. (New York: Hill and Wang, 1983).

28. William Cronen, "A Place for Stories: Nature, History, and Narrative," *Journal of American History* 78.4 (1992): 1347–76.

29. Limerick, "Unleashing" 64–66; Cronon, "A Place" 1347–76.

30. W. L. Halvorson and G. E. Davis, "Long-term Research in National Parks: From Beliefs to Knowledge," in *Science and Ecosystem Management in the National Parks*, eds. W. L. Halvorson and G. E. Davis (Tucson: University of Arizona Press, 1996) 3–10.

31. Donald Worster, *The Wealth Of Nature: Environmental History And The Ecological Imagination* (New York: Oxford University Press, 1993) 46–50

32. Cronon, "A Place" 1347–76.

33. Donald Worster, "Nature." See chapter 5.

34. Patricia Nelson Limerick, "The Adventures of the Frontier in the Twentieth Century," *The Frontier in American Culture: an Exhibition at the Newberry Library, August 26, 1994–January 7, 1995*, ed. James R. Grossman (Chicago: The Library; Berkeley: University of California Press, 1994).

35. Louise Fortmann and Sally Fairfax, "American Forestry Professionalism in the Third World: Some Preliminary Observations," *Economic and Political Weekly* 12 August 1989: 1839–44.

36. Stephen J. Pyne, *Fire In America: A Cultural History Of Wildland And Rural Fire* (Princeton, N.J.: Princeton University Press, 1982).

37. John McPhee, "Balloons of War," *The New Yorker* 29 Jan 1996, 52–61.

38. Pyne, *Fire*.

39. Cronon, "A Place" 1347–76.

40. Donald Worster, *An Unsettled Country: Changing Landscapes of the American West*, 1st ed. (Albuquerque: University of New Mexico Press, 1994) xii, 5.

41. Patricia Nelson Limerick, "What on Earth is the New Western History?" in *Trails* 87–88.

42. Limerick, "What on Earth" 81–88.

THE CONTRIBUTORS

FORREST G. ROBINSON is a Professor of American Studies at the University of California, Santa Cruz. His books on the American West include *Wallace Stegner* (with Margaret Robinson); *In Bad Faith: The Dynamics of Deception in Mark Twain's America*; *Having It Both Ways: Self-Subversion in Western Popular Classics*; and *The Cambridge Companion to Mark Twain.*

JEROME FRISK studied philosophy at Pomona College, comparative religion at Harvard Divinity School and holds a Ph.D. in History of Consciousness from the University of California, Santa Cruz. His contribution to this journal is a chapter from his dissertation on the western origins of American environmentalism. He has presented numerous papers on multicultural and environmental issues at Melus, WLA, and MLA conferences. He currently teaches Global Studies at Stevenson College, UCSC.

KRISTA COMER took her Ph.D. from Brown University's Department of American Civilization in 1996. Her first book, *Women Writers, The New West, and the Politics of Landscape*, is forthcoming from University of North Carolina Press. Forthcoming essays will appear in *Updating the Literary West* (Texas Christian University Press), in *Breaking Boundaries: New Perspectives on Women's Regional Fiction* (University Press of Iowa), and *Frontiers: Ecofeminism, A Special Issue.* Ms. Comer teaches at Rice University in the Women's Studies and English Departments.

CARL GUTIÉRREZ-JONES is an Associate Professor of English at the University of California, Santa Barbara. He is the author of *Rethinking the Borderlands: Between Chicano Culture and Legal Discourse* (University of California Press, 1995).

STEPHEN TATUM is an Associate Professor and Chair of the English Department at the University of Utah. His book, *Inventing Billy the Kid*, was recently republished by the University of Arizona Press.

SALLY K. FAIRFAX is Professor of Natural Resources Law and Policy in the Department of Environmental Science, Policy, and Management and in the Department of Environmental Planning at the University of California at Berkeley. Most of her work appears in law reviews. She is co-author, with Carolyn Yale, of *The Federal Lands* (Island Press). She is also author of the second edition of Samuel Trask Dana's classic text, *Forest and Range Policy*. Her most recent work, *State Trust Lands*, co-authored with Jon Souder, was published in 1996 by University Press of Kansas.

LYNN HUNTSINGER is Associate Professor in the Department of Environmental Science, Policy, and Management at the University of California, Berkeley. She has published numerous articles about range and forest management. Her most recent work is on the effects of historic changes in management regimes in the Yurok Forest in northwestern California.

INDEX